McGRAW-HILL's

POSTAL EXAMS 473/473C

Mark Alan Stewart

McGRAW-HILL

New York   Chicago   San Francisco   Lisbon   London   Madrid
Mexico City   Milan   New Delhi   San Juan   Seoul
Singapore   Sydney   Toronto

Library of Congress Cataloging-in-Publication Data

Stewart, Mark A. (Mark Alan), date.
    McGraw-Hill's postal exams 473/473c / Mark Alan Stewart.
        p.   cm.
    ISBN-13: 978-0-07-147509-9
    ISBN-10: 0-07-147509-5
    1. United States Postal Service—Examinations—Study guides.
2. Postal service—United States—Examinations, questions, etc.
I. Title.

    HE6499.S755   2007
    383'.1076—dc22   2006026034

ISBN-13: 978-0-07-147509-9

ISBN-10: 0-07-147509-5

This book was set in Times New Roman by Patricia Wallenburg.

Printed and bound by Quebecor/Dubuque.

McGraw-Hill books are available at special quantity discounts to use as premiums and sales promotions, or for use in corporate training programs. For more information, please write to the Director of Special Sales, McGraw-Hill Professional, Two Penn Plaza, New York, NY 10121-2298. Or contact your local bookstore.

CONTENTS

How to Use This Book

This book is designed primarily to help those who are interested in employment with the U.S. Postal Service learn about available jobs and their requirements, and, in particular, to learn about Test 473, the test required for most positions. Specific strategies and practice drills and exams are provided to help you do well on the exam—and succeed in gaining employment with the U.S. Postal Service.

Here are a few hints on how to best start using this book.

First, read Chapter 1 to learn about jobs in the U.S. Postal Service and how to apply for them.

Second, learn all about Test 473—its organization, types of questions, scoring, and so on.

Then, equipped with this basic general knowledge, learn more about each of the four main sections of Test 473 by reading (and studying) Chapters 3, 4, 5, and 6. Each of these chapters discusses the types of questions included in one part of the test and provides both specific tips for answering the questions and general strategies to use when working on that particular section. Practice drills help to ensure that you understand how to answer the questions in each section.

Finally, take a practice test, or maybe two tests. Score them and determine what your weak points are: Address Checking, Forms Completion, or Coding and Memory. Then go back to the chapter that discusses that particular part of the test and review the material to be sure you know exactly what the questions are asking and what approaches you should take in attempting to answer them correctly.

Then, take another practice test and repeat the procedure. By the time you have completed several practice tests—seven are given in this book—you should be very familiar with the test and well on your way to scoring well.

Good luck.

USPS JOBS AND TAKING TEST 473

Working for the U.S. Postal Service in Entry-Level Jobs

Eligibility, Requirements, and Benefits

The U.S. Postal Service (USPS) is one of the nation's largest civilian employers, currently employing more than 700,000 people in career positions throughout the country. A career position with the Postal Service can be rewarding work: the compensation and benefits packages are among the best you'll find anywhere, and you'll enjoy the additional satisfaction of knowing that you are part of a long tradition of providing vital services to the country and its people.

Understandably, Postal Service employment is attractive to many, many people, and the market for Postal Service career jobs is *very* competitive. Application exams such as *Test 473* are one means that the Postal Service uses to screen applicants and identify those who are best qualified for various positions. Test 473 is officially known as *Test 473 for Major Entry-Level Jobs* and is also referred to as the *473 Battery Exam*. (It replaces the old 470 Battery Exam.)

If you're applying for a job that requires you to take one of the exams given by the Postal Service, it's imperative that you gain a competitive edge by preparing thoroughly for the exam. This is especially true for Test 473 because more applicants take this exam than any of the other Postal Service exams. That's why we've created a book dedicated almost entirely to helping you do just that.

The official U.S. postal system was created during the American Revolution, primarily to facilitate the delivery of important messages among various divisions of the Revolutionary army. Meeting in July of 1775, the Second Continental Congress named Benjamin Franklin, who had been instrumental in devising the system's framework and recommending it to the Congress, as the postal system's initial Postmaster General.

Before we examine the test itself in Chapter 2, learn how to get ready for it in Chapters 3 through 6, and practice sample tests in Chapters 7 through 13, let's take a look at the various career jobs with the Postal Service. All of these career jobs require applicants to take either Test 473 or another test. A bit later in this chapter, you'll learn about the specific employment benefits offered by the Postal Service and the eligibility requirements for career employment with the Postal Service.

Postal Jobs Requiring Test 473 Scores

Applicants for most types of delivery, distribution, and retail jobs with the USPS must take Test 473 (or Test 473-C for City Carriers). There are four positions that fall into this category:

- City Carrier
- Mail Processing Clerk

■ Mail Handler
■ Sales, Services, and Distribution Associate

Applicants for permanent, or *career*, positions as City Carrier, Mail Processing Clerk, Mail Handler, or Sales, Services, and Distribution Associate must take and pass Test 473 in order to qualify for these positions. New employees in these four positions are usually paid an *hourly wage* and work on a somewhat flexible schedule, which varies depending on the work flow, especially the volume of mail during a particular day or season. Following is a brief description of each of these four positions.

Note: The Postal Service also offers temporary, or so-called casual, job positions in the same four categories. A casual job position may last from a few weeks up to a maximum of 90 days, usually during the Christmas holiday season. Applicants for casual positions do *not* need to take Test 473 or any other exam.

City Carrier

Job Description
This is the USPS job that is in most demand. City Carriers deliver and collect mail, either on foot or by vehicle (or both), and sort and organize mail for delivery, usually in the mornings. Carriers serving residential areas deliver mail once during the day, but some carriers serving commercial areas deliver mail twice during the day. Carriers also collect payments for cash on delivery (C.O.D.) parcels and obtain receipts for certified, insured, and registered mail.

Qualifications
The job of City Carrier is physically demanding. To perform the job, you must be able to

■ Carry mailbags weighing up to 35 pounds on your shoulders
■ Unload parcels and mail containers and trays weighing up to 70 pounds
■ Stand, walk, and reach for several hours at a time
■ Perform the duties just listed under various weather conditions

Testing Requirement
All applicants for the job of City Carrier must take Test 473 or 473-C.

Other Requirements
You must have a valid state driver's license. You must also show that you have at least two years of driving experience and a safe driving record.

Mail Processing Clerk

Job Description
Mail Processing Clerks operate, monitor, troubleshoot, and maintain automated mail-processing equipment, bar-code sorters, and optical bar-code readers. Mail Processing Clerks may also perform manual sorting, organizing, and bundling of mail; transfer mail from one area to another; and load mail into bins and trucks.

Qualifications
The job of Mail Processing Clerk can be somewhat physically demanding. To perform the job, you must be able to stand and reach continuously for hours at a time. You might also need to lift and transport heavy bundles and containers.

Testing Requirement

All applicants for the job of Mail Processing Clerk must take Test 473.

Mail Handler

Job Description

Mail Handlers load and unload containers of mail. Mail Handlers also transport mail, either manually or by forklift, to different areas of the same facility. Mail Handlers may also open and empty containers of mail.

Qualifications

The job of Mail Handler is physically demanding. To perform this job, you must be able to repeatedly lift and carry bundles, parcels, and containers weighing up to 70 pounds as well as push heavy rolling containers. You may also need to know how to operate a forklift.

Testing Requirement

All applicants for the job of Mail Handler must take Test 473.

Sales, Services, and Distribution Associate

Job Description

Sales, Services, and Distribution Associates provide direct sales and customer support services in a retail environment and perform distribution of mail.

Qualifications

You must successfully complete an on-the-job training program. There are no special physical demands for this job.

Testing Requirement

All applicants for the job of Sales, Services, and Distribution Associate must take Test 473.

> The U.S. Postal Department first began providing free city delivery by salaried postal carriers in 1863. Prior to that year, customers had picked up their mail at their local post office. From 1864 to 1880, the number of cities providing free delivery increased from 65 to nearly 800. However, it wasn't until the early 1900s that the use of mail slots and curbside mailboxes came into use. Until then, carriers hand-delivered mail to all their customers. Today there are more than 230,000 city mail carriers in the United States.

Jobs Requiring Scores from Other Postal Exams

The four positions described in the preceding section are the ones for which applicants must take Test 473 (or Test 473-C for City Carriers). If you're interested in a USPS job other than one of these four, you might need to take a different exam. The two positions falling into this category that are most in demand are

- Rural Carrier Associate
- Data Conversion Operator

Like other delivery and distribution workers, these employees usually start by earning an *hourly wage* and work on a flexible schedule that varies according to work flow. Following is a brief description of each of these two positions.

Rural Carrier Associate

Job Description

Rural Carrier Associates sort mail into delivery sequence, load the mail into a delivery vehicle, and deliver and collect mail by vehicle at designated addresses in a prescribed rural area. They also collect payments for cash on delivery (C.O.D.) parcels and obtain receipts for certified, insured, and registered mail.

Qualifications

To perform the job of Rural Carrier Associate, you must be able to handle bundles and parcels weighing up to 70 pounds. Also, you must have a valid state driver's license, at least two years of driving experience, and a safe driving record.

Testing Requirement

All applicants for the job of Rural Carrier Associate must take *Test 460, "Rural Carrier Associate Exam."*

Data Conversion Operator

Job Description

Data Conversion Operators use a computer terminal to prepare mail for automated sorting equipment. They read typed and handwritten addresses from letter images on the terminal screen, then select and type essential information so that a bar code can be applied to the letter.

Qualifications

To qualify for this job, you must be proficient in typing and data entry, as determined by a performance test (*Test 710,* described briefly here).

Testing Requirement

All applicants for the job of Data Conversion Operator must take *Test 710, "Clerical Abilities Exam."* This exam measures the per-minute rate at which you can accurately type a certain number of specified numbers and letters.

USPS Employment Eligibility Requirements

To be eligible for USPS employment, you must be 18 years of age at the time your employment would commence (or 16 years of age if you have a high school diploma), and you must be either a U.S. citizen or a permanent resident alien. Here are some additional requirements for USPS employment:

- You must demonstrate basic competence in the English language, as demonstrated through Test 473 or some other written examination and through job interviews.
- You must submit to a medical assessment, which provides information about your physical and mental ability to perform various jobs.

▓ You must submit to a urine drug screen to ensure that you are drug-free.

▓ You must provide the name of your current employer (if any) and the names of all your previous employers dating back 10 years (but not further back than your sixteenth birthday).

Before deciding whether to employ you, the USPS will conduct a preliminary criminal-conviction check. Should the USPS decide to hire you, it will then conduct a more thorough criminal background check.

Additional eligibility requirements apply only to certain applicants or for certain jobs:

▓ If you've served actively in the U.S. military, you'll need to complete and submit *DD Form 214*, "Certificate of Release and Discharge from Active Duty."

▓ If you're a male born in 1960 or later, you must be registered with the Selective Service System (for the U.S. military draft).

▓ If you're applying for a job that involves driving, your driving record must show that you are a safe driver.

USPS Compensation and Employment Benefits

The U.S. Postal Service provides compensation packages to its employees that are very competitive with those offered by most private-sector employers. New Postal Service employees in career positions are usually paid an *hourly wage*. In 2006, the beginning wage for entry-level career positions was between $15 and $20 per hour. Overtime pay is provided at the rate of one-and-a-half times the regular wage beyond 8 hours during any workday *or* beyond 40 hours during a workweek. Employees who work night shifts or on Sundays receive premium pay as well. Most employees receive regular wage or salary increases.

For most job seekers, the first question about any particular job that comes to mind is, "How much does the job pay?" But other questions soon come to mind as well—for example:

Is health insurance provided?
How many days off do I get each year?
Is a 401(k) or similar savings program available?

One of the attractions of working for the USPS is the generous benefits package offered to employees. Here's a brief description of those benefits. Keep in mind that there may be a waiting period for some benefits, and that some benefits may be available only to full-time or career USPS employees.

Health Insurance

A variety of health-insurance plans, including HMOs (health maintenance organizations) and traditional health-insurance plans, are available to qualifying USPS employees through the Federal Health Benefits (FEHB) Program. Most of the costs are paid by the Postal Service. The portion of the costs paid for by the employee (in the form of premiums) offsets the employee's taxable income.

Social Security and Medicare

Both types of coverage are provided to all USPS employees.

Retirement Benefits

Through a federal program, the USPS provides a defined-benefit annuity program, which guarantees a certain level of income during retirement, as well as disability benefits to qualifying employees.

Life Insurance

A basic life-insurance plan paid for entirely by the Postal Service is provided to qualifying USPS employees, who also have the option to purchase additional coverage by payroll deduction. All coverage is provided through the Federal Employees Group Life Insurance (FEGLI) Program.

Thrift Savings Plan (TSP)

Qualifying USPS employees may participate in a Thrift Savings Plan (TSP), which is a lot like the 401(k) plans provided by private-sector employers. Under this plan, the employer (the USPS) matches the employee's TSP contribution each year up to a certain percentage (currently 5 percent) of the employee's compensation. The TSP provides a vehicle for tax-deferred retirement savings, and plan contributions reduce the employee's taxable compensation.

Flexible Spending Account (FSA)

Qualifying postal employees may participate in the Postal Service's Flexible Spending Account (FSA) Program. Under this program, an employee can make tax-free contributions up to a certain amount each year to an FSA account. The employee may withdraw FSA funds to pay for qualifying health and child-care expenses at any time without tax or penalty.

Vacation and Sick Leave

During the first three years of employment, qualifying employees are allowed a total of 13 days of vacation and sick leave per year. After three years of employment, the total number of days allowed for leave each year increases to 20, and after 15 years, the total number increases to 26. Full-time employees are also allowed 13 *additional* days of sick leave per year as insurance against loss of income as a result of illness or accident.

Holidays

The USPS currently observes 10 holidays, so all USPS employees receive 10 days off each year for holidays.

U.S. mail delivery to the western states initially was done by stagecoach—a slow and undependable means. Then, in the mid-1800s, a group of enterprising businessmen obtained a contract with the U.S. Postal Department to provide the "Pony Express," a nonstop chain of riders, each covering up to 100 miles a day and changing horses every 10 to 15 miles at relay stations. The Pony Express decreased delivery time from Missouri to the West by more than half, but it operated only from 1860 to 1861, when the transcontinental telegraph line immediately rendered the service obsolete.

All About Test 473

Test 473 is an entry-level test designed by the U.S. Postal Service (USPS) to measure general aptitude and suitability for certain types of postal work. It is *not* a test of factual knowledge.

This chapter of the book will answer most of your questions about Test 473. First, you'll familiarize yourself with the format and various parts of the exam. Then, you'll learn how the exam is scored. Later in this chapter, you'll learn how to apply to take the exam and what to expect on exam day. At the end of the chapter, you'll learn some basic test-taking strategies for the exam. (We'll cover specific strategies for each of the four parts of Test 473 later in this book.)

Test 473 and Test 473-C are identical exams; in other words, they are one and the same test. Sometimes the test is administered only to fill City Carrier positions, in which case the exam is called Test 473-C. So the C stands for "City Carrier."

Note: Since Test 473 and Test 473-C are exactly the same, we'll refer to both simply as Test 473 throughout the rest of this book.

Format and Description of Test 473

Test 473 consists of four separate parts, each of which is timed. Here's the basic format:

Part	Number of Scored Questions	Time Allowed
Part A: Address Checking	60 questions	11 minutes
Part B: Forms Completion	30 questions	15 minutes
Part C: Coding and Memory	72 questions (total)	13 minutes (total)
Coding Section	36 questions	6 minutes
Memory Section	36 questions	7 minutes
Part D: Personal Characteristics and Experience Inventory	236 questions (total)	90 minutes
Personal Characteristics	160 questions	
Experience	76 questions	

Following is a brief description of each of the exam's four parts.

Part A: Address Checking

Part A will present 60 correct addresses and ZIP codes, numbered 1 through 60. To the right of each address and ZIP code, another address and ZIP code will appear. The two should be the same, but the one on the right might contain one or more errors; in other words, it might not match the correct address exactly. Your job is to determine whether there are any errors and, if so, whether the error is in the address, the ZIP code, or both.

For each of the 60 items in Part A, you select one of four answer choices: (A) if the address and ZIP code are exactly the same, (B) if there's a difference in the address only, (C) if there's a difference in the ZIP code only, or (D) if there's a difference in both the address *and* the ZIP code.

Part B: Forms Completion

In Part B, your job is to answer a total of 30 questions involving a series of simulated Postal Service forms, such as mailing receipts and shipping instructions. The questions are designed to gauge your ability to complete standard Postal Service forms accurately and properly. More specifically, the questions gauge your ability to fill in the various fields (lines and boxes) on the form with the appropriate information for each field.

Expect to encounter about five different forms on Part B, each one accompanied by about 5 to 7 questions based on the form. For each of the 30 questions, you are given four answer choices: (A), (B), (C), and (D). Some questions ask where certain information should be entered on the form, while other questions ask what types of entries are appropriate for particular fields (lines or boxes) on the form.

Part C: Coding and Memory

Part C is essentially a mail-sorting exercise, in which your job is to assign various street addresses to one of four delivery routes, lettered A, B, C, and D, according to a Coding Guide. Part C is divided into two sections: a *Coding Section*, which consists of 36 addresses to be coded in 6 minutes, and a *Memory Section*, which consists of 36 addresses to be coded in 7 minutes. During the Coding Section, you can refer to the Coding Guide, but during the Memory Section, you can't. (That's why it's called the Memory Section.) You will use the same Coding Guide for both sections of Part C.

In each of the two sections of Part C, before you code the 36 scored items, you'll attempt a series of brief, timed practice exercises to familiarize yourself with the Coding Guide. Thus, the total time for Part C is greater than the 13 minutes allowed for the two scored segments.

Part D: Personal Characteristics and Experience Inventory

In Part D, you have 90 minutes to answer 236 questions. The questions in Part D are designed to assess all the various personal characteristics, preferences, and experiences that are relevant to working effectively as an employee of the Postal Service. Part D actually consists of two sections: *Personal Characteristics* (160 questions) and *Experience* (76 questions). The Personal Characteristics section contains two basic types of questions. In one type, your job is to identify the extent to which you agree or disagree with a given statement by selecting one of four answer choices: (A) strongly agree, (B) agree, (C) disagree, or (D) strongly disagree. In the other question type, you identify the frequency with which the description fits you by selecting one of four choices: (A) very often, (B) often, (C) sometimes, or (D) rarely or never. The Experience section is designed to gauge your experience in areas relevant to performing effectively as a Postal Service employee. In this section, the response choices vary from one question to the next.

Note: There is no "correct" answer to any question in Part D. However, Part D is scored. How it is scored is a well-guarded USPS secret.

How Test 473 Is Scored

Test 473 is scored on a 0 to 100 scale. You'll receive one overall score in the 0 to 100 range for your exam. A passing score is 70. However, your test score is *not* the same as the number of questions you answer correctly. Each part of the test is scored separately, and then the four scores are combined, using a complex formula that the Postal Service will not disclose. Following is a closer look at how each part is scored.

Part A: Address Checking

Your score for Part A is based on the total number of items you answer correctly, *minus* one-third point for each item you answer incorrectly. No deduction is made for items you leave unanswered or blank on your answer sheet. Part A consists of a total of 60 items. Let's assume that you answered 45 correctly and 9 incorrectly, while leaving 6 unanswered (blank). Your score for Part A would be $45 - (1/3$ of 9), or $45 - 3 = 42$. Your score of 42 would then be combined with your scores for the other three parts of the exam to determine your overall test score.

Part B: Forms Completion

Your score for Part B is based simply on the total number of items you answer correctly. No deduction is made for questions you answer incorrectly or for those that you leave unanswered (blank). Part B consists of a total of 30 items. Let's say you answered 21 questions correctly. It doesn't matter how many of the remaining 9 questions you answered incorrectly and how many you left unanswered (blank). Your score for Part B would be 21, the total number of correct answers. Your score of 21 would then be combined with your scores for the other three parts to determine your overall test score.

Part C: Coding and Memory

Your score for Part C is calculated in the same manner as that for Part A: the total number of items you answer correctly, *minus* one-third point for each item you answer incorrectly. No deduction is made for test items you leave unanswered (blank). Part C consists of a total of 72 items. So, if you answered 53 correctly and 12 incorrectly, while leaving 7 unanswered (blank), your score for Part C would be $53 - (1/3$ of 12), or $53 - 4 = 49$. Your score of 49 would then be combined with your scores for the other three parts to determine your overall test score.

Part D: Personal Characteristics and Experience Inventory

Part D is scored and does significantly affect your overall exam score. However, the scoring system for Part D is a well-guarded secret with the Postal Service. Part D consists of a total of 236 questions altogether. Without knowing how Part D is scored, the best approach is to make sure you answer each and every question you can as honestly as you can—and leave the rest to fate!

> In the early twentieth century, U.S. retailers such as Sears and Montgomery Ward owed their success largely to the advent of Parcel Post in 1913, which made possible the operation of so-called catalog businesses. Today, the size limit for any parcel mailed from any U.S. Post Office to any destination in the United States is 130 inches (combined length and girth), and the weight limit is 70 pounds.

Applying to Take Test 473

Before you can apply for any specific Postal Service job, you must first take and pass the appropriate exam, such as Test 473. But, you cannot simply walk into an exam office anytime you wish and take one of the exams. That's not how it works. First, you must determine *when* and *where* the exam that you wish to take is next being offered in your geographical area.

Vacancy Announcements

Regional postal districts schedule exams only on an *as-needed* basis. This means that they administer a particular exam—such as Test 473—only when they anticipate openings for jobs that require applicants to take that exam. When a postal district decides to provide testing for anticipated job openings, the district will issue an *announcement* indicating a time period—for example, July 1 through September 30—during which anyone who is interested may apply to take a particular exam, such as Test 473, at that district's exam office. Each announcement is identified by a unique *announcement number*. You'll need the specific announcement number when you apply to take the exam.

There are many ways to find out when Test 473 will be offered next in the city or region where you wish to work. Following are the best places to find vacancy announcements:

- The employment area of the official USPS Web site (www.usps.com/employment)
- USPS vacancy-announcement telephone "hotlines," which are recorded announcement messages
- Bulletin boards at U.S. Post Offices
- Bulletin boards at state employment development offices
- Community job-resource and vocational-training centers

Note: Beware of classified ads in newspapers that charge fees for providing information about Postal Service employment (or any U.S. government jobs, for that matter). These ads are placed by scam artists who are out to make a quick buck by selling information that is already available to the general public for free.

Postal Exam Telephone Hotline Numbers

To apply to take any Postal Service exam, you need a specific vacancy-announcement number. You can view current vacancy-announcement numbers for all U.S. states and territories at the USPS Web site (www.usps.com). You can also obtain vacancy-announcement numbers by calling the appropriate hotline telephone number in your region. These hotlines connect you with recorded messages that provide vacancy-announcement numbers and testing dates. Some also provide telephone numbers to call in order to speak with a USPS administrative employee in that region, in case you have additional, unanswered questions.

A list of postal exam hotlines for all states, except for Alaska, Rhode Island, and Vermont, which do not provide hotlines, is given in the appendix. These telephone numbers are valid at the time of publication of this book, but they are subject to change at any time, of course.

Many of these hotlines are toll-free (1-800 or 1-877) numbers. Some numbers cover the entire state, while others cover only certain regions or cities, or, in the case of some large metropolitan areas, certain areas within cities. If you don't see a hotline number that covers your city or town, or if the phone number listed is no longer correct, try calling the number for the nearest city.

Note: Just for fun, try calling some of the hotline numbers around the country (as long as you don't pay for the phone calls), so that you can listen to a variety of regional accents. For example, you'll no doubt discover that the recorded voice for New York City's outer boroughs district (Brooklyn, Queens, and Staten Island) sounds a lot different from the one for Savannah, Georgia!

How to Apply to Take the Exam

You can apply to take Test 473 in either of two ways:

- By telephone, through a toll-free number provided by the USPS
- Online, at the official USPS Web site (www.usps.com)

Regardless of which method you use, there is absolutely no fee or charge to apply for or to take Test 473 or any other postal exam. You know what they say: the best things in life are free!

Applying by Telephone

If you have a touch-tone phone (and you probably do), you can apply to take the test by calling the Postal Service's toll-free number. At the time of publication of this book, the number is 1-866-999-8777. Once you dial the number, you'll need to use your telephone keypad to proceed through a series of menu choices. You'll be able to enter some information, such as the vacancy-announcement number and your social security number, using your telephone keypad. You'll need to provide certain other information (such as your name and address) by voice; in doing so, be sure to speak slowly and clearly so that the automated voice recording system receives the correct information from you. The automated system will ask you to spell out certain words, which can be somewhat time-consuming. Expect the telephone application process to take between 8 and 15 minutes.

Applying Online via the Official USPS Web Site

If you have Internet access, you can apply via the employment area of the Postal Service's official Web site (www.usps.com/employment). You can also access the employment area of the site from the USPS home page (www.usps.com) by clicking on the "Jobs" link. Once you're at the Jobs page of the site, follow the link to "Mail Processing Jobs," and then to the specific type of job that interests you.

To apply online to take Test 473, follow these links:

If you know the vacancy-announcement number you wish to use for your application, you can enter the number and then proceed with the application. If you don't have a vacancy-announcement number, you can click on "Continue," at which point you can select a state (e.g., New York) and view a complete list of vacancy-announcement numbers in that state; the list is organized alphabetically by city. Click on the vacancy-announcement number you wish to use and then proceed with your application.

To begin the online application process, you'll be presented with a brief, two-tier survey that asks about your interest in and suitability for Postal Service work generally and then for specific types of postal work (retail, mail processing, or carrier). You answer the survey questions by selecting "yes" or "no" for each one. The purpose of this survey is simply to help you determine whether Postal Service work is suitable for you. It is important to understand that your answers do *not* affect your eligibility to apply for postal jobs or for any of the tests, nor do they affect the employee selection process. In fact, the survey is entirely optional; if you wish, you can skip both levels of the survey by clicking on "Continue application."

Once you arrive at the application form itself, you'll simply need to enter your name, mailing address, and ZIP code. You may also enter your phone number and e-mail address, although both are optional.

That's all there is to applying for the test. Assuming that you have all the information you need at hand, applying online should take only two to four minutes, which is much quicker than applying by telephone.

Note: The Postal Service has permanently discontinued the use of *paper*-based forms for applying to take its employment exams. The two application methods just described are the only ones available now.

The total number of post offices in the United States reached a maximum of 76,945 in 1901. Since then, despite a growing U.S. population and an ever-increasing volume of mail, the number of post offices in the United States has declined steadily, primarily because of the increasing use of rural carrier routes as replacements for small post offices. Today, rural carriers serve more than 33 million U.S. homes and businesses.

After You Apply for the Exam—the Scheduling Notice

About two weeks after you apply to take the exam (using one of the two methods just described), a *scheduling notice* will be mailed to you at the address you provided in your application. The notice will indicate your scheduled testing date, time, and location (the address of the exam office where you are to report for the test). The notice indicates the time by which you must report to the test site, not the time that testing actually begins. Your testing date will probably be about six weeks from when you receive the notice (eight weeks after you applied for the test), but the time might be even longer. The packet that you'll receive will actually contain two separate items:

- Your *admission pass*, which tells you when and where to report for the test
- A 15-page booklet about the exam that contains the following information:
  - Some sample questions similar to the ones on each part of the exam
  - Instructions about what to bring with you to the exam office on the day of your exam
  - The same two-tier survey that the USPS Web site provides during the online application process
  - A brief description of each part of the test, along with some basic test-taking suggestions

Exam Accommodations for Persons with Qualifying Disabilities

Under the Rehabilitation Act of 1973, the U.S. Postal Service must find ways to accommodate qualified individuals with disabilities, where appropriate, during the examination process (as well as on the job). Under the act, a *disability* is defined as "a physical or mental impairment that substantially limits a major life activity," which includes functions such as hearing, seeing, walking, speaking, caring for self, performing manual tasks, and breathing.

If you are a Postal Service applicant and you believe that you are a qualified individual with a disability who requires accommodation during the application process (including a Postal Service exam), you are responsible for making your needs known as early as possible. Request accommodation in advance by contacting the official, or local, manager of human resources of the examination administration office in the city or region where you plan to take the exam. Explain the nature of your limitations and the accommodation you need. (This request can also be made by someone else on your behalf.)

If your disability is not obvious, you may be required to provide documentation from an appropriate professional to clearly explain the nature and/or impact of the disability and your need for reasonable accommodation during the application process, including the test.

For more information, see USPS Publication 316, "Reasonable Accommodation in the U.S. Postal Service: A Guide for Employees and Applicants."

The Day of the Exam

On exam day, there are two very important points you must remember:

- *Don't be late!* Be sure to leave for the test site early enough so that you are sure you won't be late. Keep in mind that if you arrive any later than the reporting time indicated on your scheduling notice—even only by a minute or two—you won't be allowed to take the exam.
- *Don't forget your admission pass and a picture I.D.* You won't be admitted to the testing site or allowed to take the exam without these two items. Also be sure to take at least two sharpened No. 2 pencils along. Don't count on the exam supervisor or another test taker to have extra pencils in case you forget yours.

We cannot emphasize the preceding points strongly enough. After all, if you're not allowed to take the test, you'll need to start the application process all over again, delaying your possible employment by the USPS by at least two months. If the application period has expired, you'll need to wait until the next vacancy announcement, which might not occur until the next year or even later, before applying again take the exam.

Note: On exam day, be sure to eat a good meal before you leave for the test site, and check the location of the test site given on your scheduling notice to make sure you know where it is and how to get there.

Testing Procedures and Rules

Once you and the other test takers have been admitted to the exam room and the time deadline for reporting to the test site has passed, the exam supervisor will explain the testing procedures and rules and will pass out test booklets and answer sheets. Expect these pretest procedures to take at least 20 minutes.

The exam supervisor will state key procedural rules that you must follow during the test and answer any questions about them before the timed testing begins. Here are key rules that you must follow:

- All test takers begin each part of the test simultaneously, and only when the exam supervisor instructs you all to begin.
- Once you begin a particular timed part of the test, you are not allowed to work on any other part of the test. The exam supervisor will patrol the testing room to monitor for cheating.
- At the end of each timed part, the supervisor will inform all test takers that they must stop, put their pencils down, and refrain from turning to another part of the exam.
- Just before each part begins, the supervisor will announce how much time is allowed for the part, and then will announce that you may begin work on the part.
- You can leave the testing room at any time to use the restroom, stretch, get a drink of water, or for any other reason. However, the testing clock continues to run, whether or not you're working on the test.
- Test takers are subject to disqualification and expulsion for failing to follow the procedural rules, for disturbing others during the test, or for cheating.

After completion of the timed test, the exam supervisor will collect all answer sheets and exam booklets. The total running time of Test 473 is 129 minutes (2 hours, 9 minutes). Allowing for the pretest and posttest procedures, you can expect to spend up to 3 hours at the test site.

After the Test—Your Rating on the Entrance Register

After the test, your answer sheet will be sent to the National Test Administration Center for scoring. Within about four weeks, you'll be notified by mail of your test score and whether you qualify for postal employment based on the results. Any score of 70 or above on the 0 to 100 scale is considered a qualifying score for Test 473. If you fail to attain a passing score of 70 on the exam, you do not qualify to continue with the hiring process; if you still wish to pursue postal employment, you'll need to start over by applying to take the exam again during a later vacancy-announcement period.

A passing score qualifies you to continue with the hiring process, but it is no guarantee of a job with the Postal Service. Assuming that you qualify, your name will be listed on the Postal Service's *entrance register*, along with the names of all other applicants who qualified by passing the same test during the same announcement period. The register rates all such applicants numerically in descending order, except for disabled military veterans, who are placed at the top of the list (and ranked amongst themselves separately), ahead of all other applicants.

Other military veterans receive either 5 or 10 additional rating points, depending on the length of their military service and certain other factors. Among all applicants other than disabled veterans, preference is given to veterans over other applicants receiving the same final rating after veteran preference points are added. For example, among three applicants with the same rating, if one is a military veteran, that applicant will be placed ahead of the other two applicants on the register.

As job positions become available, the Postal Service selects applicants from the top of the entrance register and notifies them of how to proceed with the next step in the hiring process.

> Between 1833 and 1836, when he was in his mid-twenties, Abraham Lincoln served as postmaster of the town of New Salem, Illinois. The town's residents customarily picked up their mail, which arrived once a week, at the post office in New Salem. However, Lincoln often delivered mail personally, usually in his hat, to the homes of residents who could not pick up their mail.

Note: During the hiring process, the Postal Service is required to give preferences to military veterans under the Veterans' Preference Act of 1944.

General Test-Taking Strategies

Later in this book, you'll learn specific techniques and tips for each part of Test 473. Right now, however, let's take a look at some basic strategies that apply to most or all parts of the test.

Avoid Random Guesswork in Parts A, C, and D

On Parts A and C, 1/3 point is deducted for every incorrect answer. However, no deduction is made for unanswered questions. So, there's no advantage to making a random guess on any question in these two parts of the exam. For every question, try to at least narrow down the choices to improve your odds of a correct answer. If you're running out of time, leave the questions you don't have time for blank.

This same strategy also applies to Part D, Personal Characteristics and Experience Inventory. Even though the scoring system for Part D is unknown, you should assume that you will be penalized for answers that the test makers determine are "incorrect." So, if you run out of time before considering all 236 questions in Part D, just leave the remaining questions blank.

Consider Random Guesswork for Part B—but *Only* If You're Running Out of Time

You won't be penalized for incorrect answers in Part B, Forms Completion. In other words, in calculating your score for Part B, the test makers make no point deduction for any wrong answers. Therefore, during this part, if you haven't attempted all the questions and you are about to run out of time, by all means take random guesses at the remaining questions—the ones that you don't have time to consider. On your answer sheet, quickly fill in the blanks for those questions before the time allowed expires. Also, go back and fill in a bubble for every question you skipped without marking an answer on the answer sheet.

Don't Be Afraid to Mark Up Your Test Booklet

During the exam, you're allowed to write in your test booklet as much as you want to. In fact, just before the timed test commences, the exam supervisor will inform you and your fellow test takers that you can do so. However, nothing that you write in your test booklet will be considered in scoring your exam. All that matters to the test makers is how you've marked your answer sheet. In fact, after the exam session, the test makers will simply shred the test booklets.

You'll learn later in this book that making the right kind of marks in your test booklet can improve your accuracy and your speed during the exam. As you attempt the practice drills and tests in this book, learn to be comfortable using your pencil to mark up the pages that contain the test questions.

Develop a System for Marking Your Answer Sheet

Test 473 contains many, many questions—a grand total of 398—which means that there are a whole lot of bubbles to fill in on your answer sheet. Try imagining yourself shifting your attention away from your test booklet and to your answer sheet after answering each and every question, locating the line of bubbles that corresponds to the particular question you just answered, filling in the bubble, and then returning your attention to the test booklet. Now, imagine doing that 398 times during the course of the exam! You would waste a lot of time going back and forth between the booklet and the answer sheet, precious time that you could put to far better use actually working on the questions. More importantly, as you'll learn later in this book, it pays to focus your uninterrupted attention on the questions as much as possible.

So, rather than constantly bouncing back and forth between the test booklet and your answer sheet, mark your answers to groups of perhaps 10 or 15 questions directly in your test booklet by simply circling your letter choice (A, B, C, or D) for each one. Then, after making your selections for all questions in the group, go to the answer sheet and fill in the corresponding bubbles for that group.

However, do *not* take this strategy to its extreme and wait until you have selected your choices for all the questions in an entire part of the test before filling in the answer sheet for that part. Why not? Well, think about it. Following this strategy would spell disaster if you happened to run out of time before you were able to fill in all the bubbles on your answer sheet. Remember, the test makers won't give you any credit for marking the correct answers in your test booklet. All that matters is how you've marked your answer sheet.

Note: Later in this book, when you study each part of the test in depth, you'll learn how best to divide questions into logical groups for the purpose of marking your answer sheet.

Pace Yourself Properly, So That You Have Time to Check Your Answers

This book contains ample practice drills and tests to allow you to determine your optimal pace, the pace that allows you to consider each and every question while leaving enough time to go back and check your answers. Use the following guidelines as a starting point in finding your proper pace.

Part A: Address Checking

You have 11 minutes to answer 60 questions. Try to answer 30 questions and fill in your answer sheet for those questions during the first 4 minutes. Check the clock after the first 30 questions to see if you're on pace. If so, try to answer the remaining 30 questions and fill in the answer sheet for them in 4 minutes. That will leave you 3 minutes to go back and review your answers. Be sure to use this time to make sure you have transferred your selections from your test booklet to the answer sheet correctly.

Part B: Forms Completion

You have 15 minutes to answer 30 questions. Questions in this part are divided into approximately five groups of 5 to 7 questions per group.

Try to answer the first three groups of questions (approximately 18 questions) and fill in the answer sheet for them in 7 minutes. Check the clock to see if you're on pace. If so, try to answer the two remaining groups of questions (approximately 12 questions in total) and fill in the answer sheet for them in 5 minutes. That will leave you 3 minutes to go back and review your answers. Be sure to use this time to make sure you have transferred your selections from your test booklet to the answer sheet correctly. Also use this time to go back and reconsider any questions that you weren't sure about the first time around.

The design of U.S. postage stamps is overseen by the Citizens' Stamp Advisory Committee (CSAC), a 15-member group appointed by the Postmaster General and made up of experts in a variety of fields, ranging from history, science, and art to education, sports, and other subjects of public interest. Each year, the CSAC receives approximately 50,000 stamp proposals! For commemorative stamps, the CSAC will consider only events, persons, and themes of widespread national appeal and significance. The Postmaster General makes the final decisions on which stamps will be issued, based on the committee's recommendations.

Part C: Coding and Memory

During the scored segment of the Coding Section, you have 6 minutes to answer 36 questions. Try to answer 18 questions and fill in the answer sheet for them in 2 minutes. Check the clock to see if you're on pace. If so, try to answer the remaining 18 questions and fill in the answer sheet for them in 2 minutes. That will leave you 2 minutes to go back and review your answers. Be sure to use this time to make sure you have transferred your selections from your test booklet to the answer sheet correctly.

During the scored segment of the Memory Section, you have 7 minutes to answer 36 questions. Try to answer 18 questions and fill in the answer sheet for them in 3 minutes. Check the clock to see if you're on pace. If so, try to answer the remaining 18 questions and fill in the answer sheet for them in 3 minutes. That will leave you 1 minute to go back and review your answers. Be sure to use this time to make sure you have transferred your selections from your test booklet to the answer sheet correctly.

Part D: Personal Characteristics and Experience Inventory

You have 90 minutes to answer 236 questions, or approximately 25 seconds per question. Part D is divided into two sections: Personal Characteristics (160 questions) and Experience (76 questions)

These two sections are *not* timed separately. Try answering the questions in groups of 30, spending no more than 10 minutes on answering each group of 30 questions. (This time includes transferring your responses to the answer sheet.) At this pace, here's your time schedule for Part D:

Question Numbers	Total Time Elapsed
1–30	10 minutes
31–60	20 minutes
61–90	30 minutes
91–120	40 minutes
121–150	50 minutes
151–180	60 minutes
181–210	70 minutes
211–236	80 minutes

At the pace of 30 questions every 10 minutes, you'll have 10 minutes to go back and check your answers to the questions in Part D. If you don't think that's enough time, adjust the schedule so that you work through the questions at a slightly faster pace.

Note: Our suggested pace for each of the four parts is merely a starting point for you. As you attempt the practice tests later in this book, adjust your pace according to what works best for you.

Address Checking

Part A of Test 473 is called *Address Checking*. This part of the exam will present 60 *correct* addresses and ZIP codes, numbered 1 through 60. To the right of each address and ZIP code, another address and ZIP code will appear. The two should be the same, but the one on the right may contain one or more errors; in other words, it might not match the correct address on the left exactly. Your job is to determine whether there are any errors and, if so, whether the error is in the address, the ZIP code, or both.

The official directions for Part A, Address Checking, are essentially as follows:

Directions

Part A of this test consists of 60 items for you to complete in 11 minutes. You will be shown a **Correct List** of addresses and ZIP codes alongside a **List to Be Checked**. The two lists should contain the same addresses and ZIP codes, except that the **List to Be Checked** may contain errors.

Each row of information consists of one item. For each item, compare the address and ZIP code in the **Correct List** with the address and ZIP code in the **List to Be Checked**. Determine whether there are **No Errors**, an error in **Address Only**, an error in **ZIP Code Only**, or an error in **Both** the address and the ZIP code. Select an answer from the following four choices:

A. No Errors	B. Address Only	C. ZIP Code Only	D. Both

Mark your answer (A, B, C, or D) on your answer sheet.

Here's how the Correct List and the List to Be Checked will appear in your test booklet. This sample provides five address pairs (numbered 1 through 5), but keep in mind that you'll see 60 pairs (numbered 1 through 60) on the actual test.

	Correct List			List to Be Checked	
	Address	*ZIP Code*		*Address*	*ZIP Code*
1.	400 Racine Rd. Milwaukee, WI	53205		400 Racine Dr. Milwaukee, WI	53205
2.	12 Estuary Court Springfield, MO	65804		12 Estuary Court Springfield, MO	65804
3.	20040 S. Parkway Blvd. Albany, NY	12209-0887		20040 S. Parkway Blvd. Albany, NY	12209-0337
4.	8967 F Street, Suite 128 Pensacola, FL	32501		8967 F Street, Suite 128 Pensecola, FL	32501
5.	PO Box 56824 Sacramento, CA	95832-0166		PO Box 56824 Sacramento, CO	95823-0166

This sample list illustrates the following key features of the Address Checking format:

■ State names are always given in their abbreviated two-letter form.
■ Some ZIP codes contain only five digits, while others include the four-digit extension as well.
■ Most addresses refer to streets, but a few of the 60 addresses will be Post Office (PO) Box numbers instead.
■ Some addresses will include units such as a suite or apartment number, but most will not.
■ All 60 items are U.S. addresses. No foreign addresses appear in Part A (or in any other part of Test 473).

The correct answer to Item 1 is **B**. The address to be checked uses *Dr.* in place of *Rd.* The two ZIP codes match exactly. So, there is an error in the address only.

The correct answer to Item 2 is **A**. The address and ZIP code to be checked match the correct address and ZIP code exactly, and so there are no errors.

The correct answer to Item 3 is **C**. The two addresses match exactly. However, the ZIP code to be checked does not match the correct ZIP code. (Notice that 88 in the four-digit extension has been replaced with 33.) So, there is an error in the ZIP code only.

The correct answer to Item 4 is **B**. The correct city name (*Pensacola*) is changed to *Pensecola* in the address to be checked. (An *a* has been replaced by an *e*.) The two ZIP codes match exactly. So, there is an error in the address only.

The correct answer to Item 5 is **D**. The address to be checked changes the two-letter state abbreviation *CA* to *CO*. The ZIP code to be checked switches the *2* and *3*. So, there is an error both in the address and in the ZIP code.

Types of Errors to Look For

In the preceding examples, you saw several different kinds of errors in the List to Be Checked. These are just some of the types of errors you'll encounter on your exam. Here's a complete list of what to look for in the List to Be Checked.

Names

■ Misspelling the name of a street or city (for example, changing Johnson to Johnston)
■ Changing the name of a street or city (for example, Fairmont to Fairview)
■ Changing a street type (for example, Road to Drive or Avenue to Street)
■ Abbreviating a word (for example, *Suite* to *Ste.* or *Drive* to *Dr.*) or changing an abbreviation to the completed word (for example, changing *Rd.* to *Road* or *Hwy.* to *Highway*)

Numbers

■ Switching two digits in a street address, ZIP code, or other number (for example, changing 11791 to 11719)
■ Adding or omitting a digit in a number (for example, changing 43 to 430)
■ Changing one digit in a number (for example, 583 to 588)

Sometimes, you'll find more than one error in an address (apart from the ZIP code). Here's an example in which there's an error on both the first address line and the second address line:

Correct List	List to Be Checked
4980 West 13th Ave. Wheat Ridge, CO 80033	4980 East 13th Ave. White Ridge, CO 80033

Most often, however, an address will contain one error at most.

Types of Errors *Not* to Look For

Punctuation

Punctuation is not tested. Abbreviations such as *Ave.*, *Blvd.*, and *Ste.* may or may not be followed by a period, but you won't find any punctuation discrepancies between the correct addresses and the addresses to be checked. So don't waste time looking for them.

Capitalization

Capitalization is not tested. Don't waste time looking for capitalization errors (for example, *Los angeles* or *main Street*) in the List to Be Checked, because you won't find any.

Incorrect ZIP Codes

You do not need to know which ZIP codes go with which cities. In each address, the five-digit ZIP code will be an actual ZIP code for the city that's named. You're not being tested on whether ZIP codes are proper matches for cities—just on whether the ZIP codes in the right-hand list match the ones in the left-hand list.

Types of Errors That Are Easily Overlooked

Cities—Spelling Errors

You'll recognize many, if not most, of the cities in the list. Spelling errors such as *New Yorck*, *Los Angels*, *Chicogo*, and *Miamie* will jump off the page at you. However, spelling errors involving some other well-known cities are remarkably easy to overlook, especially if the misspelled version "sounds" correct if you read it phonetically. For example, many test takers would miss the spelling errors in the right-hand column below:

Correct List
Duluth, MN
Boise, ID
Minneapolis, MN
Cincinnati, OH
Ann Arbor, MI

List to Be Checked
Deluth, MN
Boisie, ID
Mineapolis, MN
Cincinatti, OH
Anne Arbor, MI

Also, expect to see some cities and towns that are less well known or have unusual names. Inspect the spelling of these city and town names *very* carefully. Many test takers will overlook spelling errors such as the ones in the right-hand column below:

Correct List
Kalamazoo, MI
Pocatello, ID
Puyallup, WA
Juneau, AK
Schenectady, NY
Elkhart, IN

List to Be Checked
Kalamozoo, MI
Pocattelo, ID
Pullayup, WA
Juno, AK
Schenektady, NY
Elkardt, IN

Street Names That Look or Sound Similar

In the List to Be Checked, be on the lookout for pairs of street names that look or sound a lot alike, but aren't exactly the same. Here are some typical examples:

Correct List
9th Street
Fifth Ave.
Johnson Drive
Harrington Bridge Road

List to Be Checked
90th Street
Fourth Ave.
Johnstown Drive
Harrington Ridge Road

Note: On the exam, you won't see discrepancies such as the one between *9th Street* and *Ninth Street*. Why not? Because there's no error either way—they're just two different ways of naming the same street.

Street Names—Compass Directions

Pay close attention to street-name compass directions: North (N.), South (S.), East (E.), and West (W.), and also NE, NW, SE, and SW. You're sure to encounter at least two or three errors involving compass directions, as in the following examples:

Correct List	List to Be Checked
233 N. 22nd Street	233 S. 22nd Street
19920 SW Radcliffe Road	19920 SE Radcliffe Road
55 Boundary Blvd. NE	55 Boundary Blvd. SE
5757 South Yucca Avenue	5757 North Yucca Avenue
112 Illinois Drive, Suite 234	112 E. Illinois Drive, Suite 234

Street Names—Is It a "Road" or a "Drive"?

Pay close attention to whatever follows a street name on the first line of an address, such as the words listed below.

Most Common	Less Common
Street (St.)	Court (Ct.)
Road (Rd.)	Circle (Cir.)
Drive (Dr.)	Lane (Ln.)
Boulevard (Blvd.)	Way
Avenue (Ave.)	Terrace
	Place
	Suite (Ste.)
	Apartment (Apt.)

Look especially for *Rd.* (*Road*) confused with *Dr.* (*Drive*) and for *Ct.* (*Court*) confused with *Cir.* (*Circle*). Abbreviated versions are easier to overlook because they're briefer. Here are some examples of these sorts of errors:

Correct List	List to Be Checked
9230 W. Granger Rd.	9230 W. Granger Dr.
25 Babcock Ct.	25 Babcock Cir.
767 N. Yamhill Ridge	767 N. Yamhill Road
112 Timpuhaqua Lake	112 Timpuhaqua Lane
340 Lookout Mountain	340 Lookout Mountain Rd.

Remember: You won't be tested on punctuation, so there's no need to inspect for periods (or missing periods) after abbreviations.

Is It "Kansas City, KS" or "Kansas City, MO"?

Some well-known cities share their names with cities in one or more other states. One of the test maker's favorite ploys is to list the same city, but different states. If you're not careful, you can easily overlook this type of error, especially if the city and state in the List to Be Checked is well known, as in the following examples:

From the year 1900 to the year 2000, the annual volume of U.S. mail increased almost 30-fold, from 7,129,990,000 pieces in 1900 to 207,882,200,000 (almost 208 billion) pieces in 2000. However, the same time period saw a decline in the total number of U.S. Post Offices—from 76,688 in 1900 to 27,876 in 2000.

Correct List
Kansas City, MO
Miami, OH
Rochester, MN
Portland, ME

List to Be Checked
Kansas City, KS
Miami, FL
Rochester, NY
Portland, OR

Address-Checking Strategies

Check Each Part of Each Address Separately

An address and ZIP code may consist of as many as seven distinct parts:

- The number preceding a street name (or the P.O. Box number)
- The street name
- Apartment or suite number (if any)
- City
- Two-letter state abbreviation
- Five-digit ZIP code
- Four-digit ZIP code extension (if any)

Many test takers will read an entire two-line address before inspecting the address to be checked, and all nine digits of a nine-digit ZIP code before inspecting the ZIP code to be checked. The problem with this method is that it can be difficult to remember all that information, and so the possibility of making an address-checking mistake is high. So, for each address, you should check each element of the preceding list separately and in the order listed. For example, first check the number preceding a street name or the number of a P.O. box. Then proceed down the list, finally checking the ZIP code extension if there is one.

In addition to decreasing the chances of overlooking an error, checking each part separately will save you time. How? Once you find an error in an address, there's no need to check the other parts of the address. For example, consider the following address:

Correct List
39810 West Gambol Street, Ste. 9
Scottsbluff, NE

List to Be Checked
39801 West Gambol Street, Ste. 9
Scottsbluff, NE

By initially inspecting only the very first part of this address, the number preceding the street name (in this example, 39810 and 39801), you discover right away that there's an error in the address to be checked (right column), and so you can ignore the rest of the address's first line and the entire second line. It doesn't matter whether there are any other address errors. You know that there's at least one error in the address, *and that's all you need to know*. The correct answer choice must be either B or D, and all that's left for you to do is check the ZIP code. That's a real time saver!

Similarly, for ZIP codes that contain nine digits, you should focus initially just on the first five digits. For example, consider this pair of ZIP codes:

Correct List	**List to Be Checked**
69361-0633	69391-0633

Focus initially on just the first five digits, and you'll immediately see an error (in this example, 69361 and 69391). This means that you can ignore the four-digit extension. It doesn't matter whether the extension contains any errors. You know there's at least one error in the ZIP code, *and that's all you need to know*.

Use Your Fingers to Point to Addresses as You're Checking Them

When you first learned to read in school, your teacher probably told you not to use your finger to help you read. Well, forget that advice for Test 473! As you check each part of an address, use your left-hand index finger (or pencil) to point to the correct address, and your right-hand index finger (or pencil) to point to the address to be checked. Put your fingers right on the paper, just below the part you're checking. This method helps you focus, and it ensures that you compare matching parts of the same address.

Mark Errors with Your Pencil as You Find Them

In the address to be checked, circle or underline errors as you find them. When you go back and check all your answers, you can easily check what you've marked against the correct version.

Do you know what each digit in a ZIP code means? The first digit in any five-digit ZIP code denotes a broad geographical region, from 0 (zero) for the Northeast to 9 for the Far West. The second and third digits pinpoint population and transportation hubs, while the fourth and fifth digits designate small post offices or postal zones in larger zoned cities. The additional four digits pinpoint an even smaller geographic segment. The sixth and seventh numbers denote a group of streets or blocks, post office boxes, or office buildings, or even a single large office or apartment building. The final two digits denote even smaller segments, such as a city block; a single building, floor, or department; or a specific P.O. Box number. By the way, the five-digit ZIP code has been in use since the early 1960s. The ZIP + 4 system has been in use since 1983.

Mark Your Answer Choices in Groups on the Answer Sheet

Marking your answer sheet after each one of the 60 test items means that you'll be constantly moving back and forth between your test booklet and your answer sheet. This can be time-consuming and distracting, and it can also contribute to eyestrain. Instead, check addresses in groups of perhaps 10 at a time, and then fill in your answer sheet for each address group as you go:

- Look for errors in lines 1 through 10, marking errors in your test booklet as you find them. Then, fill in numbers 1 through 10 on your answer sheet.
- Repeat this procedure for lines 11 through 20.
- Repeat this procedure for lines 21 through 30.
- Repeat this procedure for lines 31 through 40.
- Repeat this procedure for lines 41 through 50.
- Repeat this procedure for lines 51 through 60.

Pace Yourself So You Have Enough Time to Check Your Answers

You have 11 minutes to check 60 addresses. That's more than enough time. In fact, most test takers can finish in half that time. So, pace yourself so that you can finish in about 6 minutes (that includes filling in the answer sheet). Then, use the remaining 5 minutes to go through all 60 items again. Correct any mistakes you made the first time through.

Address-Checking Practice Drills

Now it's time to put the strategies you've learned in this chapter to work. Here you'll find five practice drills. The first three are simpler than the Address Checking portion of the actual exam. Practice Drills 1 through 3 are each designed to help you improve your speed and accuracy in performing a certain aspect of address checking. After attempting Drills 1 through 3, you'll be ready for Drill 4, a shortened version of the Address Checking section of the exam, and then finally for Drill 5, which is exactly like Part A (Address Checking) of the actual exam.

Note: During each practice drill, it's important that you limit yourself strictly to the suggested time limit. Only in Practice Drill 5 are the number of questions and the time limit the same as on the actual exam.

An answer key for each drill is given at the end of the chapter.

Practice Drill 1

Directions: Practice Drill 1 consists of 50 items for you to complete in 5 minutes. You will be shown a **Correct List** of addresses (but no cities, states, or ZIP codes) alongside a **List to Be Checked**. For each item, compare the two addresses. If there are no errors, circle **NO ERROR**. If there are any errors, circle **ERROR**.

Note: The format of this Practice Drill is not the same as the Address Checking format on Test 473. This drill is designed to help build confidence, speed, and accuracy in address checking.

Number of Items: 50

Time: 5 minutes

	Correct List	**List to Be Checked**		
1.	506 Ranger Rd.	506 Range Rd.	ERROR	NO ERROR
2.	1101 W. Fairlawn	11010 W. Fairlawn	ERROR	NO ERROR
3.	1202 Fourth Avenue	1202 Fourth Avenue	ERROR	NO ERROR
4.	31 Denke Lane	31 Denke Lane	ERROR	NO ERROR
5.	40090 Hwy. 7 NE	40090 Hwy. 7 SE	ERROR	NO ERROR
6.	82688 Chapparal Rd.	82688 Chapparal Rd.	ERROR	NO ERROR
7.	577 Chase Circle	575 Chase Circle	ERROR	NO ERROR
8.	33210 North Lindsay	33210 North Lindsay	ERROR	NO ERROR
9.	PO Box 71101	PO Box 7101	ERROR	NO ERROR
10.	20 Cherot County Rd.	20 Chevot County Rd.	ERROR	NO ERROR
11.	1373 Jasper Loop #14	1373 Jasper Loop #14	ERROR	NO ERROR
12.	9505 Greenwood St.	9505 Greenwood St.	ERROR	NO ERROR
13.	90 Camino Palmera	90 Camino Palmera	ERROR	NO ERROR
14.	409 N. Atlantic Drive	409 N. Atlantis Drive	ERROR	NO ERROR
15.	141 E. Santa Lucia Ct.	141 E. Santa Lucia Ct.	ERROR	NO ERROR
16.	11223 Baskerville Avenue	11223 Baskerville Drive	ERROR	NO ERROR
17.	12 Saint Croix Way #113	12 Saint Croix Way #13	ERROR	NO ERROR
18.	19 N. 22nd Street	19 N. 32nd Street	ERROR	NO ERROR
19.	22944 Roosevelt Parkway NE	22944 Roosevelt Parkway NE	ERROR	NO ERROR
20.	250 Henry Dade Blvd.	250 Henry Dave Blvd.	ERROR	NO ERROR
21.	508 Ralston Place, Suite 18	508 Ralston Place, Floor 18	ERROR	NO ERROR
22.	1209 Spiegel Park, West Tower	1209 Spiegel Park, West Tower	ERROR	NO ERROR
23.	1807 Lawrence Court	1807 Lawrence Court	ERROR	NO ERROR
24.	198 Country Club Way	198 County Club Way	ERROR	NO ERROR
25.	Post Office Box 39397	Post Office Box 39397	ERROR	NO ERROR
26.	575 Rainbow Terrace	757 Rainbow Terrace	ERROR	NO ERROR
27.	30 Bandon Cir. #27	30 Bandon Ct. #27	ERROR	NO ERROR
28.	6611 Avenue of the Pines	6111 Avenue of the Pines	ERROR	NO ERROR
29.	301 1st Street, Suite 311	301 1st Street, Suite 311	ERROR	NO ERROR
30.	62120 North State Highway	62120 North State Highway	ERROR	NO ERROR
31.	199 Andreson Road, Apt. 21	199 Anderson Road, Apt. 21	ERROR	NO ERROR
32.	84 Dickerson Drive	84 Dickerson Drive	ERROR	NO ERROR

continued on next page

	Correct List	List to Be Checked		
33.	1260 Rowling Hills Estates	1260 Rolling Hills Estates	ERROR	NO ERROR
34.	7061 S. Louis St., Apt. 606	7061 St. Louis St., Apt. 606	ERROR	NO ERROR
35.	83 Cleveland Heights Circle	88 Cleveland Heights Circle	ERROR	NO ERROR
36.	2705 East 49th Avenue, Suite 2	2705 East 49th Avenue, Suite 2	ERROR	NO ERROR
37.	239 W. 134th St.	239 W. 139th St.	ERROR	NO ERROR
38.	22124 Chelsea Ave. #23	22124 Chelsea Ave. #23	ERROR	NO ERROR
39.	663 S. Quebec St.	663 S. Quebec St.	ERROR	NO ERROR
40.	2280 Barrows Road	2280 Barrows Road	ERROR	NO ERROR
41.	9 S. Hampshire Avenue	90 S. Hampshire Avenue	ERROR	NO ERROR
42.	961 Shady Creek Ln.	961 Shady Creek Ln.	ERROR	NO ERROR
43.	8323 SW Oahu Blvd.	8233 SW Oahu Blvd.	ERROR	NO ERROR
44.	P.O. Box 158	P.O. Box 158	ERROR	NO ERROR
45.	8728 Front Street	8728 Flint Street	ERROR	NO ERROR
46.	12413 Marcus Road	12413 Marcus Road	ERROR	NO ERROR
47.	7283 South P Ave.	7283 North P Ave.	ERROR	NO ERROR
48.	49 Peugot Circle Apt. 7	49 Peugot Circle Apt. 7	ERROR	NO ERROR
49.	24100 U.S. Highway 24	24100 U.S. Highway 42	ERROR	NO ERROR
50.	467 Ziegler Drive #9	467 Ziegler Drive #9	ERROR	NO ERROR

Practice Drill 2

Directions: Practice Drill 2 consists of 50 items for you to complete in 5 minutes. You will be shown a **Correct List** of addresses (city, state, and ZIP code only) alongside a **List to Be Checked**. For each item, compare the two addresses. If there are no errors, circle **NO ERROR**. If there are any errors, circle **ERROR**.

Note: The format of this Practice Drill is *not* the same as the Address Checking format on Test 473. This drill is designed to help build confidence, speed, and accuracy in address checking.

Number of Items: 50

Time: 5 minutes

	Correct List	List to Be Checked		
1.	Crane Hill, AL 35053	Crane Hill, AL 35053	ERROR	NO ERROR
2.	Panhandle, TX 79068	Panhandle, FL 79068	ERROR	NO ERROR
3.	Ashwaubenon, WI 54304	Ashwaubonon, WI 54304	ERROR	NO ERROR
4.	Kalskag, AK 99607	Kalskag, AK 96607	ERROR	NO ERROR
5.	Las Cruces, NM 88005	Las Cruces, MN 88005	ERROR	NO ERROR
6.	Bodega Bay, CA 94923	Bodega Bay, CA 94923	ERROR	NO ERROR
7.	Sandborn, IN 47578	Sandborn, IN 47758	ERROR	NO ERROR
8.	East Longmeadow, MA 01028	East Longmeddow, MA 01028	ERROR	NO ERROR
9.	Efland, NC 27243	Elfand, NC 27243	ERROR	NO ERROR
10.	Pocono Pines, PA 18350	Pocono Pines, PA 18350	ERROR	NO ERROR
11.	Seatac, WA 98158	Seattle, WA 98158	ERROR	NO ERROR
12.	Sarasota, FL 34233	Sarasota, FL 34233	ERROR	NO ERROR
13.	Medina, NY 14103	Medina, NY 19103	ERROR	NO ERROR
14.	Jerico Springs, MO 64756	Jerico Springs, MO 64756	ERROR	NO ERROR
15.	Telluride, CO 81435	Telluride, CO 81455	ERROR	NO ERROR
16.	Decatur, IL 62521	Decatur, IL 62521	ERROR	NO ERROR
17.	Ocean City, NJ 08226	Ocean City, NJ 08226	ERROR	NO ERROR
18.	Allenhurst, GA 31301	Allenhurst, CA 31301	ERROR	NO ERROR
19.	Research Triangle, NC 27713	Research Triangle, NC 27713	ERROR	NO ERROR
20.	Billings Heights, MT 59105	Billings Heights, MT 59105	ERROR	NO ERROR
21.	Niagara, ND 58266	Niagara, ND 58662	ERROR	NO ERROR
22.	Norwich, VT 05055	Norwitch, VT 05055	ERROR	NO ERROR
23.	Henderson, IA 51541	Henderson, LA 51541	ERROR	NO ERROR
24.	Broken Bow, NE 68822	Broken Bow, NE 68822	ERROR	NO ERROR
25.	Castaic, CA 91384	Castaic, CA 91384	ERROR	NO ERROR
26.	Poland, OH 44514-0098	Poland, OH 44514-0998	ERROR	NO ERROR
27.	McCombs, KY 41454-4772	McCombs, KY 41545-4772	ERROR	NO ERROR
28.	Gardnerville, NV 89410-1029	Gardnerville, NV 89410-1029	ERROR	NO ERROR
29.	Lawton, KS 66781-4463	Lawton, KY 66781-4463	ERROR	NO ERROR
30.	Hillsboro, NH 03244-5522	Hillsboro, NH 03244-5522	ERROR	NO ERROR
31.	Tupelo, MS 38801-0011	Tupelo, MO 38801-0011	ERROR	NO ERROR

continued on next page

	Correct List	**List to Be Checked**		
32.	Knoxville, TN 37924-2875	Knoxville, TN 37924-2875	ERROR	NO ERROR
33.	East Syracuse, NY 13057-3005	East Syracuase, NY 13057-3005	ERROR	NO ERROR
34.	Shelbyville, MI 49344-2626	Shelbyville, MI 49344-2626	ERROR	NO ERROR
35.	Fort Ritchie, MD 21719-7844	Fort Ritchie, MD 21719-7834	ERROR	NO ERROR
36.	Mount Lookout, WV 26678-1456	Mount Lookout, WV 26678-1456	ERROR	NO ERROR
37.	Coventry, RI 02816-8641	Coventry, RI 02861-8641	ERROR	NO ERROR
38.	Beaverton, OR 97005-1946	Beaverton, OR 97002-1946	ERROR	NO ERROR
39.	Charleston, SC 29418-7735	Charleston, SC 29418-7735	ERROR	NO ERROR
40.	Cape Neddick, ME 03902-3779	Cape Neddick, ME 03902-3779	ERROR	NO ERROR
41.	Sioux Falls, SD 57104-2282	Sioux Falls, SC 57104-2282	ERROR	NO ERROR
42.	Tucson, AZ 85708-1739	Tuscon, AZ 85708-1739	ERROR	NO ERROR
43.	Pocatello, ID 83201-9472	Pocatello, ID 83201-9472	ERROR	NO ERROR
44.	Honolulu, HI 96814-2847	Honolulu, HI 96814-2877	ERROR	NO ERROR
45.	Bessemer, AL 35020-3048	Bessemer, AL 35020-3048	ERROR	NO ERROR
46.	Avon, CT 06001-2992	Avon, VT 06001-2992	ERROR	NO ERROR
47.	Thayne, WY 12783-2987	Thayne, WY 12783-2987	ERROR	NO ERROR
48.	Hockessin, DE 19707-0449	Hocksesin, DE 19707-0449	ERROR	NO ERROR
49.	Fairfax, VA 22031-1166	Fairfax, VA 22031-1166	ERROR	NO ERROR
50.	Bountiful, UT 84010-8855	Bountiful, UT 84010-8855	ERROR	NO ERROR

Practice Drill 3

Directions: Practice Drill 3 consists of 50 items for you to complete in 8 minutes. You will be shown a **Correct List** of addresses (including ZIP codes) alongside a **List to Be Checked**. For each item, compare the two addresses. If there are no errors, circle **NO ERROR**. If there are any errors, circle **ERROR**.

Note: The format of this Practice Drill is *not* the same as the Address Checking format on Test 473. This drill is designed to help build confidence, speed, and accuracy in address checking.

Number of Items: 50

Time: 8 minutes

	Correct List	**List to Be Checked**		
1.	4948 Goode Ave. Big Rapids, MI 49307	4948 Goode Ave. Big Rapids, MN 49307	ERROR	NO ERROR
2.	12 Fandango Blvd. #4 Plano, TX 75024	12 Fandango Blvd. #4 Plano, TX 75024	ERROR	NO ERROR
3.	204 Front Street Asbury, WV 24916	204 First Street Asbury, WV 24916	ERROR	NO ERROR
4.	228 Fernview Court Cleveland, AL 35049	228 Fernview Court Cleveland, AL 32049	ERROR	NO ERROR
5.	12 Barker's Pass Road Binghamton, NY 13905	12 Barker's Pass Road Binghamton, NY 13905	ERROR	NO ERROR
6.	9088 Blanchard Court, Apt. 14 Ukiah, CA 95482	9088 Blanchard Court, Apt. 14 Ukiah, CA 95482	ERROR	NO ERROR
7.	17-B 12th Street Anderson, IN 46012	17-B 12th Street Anderson, MN 46012	ERROR	NO ERROR
8.	Post Office Box 2257 Worcester, MA 01603	Post Office Box 2557 Worcester, MA 01603	ERROR	NO ERROR
9.	590 Friar Court, Suite 8 Tamassee, SC 29686	590 Friar Court, Suite 8 Tamassee, SC 29686	ERROR	NO ERROR
10.	5099 S. 82nd Ave. Suite 12 Philadelphia, PA 19114	50996 82nd Ave. Suite 12 Philadelphia, PA 19114	ERROR	NO ERROR
11.	440 Highland Park Bellevue, WA 98005	440 Highland Park Bellevue, WA 98005	ERROR	NO ERROR
12.	39 Koloa Street Kekaha, HI 96752	39 Koloa Street Kekaha, HI 96752	ERROR	NO ERROR
13.	45 Flatbush Court, Apt. 8 Bronx, NY 10473	45 Flatbush Court, Apt. 8 Bronx, NY 10473	ERROR	NO ERROR
14.	550 Gracie Street Florissant, MO 63031	550 Grace Street Florissant, MO 63031	ERROR	NO ERROR
15.	44040 Overpass Road, Suite 220 Denver, CO 80219	44040 Overpass Road, Suite 220 Denver, CO 80219	ERROR	NO ERROR
16.	3005 West 123rd Street Wilmington, DE 19805	3005 West 123rd Street Wilmington, DE 19895	ERROR	NO ERROR
17.	2003 Industry Park #300 East Orange, NJ 07017	2003 Industry Park #300 East Orange, NJ 07017	ERROR	NO ERROR
18.	28 Third Street Boulder City, NV 89005	28 Third Street Boulder City, NY 89005	ERROR	NO ERROR
19.	68800 E. Brookline Blvd. Arlington, VA 22209	68880 E. Brookline Blvd. Arlington, VA 22209	ERROR	NO ERROR

continued on next page

	Correct List	List to Be Checked		
20.	6613 Jefferson Street Jackson, MS 39211	6613 Jefferson Street Jackson, MS 39211	ERROR	NO ERROR
21.	72 Butte Drive Blaisdell, ND 58718	72 Butte Road Blaisdell, ND 58718	ERROR	NO ERROR
22.	2570 Wagon Wheel Road Stockbridge, VT 05772	2570 Wagon Wheel Road Stockbridge, VT 05772	ERROR	NO ERROR
23.	3009 E. 7th Street, Ste. 12 Iowa Falls, IA 50126	3009 E. 7th Street, Apt. 12 Iowa Falls, IA 50126	ERROR	NO ERROR
24.	10039 S. State Street Layton, UT 84040	10039 S. State Street Layton, UT 84040	ERROR	NO ERROR
25.	12010 S. Beverly Boulevard Los Angeles, CA 90019	12110 S. Beverly Boulevard Los Angeles, CA 90019	ERROR	NO ERROR
26.	78833 Perimeter Drive SW Columbus, OH 43220-0988	78833 Perimeter Drive SW Columbus, OH 43220-0998	ERROR	NO ERROR
27.	355 Ridge Circle Louisville, KY 40205-3627	355 Ridge Circle Louisville, KY 40205-3627	ERROR	NO ERROR
28.	6672 Crestline Avenue Marietta, GA 30064-1662	6672 Crestline Avenue Marietta, GA 30064-1662	ERROR	NO ERROR
29.	30410 Commerce Center Drive Overland Park, KS 66204-2059	30410 Commercial Center Drive Overland Park, KS 66204-2059	ERROR	NO ERROR
30.	505 S. College Ave., Apt. 201 Amherst, NH 03031-7266	505 S. College Ave., Apt. 201 Amherst, NY 03031-7266	ERROR	NO ERROR
31.	900 N. 12th Street Moccasin, MT 59462-3399	909 N. 12th Street Moccasin, MT 59462-3399	ERROR	NO ERROR
32.	93 Erma Terrace Nashville, TN 37212-2256	93 Erma Terrace Nashville, TN 37212-2256	ERROR	NO ERROR
33.	835 Briarwood Lane Astoria, NY 11102-9045	835 Briarwood Lane Astoria, NY 11102-9045	ERROR	NO ERROR
34.	P.O. Box 203 Dearborn Heights, MI 48127-1010	P.O. Box 203 Dearborn Heights, MI 48121-7010	ERROR	NO ERROR
35.	311 Marsh Street #9 Saint Charles, MD 20602-5442	321 Marsh Street #9 Saint Charles, MD 20602-5442	ERROR	NO ERROR
36.	550 Nash Street Nekoosa, WI 54457-0206	550 Nash Street Nekoosa, WI 54457-0206	ERROR	NO ERROR
37.	35 LaPorte Court West Greenwich, RI 02817-9267	35 LaPonte Court West Greenwich, RI 02817-9267	ERROR	NO ERROR

continued on next page

	Correct List	List to Be Checked		
38.	3900 Whisper Ridge Road Portland, OR 97204-3682	3900 Whisper Ridge Road Portland, OR 97204-3682	ERROR	NO ERROR
39.	12009 Carolina Parkway Winston Salem, NC 27106-6221	12009 Carolina Parkway Winston Salem, NC 27106-6221	ERROR	NO ERROR
40.	5 Straggler Way Kittery Point, ME 03905-0047	5 Straggler Way Kittery Point, ME 03905-0047	ERROR	NO ERROR
41.	6688 E. Franklin Drive West Monroe, LA 71291-7117	6688 W. Franklin Drive West Monroe, LA 71291-7117	ERROR	NO ERROR
42.	30059 E. 13th Avenue Mesa, AZ 85204-6423	30059 E. 13th Avenue Mesa, AZ 85204-6423	ERROR	NO ERROR
43.	9482 Canyon View Rd. American Falls, ID 83211-8410	9482 Canyon View Rd. America Falls, ID 83211-8410	ERROR	NO ERROR
44.	39 Citrus Grove Lane Daytona Beach, FL 32118-3775	39 Citris Grove Lane Daytona Beach, FL 32118-3775	ERROR	NO ERROR
45.	454 Willow Glen Road Pell City, AL 35125-0099	454 Willow Glen Road Pell City, AL 35125-0099	ERROR	NO ERROR
46.	8898 N. Chase Avenue W. Hartford, CT 06107-9258	8898 N. Chase Avenue W. Hartford, CT 06107-9258	ERROR	NO ERROR
47.	13 Miners Bluff Cokeville, WY 83114-3405	13 Miners Bluff Coleville, WY 83114-3405	ERROR	NO ERROR
48.	3882 Lake Bridge Blvd. Arlington Heights, IL 60004-3389	3882 Lake Bridge Blvd. Arlington Heights, IL 60004-3689	ERROR	NO ERROR
49.	30 Sunrise Terrace Albuquerque, NM 87122-3029	30 Sunrise Terrace Albuquerque, NM 87122-3029	ERROR	NO ERROR
50.	40020 Great Prairie Highway Omaha, NE 68112-0281	40020 Grand Prairie Highway Omaha, NE 68112-0281	ERROR	NO ERROR

Practice Drill 4

Directions: Practice Drill 4 consists of 50 items to be completed in 8 minutes. You will be shown a **Correct List** of addresses (city, state, and ZIP code only) alongside a **List to Be Checked**.

Each row of information consists of one item. For each item, compare the city, state, and ZIP code in the **Correct List** with the city, state, and ZIP code in the **List to Be Checked**. Determine whether there are **No Errors**, an error in **Address Only**, an error in **ZIP Code Only**, or an error in **Both** the address and the ZIP code. Select an answer from the following four choices:

A. No Errors	B. Address (City and State) Only	C. ZIP Code Only	D. Both

Mark your answer (A, B, C, or D) on the answer sheet at the end of this chapter.

Note: The format of this Practice Drill is similar to the Address Checking format on Test 473, *but it contains only 50 items to be checked.* This drill is designed to help build confidence, speed, and accuracy in address checking and to familiarize you with the format of Part A.

Number of Items: 50

Time: 8 minutes

A. No Errors	B. Address (City and State) Only	C. ZIP Code Only	D. Both

	Correct List		List to Be Checked	
	Address (City and State)	*ZIP Code*	*Address (City and State)*	*ZIP Code*
1.	Heber City, UT	84032	Heber City, VT	84022
2.	Needham, MA	02194	Needam, MA	02194
3.	Waterbury, CT	06710	Waterbury, CT	06710
4.	Keystone, AL	35007	Keystone, AR	35007
5.	Tulsa, OK	74128	Tulsa, OK	72128
6.	Fort Defiance, VA	24437	Fort Defense, VA	23437
7.	Johnstown, PA	15905	Johnston, PA	15905
8.	Monrovia, CA	91016	Monrovia, CA	31016
9.	Glendale, AZ	85302	Glenboro, AZ	85302
10.	Bloomsbury, NJ	08804	Bloomsbury, NJ	08804
11.	Marion, OH	43302	Marian, OH	43302
12.	East Montpelier, VT	05651	East Mountpelier, VT	05650
13.	Madison, WI	53703	Madison, WI	53203
14.	Grover, WY	83122	Grover, WY	83122
15.	Burlington, ME	04417	Burlington, MN	04417
16.	Belleville, IL	62221	Belleview, IL	62221
17.	Idaho Falls, ID	83406	Idaho Falls, ID	86403
18.	New Smyrna Beach, FL	31268	New Smyra Beach, FL	31268
19.	Oklahoma City, OK	73169	Oklahoma City, OH	73169
20.	Garland, TX	75040	Garner, TX	75004
21.	Minden, NV	89423	Minden, NM	89423
22.	Pocahontas, TN	38061	Pocahontas, TN	38061

continued on next page

A. No Errors	B. Address (City and State) Only	C. ZIP Code Only	D. Both

	Correct List		List to Be Checked	
	Address (City and State)	*ZIP Code*	*Address (City and State)*	*ZIP Code*
23.	Vergennes, IL	62994	Virginias, IL	62294
24.	Oldham, SD	57051	Oldham, ND	57011
25.	Seneca, OR	97873	Seneca, OR	87873
26.	South Webster, OH	45682-3878	South Western, OH	45682-3787
27.	Laurel Springs, NC	28644-1635	Laurel Spring, NC	28644-1635
28.	Bethlehem, KY	40007-9336	Bethlehem, KS	40077-9336
29.	Fort Leavenworth, KS	66027-0733	Fort Leavenworth, KY	66027-0733
30.	Roslyn Heights, NY	11577-1261	Roslyn Heights, NY	11577-1261
31.	Emigrant, MT	59027-8358	Emmigrant, MT	59027-8358
32.	Ewa Beach, HI	96706-5519	Ewe Beach, HI	96706-5559
33.	Beaux Arts, WA	98004-0897	Beaux Arts, WA	99804-0897
34.	Fraser, MI	48026-1874	Fraser, MI	48026-1874
35.	Cheltenham, MD	20623-3286	Cheltingham, MD	20623-3285
36.	Elkhart Lake, WI	53020-2763	Elkhart Lake, WA	53020-2763
37.	Pawtucket, RI	02860-2346	Pawtucket, RI	03860-2346
38.	Skagway, AK	99840-1163	Skagway, AK	99840-1193
39.	Cologne, MN	55322-3967	Cologne, MT	55322-3967
40.	Cheshire, CT	06410-9226	Cheshiere, CT	06410-9266
41.	Belle Chasse, LA	70037-5673	Belle Chase, LA	70037-5673
42.	Kennesaw, GA	30144-4744	Kennesaw, GA	30144-4744
43.	Soda Springs, ID	83276-1990	Soda Springs, IN	83276-0990
44.	Salisbury, NH	03268-3821	Salsbury, NH	03268-3821
45.	Carthage, AR	71725-1967	Cartilage, AR	71275-1967
46.	Colcord, WV	25048-3452	Concord, WV	25048-3452
47.	Arvada, CO	80004-0764	Arveda, CO	80004-0764
48.	Arroyo Seco, NM	87514-1468	Arroyo Seco, NM	87514-1688
49.	Audubon, IA	50025-7584	Adeubon, IA	50525-7584
50.	Indianapolis, IN	46203-1425	Indianapolis, IN	46203-1425

Practice Drill 5

Directions: Practice Drill 5 is just like the actual test, Part A (Address Checking). It consists of 60 items for you to complete in 11 minutes. You will be shown a **Correct List** of addresses and ZIP codes alongside a **List to Be Checked**. The two lists contain the same addresses and ZIP codes, except that the **List to Be Checked** may contain errors.

Each row of information consists of one item. For each item, compare the address and ZIP code in the **Correct List** with the address and ZIP code in the **List to Be Checked**. Determine whether there are **No Errors**, an error in **Address Only**, an error in **ZIP Code Only**, or an error in **Both** the address and the ZIP code. Select an answer from the following four choices:

A. No Errors	B. Address Only	C. ZIP Code Only	D. Both

Mark your answer (A, B, C, or D) on the answer sheet provided at the end of the chapter.

Number of Items: 60

Time: 11 minutes

A. No Errors	B. Address Only	C. ZIP Code Only	D. Both

	Correct List		**List to Be Checked**	

	Address	*ZIP Code*	*Address*	*ZIP Code*
1.	959 Yucca Rd. Tucson, AZ	85711	595 Yucca Rd. Tucson, AZ	85711
2.	8072 Goodrich St. Philadelphia, PA	19107	8072 Goodrich Dr. Philadelphia, PA	19107
3.	126 S. Lake Ave. Muskogee, OK	74401-5518	126 S. Lake Ave. Muskegon, OK	74401-5118
4.	4270 Route 15 Cherokee Falls, SC	29702	4270 Route 15 Cherokee Falls, SC	20792
5.	PO Box 47002 Friday Harbor, WA	98250	PO Box 47002 Friday Harbor, WA	98250
6.	39 N. Tunnel Dr. #5 Butte, MT	59750-7591	39 N. Tunnel Dr. #6 Butte, MT	59750-7511
7.	150 Academy Circle Eugene, OR	97403-9637	150 Acadamy Circle Eugene, OR	97403-9637
8.	204 Flora Ct. Lancaster, NY	14086	204 Floral Ct. Lancaster, NY	15086
9.	921 S. Davis Street Alexandria, LA	71302-0005	921 S. Davis Street Alexandria, VA	71302-0005
10.	1146 Erie Ct. Cleveland, OH	44120	1146 Erie Ct. Cleveland, OH	44110
11.	662 Forbes Drive Springfield, MA	01118	622 Forbes Drive Springfield, MA	01118
12.	1333 Meridian Ave. Bartlesville, OK	74006-0880	1333 Meridian Ave. Bartlesville, OK	74066-0880
13.	61847 Patterson St. Dickson, TN	37055	61847 Paterson St. Dickson, TN	37055
14.	3130 S. Commerce Dr. Cranston, RI	02920-3258	3130 S. Commerce Rd. Cranston, RI	02920-3228
15.	4444 Lorain Rd. Yonkers, NY	10705-9170	4444 Lorain Rd. Yonkers, NY	10057-9170
16.	59 Brockton Cir. Centertown, KY	42328-7055	59 Brockton Cir. Centertown, KY	42328-7055
17.	310 3rd Avenue, Ste. C Jersey City, NJ	07305	310 33rd Avenue, Ste. C Jersey City, NJ	07305

continued on next page

A. No Errors	B. Address Only	C. ZIP Code Only	D. Both

	Correct List			List to Be Checked	
	Address	ZIP Code		Address	ZIP Code
18.	611 Woods St. Capitola, CA	95010		611 Wood St. Capitola, CA	95010
19.	4433 E. Division Blvd. Deerfield, MI	49238-3388		4433 E. Division Blvd. Deerfield, MI	49238-2288
20.	1046 W. 134th St. Jackson, MS	39204		1046 W. 134th St. Jackson, MS	39204
21.	420 NE Wake Blvd. Green Bay, WI	54313		420 N Wake Blvd. Green Bay, WI	54313
22.	82 Holland Ter. Parkersburg, WV	26101-5033		82 Holland Ter. Parksburg, WV	26110-5033
23.	18011 Sky Park Dr. Riverton, MO	65606-4085		18011 Sky Park Rd. Riverton, MO	65606-4085
24.	28 Mule Team Trail San Angelo, TX	76904		28 Mule Team Trail San Angelo, TX	76904
25.	P.O. Box 3483 Sparks, NV	89431-3483		P.O. Box 3438 Sparks, NV	89134-3483
26.	27 Ridgeline Walk #5 Huntsville, AR	72740-3658		27 Ridgeline Way #5 Huntsville, AR	72740-3658
27.	1901 E. Ball Ave. Indianapolis, IN	46204		1901 E. Ball Ave. Indianapolis, IN	42204
28.	5909 11th St. Macon, GA	31204		5909 E. 11th St. Macon, GA	31224
29.	2255 Hammond Dr. Schenectady, NY	12305		2255 Hammond Dr. Schenectedy, NY	13205
30.	6606 Boone Rd. Grand Island, NE	68801-8428		6606 Boone Rd. Grand Island, NE	68801-3428
31.	633 Sweeney Blvd., Apt. 2 San Bernardino, CA	92407-7654		633 Sweeney Blvd., Apt. 2 San Bernadino, CA	92407-7654
32.	8550 E. 2nd St. Baltimore, MD	21229-7809		8550 E. 22nd St. Baltimore, MD	21229-7809
33.	910 Marsh St. Shungnak, AK	99773		910 Marsh St. Shungnak, AL	99733
34.	2401 Lily Ln. Nashua, NH	03062-1230		2401 Lily Ln. Nashua, NH	03262-1230

continued on next page

A. No Errors	B. Address Only	C. ZIP Code Only	D. Both

	Correct List		List to Be Checked	
	Address	ZIP Code	Address	ZIP Code
35.	26 Royal Cir. Bennington, VT	05201-0984	26 Royal Cir. Bennington, VT	05201-0984
36.	2011 Freeman Ave. #10 Philadelphia, PA	19124	2001 Freeman Ave. #10 Philadelphia, PA	19124
37.	502 S. Jackson St. Amarillo, TX	79119	502 S. Jackson Dr. Amarillo, TX	79119
38.	3663 W. 6th St. Durham, NC	27705-6549	3663 W. 6th St. Durham, NC	27705-6495
39.	1450 Frazee Rd. Chicago, IL	60606-2353	1450 Frazee Rd. Chicago, IL	60606-2353
40.	4824 18th Street Buffalo, NY	14207-4545	4824 19th Street Buffalo, NY	14207-4545
41.	6505 Finney Way Lakeland, FL	33805	6505 Finney Way Lakeland, FL	33005
42.	82 Duck Creek Fort Worth, TX	76135	28 Duck Creek Fort Worth, TX	76135
43.	P.O. Box 3554 Gary, IN	46406	P.O. Box 3554 Gary, IN	46406
44.	6709 Greenbriar Road Ames, IA	50010-8983	6709 Greenbrier Road Ames, IA	50010-9893
45.	8 West Jefferson St. Independence, MO	64056	88 West Jefferson St. Independence, MO	64056
46.	324 W. 1st St. Dallas, TX	75208-8956	324 W. 1st St. Dallas, TX	75208-8955
47.	1777 Boulder Trail Akron, OH	44304	7777 Boulder Trail Akron, OH	44303
48.	601 Dade Prof. Bldg. Cape Charles, VA	23310-2435	601 Dade Prof. Bldg. Cape Charles, LA	23310-2435
49.	340 Bates Parkway Omaha, NE	68108-1016	340 Bates Parkway Omaha, NE	68108-4016
50.	1257 Third Street Boulder, CO	80302	1275 Third Street Boulder, CO	80302
51.	1135 Tremont St. New York, NY	10128	1135 Tremont St. New York, NY	10728

continued on next page

A. No Errors	B. Address Only	C. ZIP Code Only	D. Both

	Correct List		List to Be Checked	
	Address	ZIP Code	Address	ZIP Code
52.	3110 Waddell Blvd. Dubuque, IA	52002	3110 Waddel Blvd. Dubuque, IA	52002
53.	PO Box 8462 Cabot, VT	05647-8462	PO Box 84620 Cabot, VT	05672-8462
54.	1031 E. Holt Ave. Saint Louis, MO	63113-7661	1031 E. Holt Ave. Saint Louis, MO	63113-7671
55.	701 Mount Vernon Way Augusta, GA	30904	701 Mount Vernon Way Augusta, GA	30904
56.	337 N. U.S. Highway 1 Nantucket, MA	02554-7300	337 N. U.S. Highway Nantucket, MA	02554-7300
57.	3660 Scenic Loop Louisville, KY	40202	3660 Scenic Drive Louisville, KY	40220
58.	84 Box Hill Road Abilene, TX	79603-0488	84 Box Hill Road Abilene, TX	79303-0488
59.	800 Abrams Pl. #220 Albany, NY	12208-1467	800 Abrams Pl. #220 Albany, NY	12208-1467
60.	130 N. Fairview St. Naperville, IL	60564	130 N. Fairview St. Napersville, IL	60564

ANSWER SHEET

Practice Drill 4

1. A B C D	21. A B C D	41. A B C D
2. A B C D	22. A B C D	42. A B C D
3. A B C D	23. A B C D	43. A B C D
4. A B C D	24. A B C D	44. A B C D
5. A B C D	25. A B C D	45. A B C D
6. A B C D	26. A B C D	46. A B C D
7. A B C D	27. A B C D	47. A B C D
8. A B C D	28. A B C D	48. A B C D
9. A B C D	29. A B C D	49. A B C D
10. A B C D	30. A B C D	50. A B C D
11. A B C D	31. A B C D	
12. A B C D	32. A B C D	
13. A B C D	33. A B C D	
14. A B C D	34. A B C D	
15. A B C D	35. A B C D	
16. A B C D	36. A B C D	
17. A B C D	37. A B C D	
18. A B C D	38. A B C D	
19. A B C D	39. A B C D	
20. A B C D	40. A B C D	

Practice Drill 5

1. A B C D	21. A B C D	41. A B C D
2. A B C D	22. A B C D	42. A B C D
3. A B C D	23. A B C D	43. A B C D
4. A B C D	24. A B C D	44. A B C D
5. A B C D	25. A B C D	45. A B C D
6. A B C D	26. A B C D	46. A B C D
7. A B C D	27. A B C D	47. A B C D
8. A B C D	28. A B C D	48. A B C D
9. A B C D	29. A B C D	49. A B C D
10. A B C D	30. A B C D	50. A B C D
11. A B C D	31. A B C D	51. A B C D
12. A B C D	32. A B C D	52. A B C D
13. A B C D	33. A B C D	53. A B C D
14. A B C D	34. A B C D	54. A B C D
15. A B C D	35. A B C D	55. A B C D
16. A B C D	36. A B C D	56. A B C D
17. A B C D	37. A B C D	57. A B C D
18. A B C D	38. A B C D	58. A B C D
19. A B C D	39. A B C D	59. A B C D
20. A B C D	40. A B C D	60. A B C D

Answer Key

Practice Drill 1

1. Error	11. No Error	21. Error	31. Error	41. Error
2. Error	12. No Error	22. No Error	32. No Error	42. No Error
3. No Error	13. No Error	23. No Error	33. Error	43. Error
4. No Error	14. Error	24. Error	34. Error	44. No Error
5. Error	15. No Error	25. No Error	35. Error	45. Error
6. No Error	16. Error	26. Error	36. No Error	46. No Error
7. Error	17. Error	27. Error	37. Error	47. Error
8. No Error	18. Error	28. Error	38. No Error	48. No Error
9. Error	19. No Error	29. No Error	39. No Error	49. Error
10. Error	20. Error	30. No Error	40. No Error	50. No Error

Practice Drill 2

1. No Error	11. Error	21. Error	31. Error	41. Error
2. Error	12. No Error	22. Error	32. No Error	42. Error
3. Error	13. Error	23. Error	33. Error	43. No Error
4. Error	14. No Error	24. No Error	34. No Error	44. Error
5. Error	15. Error	25. No Error	35. Error	45. No Error
6. No Error	16. No Error	26. Error	36. No Error	46. Error
7. Error	17. No Error	27. Error	37. Error	47. No Error
8. Error	18. Error	28. No Error	38. Error	48. Error
9. Error	19. No Error	29. Error	39. No Error	49. No Error
10. No Error	20. No Error	30. No Error	40. No Error	50. No Error

Practice Drill 3

1. Error	11. No Error	21. Error	31. Error	41. Error
2. No Error	12. No Error	22. No Error	32. No Error	42. No Error
3. Error	13. No Error	23. Error	33. No Error	43. Error
4. Error	14. Error	24. No Error	34. Error	44. Error
5. No Error	15. No Error	25. Error	35. Error	45. No Error
6. No Error	16. Error	26. Error	36. No Error	46. No Error
7. Error	17. No Error	27. No Error	37. Error	47. Error
8. Error	18. Error	28. No Error	38. No Error	48. Error
9. No Error	19. Error	29. Error	39. No Error	49. No Error
10. Error	20. No Error	30. Error	40. No Error	50. Error

Practice Drill 4

1. D	11. B	21. B	31. B	41. B
2. B	12. D	22. A	32. D	42. A
3. A	13. C	23. D	33. C	43. D
4. B	14. A	24. D	34. A	44. B
5. C	15. B	25. C	35. D	45. D
6. D	16. B	26. D	36. B	46. B
7. B	17. C	27. B	37. C	47. B
8. C	18. B	28. D	38. C	48. C
9. B	19. B	29. B	39. B	49. D
10. A	20. D	30. A	40. D	50. A

Practice Drill 5

1. B	11. B	21. B	31. B	41. C	51. C
2. B	12. C	22. D	32. B	42. B	52. B
3. D	13. B	23. B	33. D	43. A	53. D
4. C	14. D	24. A	34. C	44. D	54. C
5. A	15. C	25. D	35. A	45. B	55. A
6. D	16. A	26. B	36. B	46. C	56. B
7. B	17. B	27. C	37. B	47. D	57. D
8. D	18. B	28. D	38. C	48. B	58. C
9. B	19. C	29. D	39. A	49. C	59. A
10. C	20. A	30. C	40. B	50. B	60. B

Forms Completion

Part B of Test 473 is called *Forms Completion*. It consists of 30 questions for you to complete in 15 minutes. In this part, your job is to answer questions involving a series of simulated Postal Service forms, such as mailing receipts and shipping instructions. The questions are designed to gauge your ability to complete standard Postal Service forms accurately and properly. More specifically, this part is designed to help you to fill in the various fields (lines and boxes) on the forms with the appropriate information for each field.

Here are some additional key facts about Part B:

- Expect to encounter about five different forms in Part B. (The total number of forms differs slightly from one exam to the next, but the average number is five.)
- Each form in Part B will be accompanied by about five to seven questions based on the form.
- The forms in Part B are not actual Postal Service forms. Rather, they are modified and, generally speaking, simpler versions of real forms.

Note: Why don't the test makers use actual, unmodified Postal Service forms on the test? Well, if real forms were used, test takers could gain an unfair advantage by studying and memorizing the forms prior to taking the test. This would defeat the purpose of Test 473, which is designed as a test of skill, not of knowledge.

Here's a form that's typical of the ones you'll see on Part B of your test. Just like the ones on the test, it's a modified, simpler version of an actual Postal Service form.

Authorization to Hold Mail	
1. Hold Mail For:	2. Beginning Date
1a. Name	3. Ending Date
1b. Street Address	4a. ☐ Do NOT resume delivery until I pick up all accumulated mail.
1c. City, State, ZIP	
	4b. ☐ Resume delivery of accumulated and new mail on ending date.
5. Customer Signature	
POSTAL USE ONLY — 6. Date Received	8. Carrier
7. Clerk	9. Route Number

Compared with the forms you'll see on your exam, this example—Authorization to Hold Mail—is average in length and complexity. Some of the forms on your exam might be longer than this one (containing more fields), while others might be briefer (containing fewer fields). The example form here illustrates the following key features of each and every form you'll encounter on Part B:

■ The form is completed by providing various types of information, ranging from numbers and names to dates and check marks.
■ Each distinct field is either a "box" or a "line" and is identified by either a number or a number-letter combination (such as "1a"). This is how all the forms on Part B will look. The questions based on each form refer to the form's boxes and lines by number or number-letter combination.
■ The fields are numbered in an organized way—from left to right (in rows) and/or from top to bottom (in columns). This feature helps you locate fields quickly according to their number as you answer the questions.

Three Types of Questions

There are three basic types of questions in Part B. All involve the identification of information and its correct placement on the forms.

Identifying Information for a Particular Field

One type of question asks you to identify information that would be appropriate for a particular field (a box or a line). Following are two examples of this type of question, based on the previous "Authorization to Hold Mail" form, along with an explanatory answer for each one. As you examine both questions, notice that most answer choices are set off by quotations marks; this tells you that the answer choice provides the actual entry for the box or line, rather than a description of the type of entry (such as a check mark).

1. Which of these would be a correct entry for Box 6?
   (A) "Jeremy Stuart"
   (B) "02/12/07"
   (C) A check mark
   (D) "Chicago, IL"

2. Which of these would be an appropriate entry for Line 1b?
   (A) "1228 Laredo Blvd."
   (B) "Marla Francici"
   (C) "Sender"
   (D) "Cleveland, OH 44189"

The correct answer to Question 1 is **B**. Box 6 of the form contains the phrase "Date Received." Therefore, the only type of entry that would be appropriate in Box 6 is a date. Only choice **B** provides an example of this type of entry, so **B** must be the correct answer.

In Question 1, do you really need to know that 02/12/07 would be the "correct" information to enter in Box 6? No, it doesn't matter. In questions like this one, your job is not to identify a factually correct answer, but rather to identify the answer choice that would make sense in a particular box or line. And, don't worry: only one of the four choices will make sense.

The correct answer to Question 2 is **A**. Line 1b of the form contains the phrase "Street Address." Notice that Line 1c asks for the city, state, and ZIP code. Therefore, the type of entry that would be appropriate in Line 1b would be a street number and name, or possibly a Post Office Box number, but not a city, state, and ZIP code. Choice **A** is the only one that provides an example of this type of entry.

Identifying the Appropriate Field for a Given Type of Information

Another basic question type asks you to identify the appropriate field (a box or line) in which to enter a given type of information. Here are two examples of this type of question, based on the "Authorization to Hold Mail" form.

3. Where should the ending date for holding mail be entered on this form?
   (A) Box 2
   (B) Box 3
   (C) Line 4b
   (D) Box 6

4. The postal clerk's name would be the correct entry for which box?
   (A) Box 4
   (B) Box 5
   (C) Box 7
   (D) Box 8

The correct answer to Question 3 is **B**. Box 3 of the form contains the phrase "Ending Date," which means that the ending date for holding mail should be entered in Box 3.

The correct answer to Question 4 is **C**. Box 7 of the form contains the phrase "Clerk." Also, notice that the bottom two rows of the form are for "Postal Use Only." Clearly, then, the name of the postal clerk should be entered in Box 7.

Identifying the Type of Information and Where to Enter It

In a third type of question, you need to figure out both what type of information to enter on the form *and* where to enter it. Here's a good example of this question type, based again on the "Authorization to Hold Mail" form.

5. How would the customer indicate that he wants delivery of mail to resume on the date that mail holding ends?

(A) Enter a check mark in Line 4a and in Line 4b

(B) Enter a check mark in Line 4a only

(C) Enter a check mark in Line 4b only

(D) Enter "Resume Delivery" in Line 3

The correct answer to Question 5 is **C**. Line 4b is the place on the form where the customer should indicate how the mail should be handled after the ending date. Line 4b should be checked in this situation because the customer wants the Postal Service to "resume delivery of accumulated mail and new mail on ending date."

> Until the mid-nineteenth century, U.S. postage rates were based on both the number of sheets in a letter and the distance that a letter traveled. The more sheets and the longer the distance, the more postage you paid. In 1845, the rate structure was revised so that additional postage based on distance was paid only for letters traveling more than 300 miles. In 1855, that distance was extended to 3,000 miles. Finally, in 1863, rate differences based on distance were eliminated entirely.

Strategies for Forms Completion

Marking the appropriate answer code (A, B, C, or D) for each test item in Part B and completing the Postal Service forms is a pretty straightforward process. Nevertheless, it is remarkably easy to make errors when filling out the forms—for example, by putting the information in the wrong box or line. It is best to use an efficient, systematic approach. Here are our best points of advice for how to complete forms like a pro during Part B.

Familiarize Yourself with the Form

Before you tackle the questions for each form, take a few seconds to look over the form to get a rough idea of its purpose and what kind of information is needed to complete it. Note whether the numbered fields are arranged in rows, columns, or a combination of rows and columns. Pay special attention to any shaded areas of the form, which often indicate who is supposed to complete certain portions of the form (for example, the sender, the recipient, or a postal worker). Getting a feel for the form first will make answering the questions based on it easier and quicker.

If a Form Confuses You, Skip It and Come Back to It Later

Some forms are simpler than others, and some are easier to understand than others. If a particular form confuses you—for whatever reason—skip over the questions based on it and answer the questions based on the other forms in Part B. Once you're done with all the other questions, you can return to the troublesome form and focus better on it, knowing that the rest of Part B is behind you.

Answer the Questions in the Order Presented

During Part A, Address Checking, it may make sense to answer questions in a sequence different from the one presented on the exam. (You'll find that the same will be true for Part C, Coding and Memory). However, this strategy does not apply to Part B. Simply handle the five to seven questions for each form in the order in which they're presented.

Mark Your Answer Choices on Your Answer Sheet in Groups

Instead of marking your answer sheet after each one of the 30 questions in Part B, wait until you've completed the group of questions based on a particular form, and then fill in your answer sheet for each group as you go.

Pace Yourself

During Part B, you have 15 minutes to answer 30 questions based on approximately five different forms. As long as you work at a steady pace, you should have no trouble finishing with time to spare. As you practice, allot about 4 minutes to each group of questions. At that pace, you'll have about 10 minutes at the end to check your work.

> The official seal of the U.S. Postal Service features a bald eagle poised for flight on a white field, above red and blue bars framing the words "U.S. Mail." A border features the words "United States Postal Service" on three sides and nine five-pointed stars at the base. The Postal Service also has a corporate logo: an eagle's head in white leaning into the wind, on a blue background.

Forms Completion Practice Drills

Now it's time to tackle some Forms Completion questions on your own. Here you'll find five Practice Drills. The instructions for these drills—and for Part B of Test 473—are essentially as follows:

Directions

You will be shown a series of forms that are similar to ones used by the U.S. Postal Service. The parts of each form are labeled (for example, 3 and 4a). Each form is accompanied by several questions that test your ability to complete the form properly. All questions in Part B come with four answer choices, lettered (A), (B), (C), and (D). For each question, choose the best answer and mark your selection (A, B, C, or D) on the answer sheet given at the end of the chapter.

Note: The forms in the earlier practice drills are a bit briefer and simpler than those in the later drills. During each Practice Drill, it's important that you limit yourself strictly to the suggested time limit: *4 minutes per drill.*

An answer key for each drill is given at the end of the chapter.

Practice Drill 1

Time limit: 4 minutes

Return Receipt (Domestic)	
SENDER: COMPLETE THIS SECTION	

1. Article Sent To:	2. Type of Service
	☐ Certified Mail ☐ Insured Mail
	☐ Registered Mail ☐ COD
3. Article Number:	☐ Express Mail

4. Check here if delivery is restricted: ☐ (extra fee)

COMPLETE THIS SECTION ON DELIVERY

5. Received By (Print Name)	6. Delivery Date

7. Delivered To (check one)
  ☐ Address shown in Item No. 1
  ☐ Other (enter address):

8. Signature	☐ Addressee
	☐ Other

1. Which of these would be a correct entry in Box 3?

    (A) "July 23, 2007"

    (B) A check mark

    (C) "309982"

    (D) "90223 J. Street"

2. Where would you indicate that the item is sent C.O.D.?

    (A) Box 4

    (B) Box 2

    (C) Box 8

    (D) Box 1

3. Which of these would be a correct entry for Box 5?

    (A) A number

    (B) A date

    (C) A printed name

    (D) A signature

4. A check mark would be a correct entry in each box EXCEPT which?

    (A) Box 6

    (B) Box 8

    (C) Box 4

    (D) Box 2

5. Which of these entries would indicate that the addressee signed the form?

    (A) A check mark next to "Address shown in Item No. 1" in Box 7

    (B) The addressee's name in Box 1

    (C) The addressee's name in Box 6

    (D) A check mark next to "Addressee" in Box 8

6. The item was delivered on November 14, 2006. Where would this be indicated?

    (A) Box 7

    (B) Box 6

    (C) Box 1

    (D) Box 3

Practice Drill 2

Time limit: 4 minutes

<table>
<tr><th colspan="3">Signature Confirmation and Receipt</th></tr>
<tr><td rowspan="4">SIGNATURE CONFIRMATION RECEIPT</td><td>TO BE COMPLETED BY SENDER</td><td>POST OFFICE USE ONLY</td></tr>
<tr><td>1a. Sent To (Name):

_____</td><td>2a. Check One:
☐ Priority   ☐ Package Service

2b. Waiver of Signature?
☐ Yes   ☐ No</td></tr>
<tr><td>1b. Address:

_____
_____</td><td>2c.

Postmark
Here</td></tr>
<tr><td>Signature Confirmation Number
4258 0092 1773 8108</td><td></td></tr>
<tr><td rowspan="2">SIGNATURE CONFIRMATION</td><td colspan="2">3. WAIVER OF SIGNATURE. I authorize that the postal delivery employee s signature suffices as proof of delivery if the item is left in a secure location.</td></tr>
<tr><td>4. Customer Signature</td><td>Signature Confirmation Number
4258 0092 1173 8108</td></tr>
</table>

7. Which of these would be a correct type of entry in Line 2b?

   (A) The delivery address

   (B) The signature confirmation number

   (C) The customer's name

   (D) A check mark

8. In which of the following would it be appropriate for the sender to enter information?

   (A) Line 2b

   (B) Box 3

   (C) Line 2c

   (D) Line 1b

9. Which of these is a correct entry in Line 1a?

   (A) "6746 N. 3rd Ave."

   (B) "33529"

   (C) "Greg Hollaway"

   (D) "(310) 555-3441"

10. Where would the customer sign this form?

    (A) Box 3

    (B) Box 4

    (C) Line 2a

    (D) Line 2c

11. Which of these is indicated by entering a check mark?

    (A) Priority mail

    (B) Insured mail

    (C) Certified mail

    (D) Waiver of receipt

Practice Drill 3

Time limit: 4 minutes

Insured Mail Receipt		
1a. Name		5.
		☐ Fragile
1b. Street, Apt., or PO Box No.		☐ Perishable
		☐ Liquid
1c. City, State, ZIP + 4, Country		6. Insurance Coverage $
Postage	2. $	
Insurance Fee	3a. $	
Special Handling Fee (Endorsement Required)	3b. $	Postmark Here
Return Receipt Fee (Except for Canada)	3c. $	
Total Postage and Fees	4. $	

12. It would be correct to enter a check mark in Box 5 for any of these EXCEPT:

    (A) The article is valuable

    (B) The article is perishable

    (C) The article is liquid

    (D) The article is fragile

13. Which of these would be an appropriate and complete entry for Box 1c?

    (A) "Mariah Patterson"

    (B) "PO Box 3427, Albany, NY 12208-1467"

    (C) "49 Hart Circle, Apt. 12"

    (D) "Albany, NY 12208-1467 U.S.A."

14. Where is the special handling fee entered on this form?

    (A) Box 6

    (B) Box 3a

    (C) Box 3a

    (D) Box 3b

15. Which of these is a correct type of entry for Box 2?

    (A) A check mark

    (B) A street address

    (C) A dollar amount

    (D) A signature

16. The item is mailed to Canada. How would this be indicated on the form?

    (A) An entry in Box 1c

    (B) An entry in Box 3b

    (C) An entry in Box 3b

    (D) A check mark in Box 5

17. The postage and fees total $4.70. Where would you enter this on the form?

    (A) Box 1b

    (B) Box 4

    (C) Box 3a

    (D) Box 2

Practice Drill 4

Time limit: 4 minutes

Receipt for Registered Mail		
TO BE COMPLETED BY CUSTOMER		
1. Sender		2. Addressee
3. Full Value of Articles (Required): $		
TO BE COMPLETED BY POST OFFICE		
4. Reg. Fee	6. Postage	8. Postal Insurance ☐ Yes ☐ No
5. Handling Fee	7. Return Receipt	9. Total Fee, Postage, and Charges
10. Received By:		11. Date Received

18. Which of these is a correct type of entry for Box 10?

(A) A check mark

(B) A name

(C) A dollar amount

(D) A time

19. In which box would a date be an appropriate entry?

(A) Box 11

(B) Box 8

(C) Box 1

(D) Box 5

20. Whose name should be entered in Box 2?

(A) The sender's

(B) The recipient's

(C) The postal clerk's

(D) The addressee's

21. In which of these boxes should a postal employee enter information?

(A) Box 1

(B) Box 2

(C) Box 3

(D) Box 4

22. The customer pays for postal insurance. How would this be indicated on the form?

(A) Enter a dollar figure in Box 5

(B) Enter a dollar figure in Box 8

(C) Enter a check mark in Box 8

(D) Enter "Yes" in Box 8

23. "Hector Martinez" would be an appropriate entry in any of these EXCEPT:

(A) Box 2

(B) Box 3

(C) Box 1

(D) Box 10

Practice Drill 5

Time limit: 4 minutes

Postage Statement – Priority Mail	
1. Permit Holder	2. Mailing Agent (if different from permit holder)
1a. Name:	2a. Name:
1b. Address:	2b. Address:
1c. Telephone Number:	2c. Telephone Number:

3a. Mailing Date:	USPS Use Only		
3b. Post Office of Mailing:	6a. Weight (Single Piece)	lb.	oz.
4. Processing Type	6b. Number of Pieces		
☐ Letters	6c. Total Weight	lb.	oz.
☐ Parcels	6d. Total Postage		
☐ Flats	7a. Employee's Name (Print)		
☐ Other: _____	7b. Employee's Signature		
5. Permit Number	7c. Date Mailer Notified		

24. Where would you indicate the date on which the mailer is notified?

    (A) Line 7c

    (B) Line 3b

    (C) Line 6d

    (D) Line 2b

25. Which of these would be a correct entry for Line 2c?

    (A) "James Wiley"

    (B) "(808) 555-9302"

    (C) "07/19/08"

    (D) A check mark

26. Where should the permit holder's name be entered on this form?

    (A) Line 7b

    (B) Line 7a

    (C) Line 2a

    (D) Line 1a

27. The mailing agent is also the permit holder. How would this be indicated?

    (A) Enter "Same" in Line 2a

    (B) Enter a check mark in Box 2

    (C) Enter the permit holder's name in Line 2a

    (D) Leave Lines 2a, 2b, and 2c blank

28. Where should a postal employee's name be printed?

    (A) Line 2a

    (B) Line 7a

    (C) Line 3b

    (D) Line 7b

29. The total weight of the article is 12 pounds, 7 ounces. How would you indicate this?

    (A) Enter "12" and "7" in Line 6c

    (B) Enter "12 lb. 7 oz." in Line 6b

    (C) Enter "12" and "7" in Line 6a

    (D) Enter "12 lb. 7 oz." in Line 6d

30. The date of mailing is May 3, 2007. Where would you indicate this?

    (A) Line 7c

    (B) Line 6a

    (C) Box 4

    (D) Line 3a

Answer Sheet

Practice Drill 1

1. Ⓐ Ⓑ Ⓒ Ⓓ   3. Ⓐ Ⓑ Ⓒ Ⓓ   5. Ⓐ Ⓑ Ⓒ Ⓓ
2. Ⓐ Ⓑ Ⓒ Ⓓ   4. Ⓐ Ⓑ Ⓒ Ⓓ   6. Ⓐ Ⓑ Ⓒ Ⓓ

Practice Drill 2

7. Ⓐ Ⓑ Ⓒ Ⓓ   9. Ⓐ Ⓑ Ⓒ Ⓓ   11. Ⓐ Ⓑ Ⓒ Ⓓ
8. Ⓐ Ⓑ Ⓒ Ⓓ   10. Ⓐ Ⓑ Ⓒ Ⓓ

Practice Drill 3

12. Ⓐ Ⓑ Ⓒ Ⓓ   14. Ⓐ Ⓑ Ⓒ Ⓓ   16. Ⓐ Ⓑ Ⓒ Ⓓ
13. Ⓐ Ⓑ Ⓒ Ⓓ   15. Ⓐ Ⓑ Ⓒ Ⓓ   17. Ⓐ Ⓑ Ⓒ Ⓓ

Practice Drill 4

18. Ⓐ Ⓑ Ⓒ Ⓓ   20. Ⓐ Ⓑ Ⓒ Ⓓ   22. Ⓐ Ⓑ Ⓒ Ⓓ
19. Ⓐ Ⓑ Ⓒ Ⓓ   21. Ⓐ Ⓑ Ⓒ Ⓓ   23. Ⓐ Ⓑ Ⓒ Ⓓ

Practice Drill 5

24. Ⓐ Ⓑ Ⓒ Ⓓ   27. Ⓐ Ⓑ Ⓒ Ⓓ   29. Ⓐ Ⓑ Ⓒ Ⓓ
25. Ⓐ Ⓑ Ⓒ Ⓓ   28. Ⓐ Ⓑ Ⓒ Ⓓ   30. Ⓐ Ⓑ Ⓒ Ⓓ
26. Ⓐ Ⓑ Ⓒ Ⓓ

Answer Key

Practice Drill 1

1. C	3. C	5. D
2. B	4. A	6. B

Practice Drill 2

7. D	9. C	11. A
8. D	10. B	

Practice Drill 3

12. A	14. D	16. A
13. D	15. C	17. B

Practice Drill 4

18. B	20. D	22. C
19. A	21. D	23. B

Practice Drill 5

24. A	26. D	28. B	30. D
25. B	27. D	29. A	

Coding and Memory

Part C of Test 473 is called *Coding and Memory*. In this part, your job is to assign various street addresses to one of four delivery routes. Think of Part C as a mail-sorting exercise, in which you must sort through a big stack of mail and put each piece in one of four bins, each marked for delivery to a specific neighborhood.

Part C is divided into two sections:

- A *Coding Section,* which consists of 36 questions to be completed in 6 minutes
- A *Memory Section,* which consists of 36 questions to be completed in 7 minutes

You will use the same Coding Guide for both sections of Part C. The first column of the Coding Guide shows the address ranges for each delivery route. The second column shows the delivery route code (A, B, C, or D) for the address ranges shown in the same row as the code. You may assume that each address range runs continuously (no numbers are skipped) from the lowest to the highest number in the range. Some of the street names appear twice, showing two different address ranges.

Coding Section

The Coding Section consists of three segments. You will use the same Coding Guide for all three segments.

- Segment 1 is an introductory exercise consisting of 4 items to be completed in 2 minutes. *Segment 1 is not scored.*
- Segment 2 is a practice exercise consisting of 8 items to be completed in 1 1/2 minutes (90 seconds). *Segment 2 is not scored.*
- Segment 3 is the actual Coding Section of the test. This segment consists of 36 items to be completed in 6 minutes. *Segment 3 is scored and counts toward your total test score.*

Memory Section

The Memory Section consists of four segments. You will use the same Coding Guide for all four segments.

- Segment 1 is a 3-minute study period, during which you will attempt to memorize the Coding Guide. *Segment 1 is not scored,* and there are no answers to mark during this segment.
- Segment 2 is a practice exercise consisting of 8 items to be completed in 1 1/2 minutes (90 seconds). *Segment 2 is not scored.*

■ Segment 3 is a 5-minute study period, during which you will attempt to memorize the Coding Guide. *Segment 3 is not scored*, and there are no answers to mark during this segment.

■ Segment 4 is the actual Memory Section of the test. This segment consists of 36 items to be completed in 7 minutes. *Segment 4 is scored and counts toward your total test score.*

Part C of the test provides a series of practice exercises preceding the 36 scored coding items and, similarly, a series of practice exercises preceding the 36 scored memory items. The same Coding Guide is used throughout Part C. So, by the time you finish the practice exercises, you'll be familiar with the Coding Guide, which will make your job during the scored portion easier.

Coding Guide

Now, here's an example of a Coding Guide. Just like the one you'll encounter on the actual test, this example uses five different street names, but some of these street names appear in two different coded categories (delivery routes).

Coding Guide	
Address Range	*Delivery Route*
300–700 Hartford Blvd. 10–25 Oswago Road 1800–6000 N. 23rd St.	A
26–40 Oswago Road 701–1000 Hartford Blvd.	B
150–250 Point Lookout Loop 50000–75000 Rose St. SW 6001–12000 N. 23rd St.	C
All mail that does not fall in one of the address ranges listed above	D

In interpreting the Coding Guide, you are to assume that no numbers within an address range are skipped. For example, in the preceding example, the range "1800–6000 N. 23rd St." includes 1800, 1801, 1802, 1803, and so forth. So, you know that *any* N. 23rd St. address within that range is included in Delivery Route A.

The preceding Coding Guide example illustrates the following key features of the Coding Guide that you'll encounter on the actual test:

■ The Coding Guide covers street addresses only. Cities, states, and ZIP codes are excluded.
■ All addresses refer to streets. No Post Office Boxes are included.
■ The Coding Guide lists five different streets altogether.
■ Three streets appear *twice* in the Coding Guide, while the remaining two streets appear only *once*.
■ Delivery Route D covers any address that does not fall into one of the delivery routes listed in categories A, B, and C.

One additional feature requires special explanation. In the Coding Guide example, notice that for street names appearing twice, the second address range starts where the first one left off. For example, the Hartford Blvd. range in Route A ends at 700, and the range in Route B begins at 701. This is how the Coding Guide on the actual test will probably organize address ranges. However, it is possible that certain numbers will be skipped between two address ranges for the same street. For example, consider the following two address ranges:

45–60 Park Drive (Delivery Route A)

75–90 Park Drive (Delivery Route C)

In this example, any address on Park Drive falling between 60 and 75, or, in other words, 61 through 74, would not be included in either delivery route, and the correct answer for any such address would be **D**.

Test Items Based on Sample Coding Guide

Now let's look at some example addresses to see how you should respond to the test items in Part C. In your test booklet, the test items will be numbered and listed as they are here (although the total number of test items varies from one segment to another). Try matching each of these eight addresses to the correct delivery route (code) in the preceding Coding Guide. Then, check the answers that follow this list of addresses.

1. 10500 N. 23rd St.
2. 422 Hartford Blvd.
3. 125 Point Lookout Loop
4. 39 Oswago Road
5. 3456 N. 23rd St.
6. 900 Harper Blvd.
7. 57075 Rose St. SW
8. 28 Oswago Road

The correct answer to Item 1 is **C**. The address 10500 N. 23rd St. falls in the range "6001–12000 N. 23rd St." (Delivery Route C).

The correct answer to Item 2 is **A**. The address 422 Hartford Blvd. falls in the range "300–700 Hartford Blvd." (Delivery Route A).

The correct answer to Item 3 is **D**. The address 125 Point Lookout Loop is *outside* the range "150–250 Point Lookout Loop," which is the only range shown in the Coding Guide for Point Lookout Loop.

The correct answer to Item 4 is **B**. The address 39 Oswago Road falls in the range "26–40 Oswago Road" (Delivery Route B).

The correct answer to Item 5 is **A**. The address 3456 N. 23rd St. falls in the range "1800–6000 N. 23rd St." (Delivery Route A).

The correct answer to Item 6 is **D**. Harper Blvd. is not one of the streets listed in the Coding Guide. Therefore, any Harper Blvd. address falls outside all the address ranges provided for Delivery Routes A, B, and C.

The correct answer to Item 7 is **C**. The address 57075 Rose St. SW falls in the range "50000–75000 Rose St. SW" (Delivery Route C).

The correct answer to Item 8 is **B**. The address 28 Oswago Road falls in the range "26–40 Oswago Road" (Delivery Route B).

Note: Did you notice that Item 6 is a bit different from any of the others? The issue in item 6 is not the *number* but rather the street *name*, which does not appear in the Coding Guide. Although this is unusual, you should expect to encounter at least one or two items that give an incorrect street name on Part C of the test. Of course, the correct answer to this type of item is always **D**.

Strategies for the Coding Section of Part C

Marking the appropriate code (A, B, C, or D) for each test item in Part C is a fairly straightforward process. Nevertheless, it's easy to make coding mistakes unless you use an efficient, systematic approach. Here are our three best points of advice for how to code like a pro during the Coding Section of Part C.

Code All Addresses for Each Street Name Separately; Start with the Street Names Appearing Only Once in the Coding Guide

Most test takers will code addresses in the order in which they're listed in the test booklet. Using this approach, a test taker must continually review the Coding Guide (either in the test booklet or from memory) from one question to the next. This is an inefficient approach that is likely to lead to mistakes. A better approach is to code all addresses for each street name separately.

Start with the street names that appear only once in the Coding Guide. (Remember, two of the five street names will be listed only once.) For example, the two street names that appear only once in the Coding Guide shown earlier in this chapter are Point Lookout Loop and Rose St. SW. Both are listed under Delivery Route C, so the correct answer to any test item naming either of these two streets must be either **C** or **D**. A good way to code the addresses based on this Coding Guide would be as follows:

Step 1: Code all Point Lookout Loop addresses.
Step 2: Code all Rose St. SW addresses.
Step 3: Code all Hartford Blvd. addresses.
Step 4: Code all Oswago Road addresses.
Step 5: Code all N. 23rd St. addresses.

Step 1
Here's how you'd perform Step 1. Fix the Point Lookout Loop address range 150–250 in your mind, and then code each test item containing only this street name (or an incorrect version of this street name). For any number between 150 and 250, the correct code is **C**. For any number outside that range and for any incorrect version of the street name, the correct code is **D**.

The following address list (numbered 1–36) illustrates how quickly and easily you can correctly code addresses for the same street if you examine them one right after another and ignore all other street names. Write the code letter to the left of the question number containing the address.

1. _____

2. _____

C 3. 201 Point Lookout Loop

4. _____

5. _____

6. _____

7. _____

8. _____

9. _____

10. _____

D 11. 40 Point Lookout Loop

12. _____

13. _____

14. _____

C 15. 199 Point Lookout Loop

16. _____

17. _____

18. _____

19. _____

D 20. 180 Point Hartford Loop

21. _____

22. _____

23. _____

24. _____

25. _____

C 26. 236 Point Lookout Loop

27. _____

28. _____

29. _____

30. _____

31. _____

32. _____

D 33. 6150 Point Lookout Loop

34. _____

35. _____

36. _____

You already have 6 of the 36 addresses coded using this system.

Step 2
In Step 2, you'd repeat this procedure for all Rose St. SW addresses.

Steps 3 through 5
Then, in Steps 3 through 5, you'd repeat the procedure for the three streets that appear twice each in the Coding Guide. For example, in Step 3, you would fix in your mind two address ranges for Hartford Blvd: 300–700 (Delivery Route A) and 701–1000 (Delivery Route B). Then, ignoring all other street names, you would code all the Hartford Blvd. addresses among the list of 36:

1. _____

B 2. 777 Hartford Blvd.

3. _____

4. _____

5. _____

6. _____

7. _____

8. _____

A 9. 460 Hartford Blvd.

10. _____

11. _____

12. _____

13. _____

14. _____

15. _____

D 16. 1010 Hartford Blvd.

17. _____

18. _____

19. _____

20. _____

A 21. 337 Hartford Blvd.

22. _____

23. _____

24. _____

A 25. 685 Hartford Blvd.

26. _____

27. _____

28. _____

29. _____

D 30. 900 Hart Blvd.

31. _____

32. _____

33. _____

34. _____

A 35. 700 Hartford Blvd.

36. _____

Code the Addresses in Your Test Booklet First

As you check each address according to the method just described, jot down the code to the left of the item number in your test booklet, as shown. After you've coded all 36 items, transcribe all 36 codes on your answer sheet.

Pace Yourself So That You Have Enough Time to Check Your Scored Answers

During the Coding Section, you have 6 minutes to code 36 addresses, numbered 1 through 36. That's plenty of time, as long as you work at a steady pace. Try to finish coding in 3 minutes, then transcribe your answers on the answer sheet, which should take no more than 2 minutes. That will leave you 1 minute to check your answers.

Strategies for the Memory Section of Part C

During the Memory Section, you have 7 minutes to code 36 addresses, numbered 37 through 72. Pace yourself so that you finish coding from memory in about 3 minutes, and then take no more than 2 minutes to fill in the answer sheet. That will leave you 2 minutes to go through all 36 items again and correct any mistakes you may have made the first time through.

The Coding Section of Part C is pretty straightforward because the Coding Guide is right there in front of you as you code each list of addresses. However, during the Memory Section, you won't have the luxury of referring to a preprinted Coding Guide as you code addresses. Instead, you must rely on your memory to do so. This is what makes the Memory Section of Part C more challenging than the Coding Section. However, by using the following simple strategies, you can easily handle this section.

Reorganize the Coding Guide in a Way That's Easy to Memorize

The Coding Guide presents the addresses and corresponding delivery routes in a clear, organized way. But, the guide doesn't organize the information in a way that's very easy to memorize. It's up to you to shuffle the information around in your mind so that it's easy to memorize it all. Let's look again at the Coding Guide you saw earlier in this lesson, and then we'll reorganize the data.

Coding Guide	
Address Range	*Delivery Route*
300–700 Hartford Blvd. 10–25 Oswago Road 1800–6000 N. 23rd St.	A
26–40 Oswago Road 701–1000 Hartford Blvd.	B
150–250 Point Lookout Loop 50000–75000 Rose St. SW 6001–12000 N. 23rd St.	C
All mail that does not fall in one of the address ranges listed above	D

Here are three suggestions for reorganizing the information in your mind so that it's easier to remember:

- In your mind, separate the two streets that are listed only once from the three other streets.
- Ignore words such as *Street*, *Road*, and *Avenue*, as well as their abbreviated forms.
- Instead of thinking about which streets and ranges match a delivery code, think first about a particular street, and then think about the street's delivery code(s).

Here's what the guide might look like after you reorganize the information in your mind in accordance with the preceding suggestions:

C 150–250 Point Lookout
C 50000–75000 Rose

Hartford
A 300–700
B 701–1000

Oswago
A 10–25
B 26–40

N. 23rd
A 1800–6000
C 6001–12000

As you can see, our revised Coding Guide is simpler and less cluttered than the original one. You can no doubt see that it's easier to memorize the information when it's presented this way than when it's presented the original way.

Use Memory Techniques Such as Association to Help Fix Street Ranges in Your Mind

Even after simplifying the Coding Guide as we've just shown, there's still a lot of information there to memorize. Many test takers try to memorize the Coding Guide simply by repeating the information silently to themselves, over and over. A much more effective technique, however, is what is known as *association*. A particular street name or number might remind you of something else—for whatever reason. Associating two things with each other in your mind can help you remember what you need to know. Here's how a test taker might use association to help memorize some of the information in the example Coding Guide that we've been studying in this lesson. (The test taker is thinking to him- or herself here.)

To help remember the streets that are listed only once in the Coding Guide:

A *rose* has thorns, which are *pointy*. So, Rose and Point Lookout are related to each other. A pointy thorn is shaped like the number *1*, just as both streets appear only *one* time in the guide, under **C**, which looks round—just the opposite of a pointy thorn.

To help remember Hartford delivery routes and address ranges:

Hartford is the name of an insurance company. Always pay your insurance premiums on time; it's a high priority—**A** or **B** priority—definitely not C. My car insurance payments are about $1,000 per year (upper limit on address range). New brakes on a car might cost $300–$700 (lower address range).

To help remember Oswago delivery routes and address ranges:

The word *Oswago* starts and ends with an *o*, or think of it as a zero. There are then two zeros, just as there are two digits in each address number.

Zero (0) is where counting numbers start, just like **A** and **B** are where the alphabet starts.

The lowest number (10) and the highest number (40) both end in a zero (just like the word *Oswago*).

The addresses are fairly equally split between the two ranges, and so I'll visualize Oswago being split right down the middle: Osw | ago. That corresponds to 25.

As these illustrations show, any association—no matter how seemingly illogical or silly—that means something to you can help you memorize the Coding Guide.

After Each Study Period, Immediately Jot Down the Address Ranges in Your Test Booklet

After each 5-minute study period, turn the page to the list of addresses you need to code, and then write down the address ranges—from your memory, of course—right on the page. It's okay to scribble in the test booklet. This is not considered cheating. Your notes should look essentially like the reorganized guide shown earlier.

Once you've reproduced your own version of the Coding Guide on paper, you don't need to code the list of addresses from memory and risk making mistakes as your mind flits from one street address to another. Instead, you've transformed the Memory Section of Part C into a simple coding exercise, just like the first section of Part C.

As You Code from Memory, Apply the Same Coding Strategies as for the Coding Section

The three coding strategies you learned earlier in this chapter also apply to the Memory Section of Part C (see the earlier discussion for more detailed descriptions):

> In colonial America, official international mail service actually began before official domestic mail service, when in 1639 a Boston tavern was designated by the General Court of Massachusetts as the official mail drop for letters received from and sent to England and certain other European countries.

- Code all addresses for each street name separately; start with the street names appearing only once in the Coding Guide.
- Code the addresses in your test booklet first. After you've finished an entire list, transcribe your answers on the answer sheet.
- Pace yourself so that you have enough time to check your scored answers.

Coding and Memory Practice Drills

Now it's time to put to work what you've learned in this chapter. Here you'll find five practice drills, each of which consists of a Coding Section followed by a Memory Section. Practice Drills 1 through 4 are each simpler than the actual exam. After attempting these four drills, you'll be ready for Drill 5, which is exactly like Part C (Coding and Memory) of the actual exam.

Note: During each practice drill, it's important that you limit yourself strictly to the suggested time limit. Only in Practice Drill 5 are the number of questions and the time limit the same as on the actual exam.

An answer key for each drill is given at the end of the chapter.

Practice Drill 1

Coding Section

Directions: Based on the following Coding Guide, match each address to a delivery route. Mark your answers on the answer sheet at the end of the chapter.

Note: The format of this Practice Drill is *not* the same as the format of Test 473. This drill is designed to help build confidence, speed, and accuracy in coding.

Number of Items: 20

Time Limit: 3 minutes

Coding Guide	
Address Range	*Delivery Route*
4400–10000 Newport Blvd.	A
21–50 Holden Court	B
150–250 Saddleback Road	C
All mail that does not fall in one of the address ranges listed above	D

	Address	Delivery Code			
1.	200 Saddleback Road	A	B	C	D
2.	49 Holden Court	A	B	C	D
3.	11900 Newport Blvd.	A	B	C	D
4.	21 Saddleback Road	A	B	C	D
5.	33 Holden Court	A	B	C	D
6.	5100 Newport Blvd.	A	B	C	D
7.	225 Saddleback Road	A	B	C	D
8.	905 Holden Court	A	B	C	D
9.	10001 Newport Blvd.	A	B	C	D
10.	5000 Saddleback Road	A	B	C	D
11.	38 Holden Court	A	B	C	D
12.	9900 Newport Blvd.	A	B	C	D
13.	50 Saddleback Road	A	B	C	D
14.	250 Holden Court	A	B	C	D
15.	44000 Newport Blvd.	A	B	C	D
16.	201 Saddleback Road	A	B	C	D
17.	101 Holden Court	A	B	C	D
18.	4170 Newport Blvd.	A	B	C	D
19.	520 Saddleback Road	A	B	C	D
20.	33 Holden Court	A	B	C	D

Memory Section

Directions: Spend 2 minutes studying the Coding Guide on page 76. Then return to this page and match each address numbered 21–40 below to a delivery route based on the Coding Guide. Mark your answer on the answer sheet at the end of the chapter. *Do **not** look back at the Coding Guide as you attempt to match the addresses on this page.*

Note: The format of this Practice Drill is not the same as the format of Test 473. This drill is designed to help build confidence, speed, and accuracy in the memory segment of Part C of the exam.

Number of Items: 20

Time Limit: 3 minutes

	Address	Delivery Code			
21.	20 Saddleback Road	A	B	C	D
22.	30 Holden Court	A	B	C	D
23.	9400 Newport Blvd.	A	B	C	D
24.	111 Saddleback Road	A	B	C	D
25.	440 Holden Court	A	B	C	D
26.	7500 Newton Blvd.	A	B	C	D
27.	205 Saddleback Road	A	B	C	D
28.	50 Holden Court	A	B	C	D
29.	9999 Newport Blvd.	A	B	C	D
30.	166 Saddleback Road	A	B	C	D
31.	12 Holden Court	A	B	C	D
32.	2200 Newport Blvd.	A	B	C	D
33.	145 Saddleback Road	A	B	C	D
34.	92 Holden Court	A	B	C	D
35.	4400 Newport Blvd.	A	B	C	D
36.	250 Saddleback Road	A	B	C	D
37.	10000 Holden Court	A	B	C	D
38.	50 Newport Blvd.	A	B	C	D
39.	200 Camelback Road	A	B	C	D
40.	35 Holden Court	A	B	C	D

Practice Drill 2

Coding Section

Directions: Based on the following Coding Guide, match each address to a delivery route. Mark your answers on the answer sheet at the end of the chapter.

Note: The format of this Practice Drill is *not* the same as the format of Test 473. This drill is designed to help build confidence, speed, and accuracy in coding.

Number of Items: 20

Time Limit: 3 minutes

Coding Guide	
Address Range	*Delivery Route*
50–130 Friendly Circle 3400–4400 Lilac Street	A
131–180 Friendly Circle 45–115 W. 13th Ave.	B
4401–5400 Lilac Street 116–145 W. 13th Ave.	C
All mail that does not fall in one of the address ranges listed above	D

Address	Delivery Code			
1. 4340 Lilac Street	A	B	C	D
2. 210 Friendly Circle	A	B	C	D
3. 115 W. 13th Ave.	A	B	C	D
4. 4901 Lilac Street	A	B	C	D
5. 120 Friendly Circle	A	B	C	D
6. 380 Lilac Street	A	B	C	D
7. 90 W. 13th Ave.	A	B	C	D
8. 135 Friendly Circle	A	B	C	D
9. 5120 Lilac Street	A	B	C	D
10. 100 E. 16th Ave.	A	B	C	D
11. 114 Friendly Circle	A	B	C	D
12. 3877 Lilac Street	A	B	C	D
13. 125 W. 13th Ave.	A	B	C	D
14. 145 Friendly Circle	A	B	C	D
15. 116 Lilac Street	A	B	C	D
16. 134 W. 13th Ave.	A	B	C	D
17. 105 Friendly Circle	A	B	C	D
18. 154 W. 13th Ave.	A	B	C	D
19. 5050 Lilac Street	A	B	C	D
20. 130 Friendly Circle	A	B	C	D

Memory Section

Directions: Spend 2 minutes studying the Coding Guide on page 79. Then, return to this page and match each address numbered 21–40 below to a delivery route based on the Coding Guide. Mark your answers on the answer sheet at the end of the chapter. *Do **not** look back at the Coding Guide as you attempt to match the addresses on this page.*

Note: The format of this Practice Drill is *not* the same as the format of Test 473. This drill is designed to help build confidence, speed, and accuracy in coding.

Number of Items: 20

Time Limit: 3 minutes

	Address	Delivery Code			
21.	121 W. 13th Ave.	A	B	C	D
22.	68 Friendly Circle	A	B	C	D
23.	5000 Lilac Street	A	B	C	D
24.	160 Friendly Circle	A	B	C	D
25.	910 Lilac Street	A	B	C	D
26.	99 W. 13th Ave.	A	B	C	D
27.	3902 Lilac Street	A	B	C	D
28.	140 French Circle	A	B	C	D
29.	5209 Lilac Street	A	B	C	D
30.	2200 W. 13th Ave.	A	B	C	D
31.	175 Friendly Circle	A	B	C	D
32.	3400 Lilac Street	A	B	C	D
33.	127 W. 13th Ave.	A	B	C	D
34.	200 Friendly Circle	A	B	C	D
35.	64 W. 13th Ave.	A	B	C	D
36.	4343 Lilac Street	A	B	C	D
37.	117 Friendly Circle	A	B	C	D
38.	135 W. 13th Ave.	A	B	C	D
39.	139 Friendly Circle	A	B	C	D
40.	4250 Lilly Street	A	B	C	D

Practice Drill 3

Coding Section

Directions: Based on the following Coding Guide, match each address to a delivery route. Mark your answers on the answer sheet at the end of the chapter.

Note: The format of this Practice Drill is *not* the same as the format of Test 473. This drill is designed to help build confidence, speed, and accuracy in coding.

Number of Items: 20

Time Limit: 3 minutes

Coding Guide	
Address Range	*Delivery Route*
9000–13000 Beaumont Pkwy. 1–15 Juniper Lane 500–700 North Laurel Rd.	A
16–30 Juniper Lane 13001–20000 Beaumont Pkwy.	B
701–800 North Laurel Rd. 120–150 San Lucas 3300–6300 Grant St. SW	C
All mail that does not fall in one of the address ranges listed above	D

	Address	Delivery Code			
1.	24 Juniper Lane	A	B	C	D
2.	11000 Beaumont Pkwy.	A	B	C	D
3.	730 North Laurel Rd.	A	B	C	D
4.	110 San Lucas	A	B	C	D
5.	15590 Beaumont Pkwy.	A	B	C	D
6.	150 North Laurel Rd.	A	B	C	D
7.	4303 Grant St. SW	A	B	C	D
8.	12 Juniper Lane	A	B	C	D
9.	6200 Beaumont Pkwy.	A	B	C	D
10.	700 North Laurel Rd.	A	B	C	D
11.	23 Juniper Lane	A	B	C	D
12.	148 San Lucas	A	B	C	D
13.	5402 Grant St. SW	A	B	C	D
14.	1268 North Laurel Rd.	A	B	C	D
15.	10 Jasper Lane	A	B	C	D
16.	9770 Beaumont Pkwy.	A	B	C	D
17.	135 San Lucas	A	B	C	D
18.	17 Juniper Lane	A	B	C	D
19.	4990 Grant St. SW	A	B	C	D
20.	11122 Beaumont Pkwy.	A	B	C	D

Memory Section

Directions: Spend 2 minutes studying the Coding Guide on page 82. Then, return to this page and match each address numbered 21–40 below to a delivery route based on the Coding Guide. Mark your answers on the answer sheet at the end of the chapter. *Do **not** look back at the Coding Guide as you attempt to match the addresses on this page.*

Note: The format of this Practice Drill is *not* the same as the format of Test 473. This drill is designed to help build confidence, speed, and accuracy in coding.

Number of Items: 20

Time Limit: 3 minutes

	Address	Delivery Code			
21.	508 North Laurel Rd.	A	B	C	D
22.	18220 Beaumont Pkwy.	A	B	C	D
23.	7 Juniper Lane	A	B	C	D
24.	5331 Grant St. SW	A	B	C	D
25.	10001 Beaumont Pkwy.	A	B	C	D
26.	640 North Laurel Rd.	A	B	C	D
27.	200 San Lucas	A	B	C	D
28.	30 Juniper Lane	A	B	C	D
29.	18700 Beaumont Pkwy.	A	B	C	D
30.	590 North Laurel Rd.	A	B	C	D
31.	6220 Grant St. SW	A	B	C	D
32.	600 Juniper Lane	A	B	C	D
33.	121 San Lucas	A	B	C	D
34.	800 North Laurel Rd.	A	B	C	D
35.	20 Juniper Lane	A	B	C	D
36.	13480 Beaumont Pkwy.	A	B	C	D
37.	140 Santa Lucia	A	B	C	D
38.	3333 Grant St. SW	A	B	C	D
39.	10200 Beaumont Pkwy.	A	B	C	D
40.	17 Juniper Lane	A	B	C	D

Practice Drill 4

Coding Section

Directions: Based on the following Coding Guide, match each address to a delivery route. Mark your answers on the answer sheet at the end of the chapter.

Note: The format of this Practice Drill is *not* the same as the format of Test 473. This drill is designed to help build confidence, speed, and accuracy in coding.

Number of Items: 20

Time Limit: 3 minutes

Coding Guide	
Address Range	*Delivery Route*
30–50 Costello Drive 200–800 W. 22nd St. 7000–9000 Nygren Blvd.	A
801–1000 W. 22nd St. 100–150 Costello Drive	B
60–90 Rancho Grande 5–15 Filipe Circle 9001–11000 Nygren Blvd.	C
All mail that does not fall in one of the address ranges listed above	D

	Address	Delivery Code			
1.	150 Costello Drive	A	B	C	D
2.	20 Rancho Grande	A	B	C	D
3.	330 W. 22nd St.	A	B	C	D
4.	10000 Nygren Blvd.	A	B	C	D
5.	11 Filipe Circle	A	B	C	D
6.	43 Costello Drive	A	B	C	D
7.	81 Rancho Grande	A	B	C	D
8.	114 W. 22nd St.	A	B	C	D
9.	8901 Nygren Blvd.	A	B	C	D
10.	106 Costello Drive	A	B	C	D
11.	15 Rancho Grande	A	B	C	D
12.	5 Filipe Circle	A	B	C	D
13.	12200 Nygren Blvd.	A	B	C	D
14.	924 W. 22nd St.	A	B	C	D
15.	47 Costello Drive	A	B	C	D
16.	80 Rancho Grande	A	B	C	D
17.	313 Filipe Circle	A	B	C	D
18.	551 W. 22nd St.	A	B	C	D
19.	7235 Nygren Blvd.	A	B	C	D
20.	126 Costello Drive	A	B	C	D

Memory Section

Directions: Spend 2 minutes studying the Coding Guide on page 85. Then, return to this page and match each address numbered 21–40 below to a delivery route based on the Coding Guide. Mark your answers on the answer sheet at the end of the chapter. *Do **not** look back at the Coding Guide as you attempt to match the addresses on this page.*

Note: The format of this Practice Drill is *not* the same as the format of Test 473. This drill is designed to help build confidence, speed, and accuracy in coding.

Number of Items: 20

Time Limit: 3 minutes

	Address	Delivery Code			
21.	980 W. 22nd St.	A	B	C	D
22.	8202 Nygren Blvd.	A	B	C	D
23.	140 Castle Drive	A	B	C	D
24.	72 Rancho Grande	A	B	C	D
25.	16 Filipe Circle	A	B	C	D
26.	101 Costello Drive	A	B	C	D
27.	88 Rancho Grande	A	B	C	D
28.	411 W. 22nd St.	A	B	C	D
29.	7070 Nygren Blvd.	A	B	C	D
30.	44 Costello Drive	A	B	C	D
31.	9000 Nygren Blvd.	A	B	C	D
32.	14 Filipe Circle	A	B	C	D
33.	139 Costello Drive	A	B	C	D
34.	71 Rancho Grande	A	B	C	D
35.	882 Nygren Blvd.	A	B	C	D
36.	828 W. 22nd St.	A	B	C	D
37.	6 Filipe Circle	A	B	C	D
38.	901 Nygren Blvd.	A	B	C	D
39.	26 Costello Drive	A	B	C	D
40.	1000 W. 22nd St.	A	B	C	D

Practice Drill 5—Coding and Memory

This Practice Drill is *exactly* like Part C of the test. The drill consists of two sections:

- A Coding Section, which consists of 36 questions to be completed in 6 minutes
- A Memory Section, which consists of 36 questions to be completed in 7 minutes

Both sections test your ability to match one-letter codes to addresses quickly and accurately. The Memory Section also tests your ability to memorize codes and their matching address ranges.

You will use the same Coding Guide for both sections of this practice drill. The first column of the Coding Guide shows each address range. The second column shows the delivery route code (A, B, C, or D) for the address ranges shown in the same row as the code. You may assume that each address range runs continuously (no numbers are skipped) from the lowest to the highest number in the range. Some of the street names appear twice, showing two different address ranges.

Coding Section
This section consists of three segments:

- **Segment 1** is an introductory exercise consisting of 4 items to be completed in 2 minutes. *Segment 1 is not scored.*
- **Segment 2** is a practice exercise consisting of 8 items to be completed in 1 1/2 minutes (90 seconds). *Segment 2 is not scored.*
- **Segment 3** is the actual Coding Section of the test. This segment consists of 36 items to be completed in 6 minutes. *Segment 3 is scored and counts toward your total test score.*

You will use the same Coding Guide for all three segments.

An answer key for all three segments is given at the end of the chapter.

Coding Section—Segment 1
Directions: Segment 1 is an introductory exercise that will familiarize you with the Coding Section and help you learn how to complete it. This segment is *not* scored. Based on the Coding Guide, match each address to a delivery route. Mark your answers on the answer sheet at the end of the chapter.

Number of Items: 4

Time Limit: 2 minutes

Coding Guide	
Address Range	*Delivery Route*
6000–12000 Old Hwy. 14 20–50 Honeysuckle Road 300–500 Frontage Blvd.	A
51–100 Honeysuckle Road 12001–16000 Old Hwy. 14	B
1–99 Sawtooth Ridge 100–500 Flores St. 501–700 Frontage Blvd.	C
All mail that does not fall in one of the address ranges listed above	D

	Address	Delivery Code			
1.	417 Flores St.	A	B	C	D
2.	51 Honeysuckle Road	A	B	C	D
3.	11400 Old Hwy. 14	A	B	C	D
4.	150 Frontage Blvd.	A	B	C	D

Coding Section—Segment 2

Directions: Segment 2 is *not* scored. It is a practice exercise that will give you experience with the Coding Section under a time constraint similar to the one during the scored Coding Section. Based on the Coding Guide, match each address to a delivery route. Mark your answers on the answer sheet at the end of the chapter.

Number of Items: 8

Time Limit: 1 1/2 minutes (90 seconds)

Coding Guide	
Address Range	*Delivery Route*
6000–12000 Old Hwy. 14 20–50 Honeysuckle Road 300–500 Frontage Blvd.	A
51–100 Honeysuckle Road 12001–16000 Old Hwy. 14	B
1–99 Sawtooth Ridge 100–500 Flores St. 501–700 Frontage Blvd.	C
All mail that does not fall in one of the address ranges listed above	D

Address	Delivery Code			
1. 519 Sawtooth Ridge	A	B	C	D
2. 82 Honeysuckle Road	A	B	C	D
3. 450 Frontage Blvd.	A	B	C	D
4. 670 Old Hwy. 14	A	B	C	D
5. 49 Honeysuckle Road	A	B	C	D
6. 99 Sawtooth Ridge	A	B	C	D
7. 510 Frontage Blvd.	A	B	C	D
8. 9001 Old Hwy. 14	A	B	C	D

Coding Section—Segment 3
Directions: Segment 3 is the *actual scored* Coding Section of the test. Based on the Coding Guide, match each address to a delivery route. Mark your answers on the answer sheet at the end of the chapter.

Number of Items: 36

Time Limit: 6 minutes

Coding Guide	
Address Range	*Delivery Route*
6000–12000 Old Hwy. 14 20–50 Honeysuckle Road 300–500 Frontage Blvd.	A
51–100 Honeysuckle Road 12001–16000 Old Hwy. 14	B
1–99 Sawtooth Ridge 100–500 Flores St. 501–700 Frontage Blvd.	C
All mail that does not fall in one of the address ranges listed above	D

	Address	Delivery Code			
1.	38 Honey Ridge Road	A	B	C	D
2.	7835 Old Hwy. 14	A	B	C	D
3.	5 Flores St.	A	B	C	D
4.	441 Frontage Blvd.	A	B	C	D
5.	31 Honeysuckle Road	A	B	C	D
6.	7 Sawtooth Ridge	A	B	C	D
7.	589 Frontage Blvd.	A	B	C	D
8.	12200 Old Hwy. 14	A	B	C	D
9.	417 Flores St.	A	B	C	D
10.	40 Honeysuckle Road	A	B	C	D
11.	29 Sawtooth Ridge	A	B	C	D
12.	20 Honeysuckle Road	A	B	C	D
13.	4600 Old Hwy. 14	A	B	C	D
14.	385 Flores St.	A	B	C	D
15.	28 Frontage Blvd.	A	B	C	D
16.	90 Honeysuckle Road	A	B	C	D
17.	16000 Old Hwy. 14	A	B	C	D
18.	119 Flores St.	A	B	C	D
19.	52 Sweet Honey Road	A	B	C	D
20.	462 Frontage Blvd.	A	B	C	D
21.	11 Chain Saw Road	A	B	C	D
22.	550 Flores St.	A	B	C	D
23.	29 Honeysuckle Road	A	B	C	D
24.	44 Sawtooth Ridge	A	B	C	D
25.	14202 Old Hwy. 14	A	B	C	D
26.	322 Frontage Blvd.	A	B	C	D
27.	363 Floral Ave.	A	B	C	D
28.	74 Honeysuckle Road	A	B	C	D
29.	21050 Old Hwy. 14	A	B	C	D
30.	20 Sawtooth Ridge	A	B	C	D
31.	601 Frontage Blvd.	A	B	C	D
32.	65 Honeysuckle Road	A	B	C	D
33.	6022 Old Hwy. 14	A	B	C	D
34.	624 Frontage Blvd.	A	B	C	D
35.	228 Flores St.	A	B	C	D
36.	120 Honeysuckle Road	A	B	C	D

Memory Section

This section consists of four segments:

- **Segment 1** is a 3-minute study period during which you will attempt to memorize the Coding Guide. *Segment 1 is not scored*, and there are no answers to mark during this segment.
- **Segment 2** is a practice exercise consisting of 8 items to be completed in 1 1/2 minutes (90 seconds). *Segment 2 is not scored*.
- **Segment 3** is a 5-minute study period during which you will attempt to memorize the Coding Guide. *Segment 3 is not scored*, and there are no answers to mark during this segment.
- **Segment 4** is the actual Memory Section of the test. This segment consists of 36 items to be completed in 7 minutes. *Segment 4 is scored and counts toward your total test score*.

You will use the same Coding Guide for all four segments.

An answer key for Segments 2 and 4 is given at the end of the chapter.

Memory Section—Segment 1

Directions: Segment 1 is a 3-minute study period during which you will attempt to memorize the Coding Guide. This segment is *not* scored, and there are no answers to mark during this segment.

Begin the 3-minute study period when you are ready.

Coding Guide	
Address Range	Delivery Route
6000–12000 Old Hwy. 14 20–50 Honeysuckle Road 300–500 Frontage Blvd.	A
51–100 Honeysuckle Road 12001–16000 Old Hwy. 14	B
1–99 Sawtooth Ridge 100–500 Flores St. 501–700 Frontage Blvd.	C
All mail that does not fall in one of the address ranges listed above	D

Memory Section—Segment 2

Directions: Segment 2 is a practice exercise that will give you experience coding addresses from memory based on the Coding Guide on the previous page. The Coding Guide is not shown during this segment. Based on the Coding Guide, match each address to a delivery route. Mark your answers on the answer sheet at the end of the chapter. This segment is *not* scored.

See the opposite page when you are ready to begin Segment 2 under timed conditions.

Number of Items: 8

Time Limit: 1 1/2 minutes (90 seconds)

	Address	Delivery Code			
1.	401 Frontier Blvd.	A	B	C	D
2.	9020 Old Hwy. 14	A	B	C	D
3.	81 Sawtooth Ridge	A	B	C	D
4.	15990 Old Hwy. 14	A	B	C	D
5.	99 Honeysuckle Road	A	B	C	D
6.	380 Frontage Blvd.	A	B	C	D
7.	100 Sawtooth Ridge	A	B	C	D
8.	239 Flores St.	A	B	C	D

Memory Section—Segment 3
Directions: Segment 3 is a 5-minute study period during which you will again attempt to memorize the Coding Guide. This segment is *not* scored, and there are no answers to mark during this segment.

Begin the 5-minute study period when you are ready.

Coding Guide	
Address Range	*Delivery Route*
6000–12000 Old Hwy. 14 20–50 Honeysuckle Road 300–500 Frontage Blvd.	A
51–100 Honeysuckle Road 12001–16000 Old Hwy. 14	B
1–99 Sawtooth Ridge 100–500 Flores St. 501–700 Frontage Blvd.	C
All mail that does not fall in one of the address ranges listed above	D

Memory Section—Segment 4

Directions: Segment 4 is the *actual scored* Memory Section of the test. The Coding Guide is not shown during this segment. Based on the Coding Guide, match each address to a delivery route. Mark your answer on the answer sheet at the end of the chapter.

Turn the page when you are ready to begin Segment 4 under timed conditions.

Number of Items: 36

Time Limit: 7 minutes

	Address	Delivery Code			
37.	305 Frontage Blvd.	A	B	C	D
38.	75 Honeysuckle Road	A	B	C	D
39.	1002 Old Hwy. 14	A	B	C	D
40.	62 Flores St.	A	B	C	D
41.	310 Frontage Blvd.	A	B	C	D
42.	3000 Sawtooth Ridge	A	B	C	D
43.	13450 Hwy. 14	A	B	C	D
44.	700 Frontage Blvd.	A	B	C	D
45.	22 Honeysuckle Road	A	B	C	D
46.	40 Sawyer Ridge	A	B	C	D
47.	500 Frontage Blvd.	A	B	C	D
48.	68 Sawtooth Ridge	A	B	C	D
49.	36 Honeysuckle Road	A	B	C	D
50.	15242 Old Hwy. 14	A	B	C	D
51.	558 Frontage Blvd.	A	B	C	D
52.	250 Flores St.	A	B	C	D
53.	80 Honeysuckle Road	A	B	C	D
54.	13890 Old Hwy. 14	A	B	C	D
55.	690 Frontage Blvd.	A	B	C	D
56.	101 Flores St.	A	B	C	D
57.	66 Honeysuckle Road	A	B	C	D
58.	6100 Old Hwy. 51	A	B	C	D
59.	487 Frontage Blvd.	A	B	C	D
60.	16 Sawtooth Ridge	A	B	C	D
61.	490 Flores St.	A	B	C	D
62.	12126 Old Hwy. 14	A	B	C	D
63.	675 Front Street	A	B	C	D
64.	45 Honeysuckle Road	A	B	C	D
65.	212 Flower St.	A	B	C	D
66.	5 Sawtooth Ridge	A	B	C	D
67.	18 Honeysuckle Road	A	B	C	D
68.	8855 Old Hwy. 14	A	B	C	D
69.	930 Frontage Blvd.	A	B	C	D
70.	333 Flores St.	A	B	C	D
71.	10 Honeysuckle Road	A	B	C	D
72.	14001 Old Hwy. 14	A	B	C	D

Answer Sheet

Practice Drill 1

Coding Section

1. (A) (B) (C) (D)
2. (A) (B) (C) (D)
3. (A) (B) (C) (D)
4. (A) (B) (C) (D)
5. (A) (B) (C) (D)
6. (A) (B) (C) (D)
7. (A) (B) (C) (D)

8. (A) (B) (C) (D)
9. (A) (B) (C) (D)
10. (A) (B) (C) (D)
11. (A) (B) (C) (D)
12. (A) (B) (C) (D)
13. (A) (B) (C) (D)
14. (A) (B) (C) (D)

15. (A) (B) (C) (D)
16. (A) (B) (C) (D)
17. (A) (B) (C) (D)
18. (A) (B) (C) (D)
19. (A) (B) (C) (D)
20. (A) (B) (C) (D)

Memory Section

21. (A) (B) (C) (D)
22. (A) (B) (C) (D)
23. (A) (B) (C) (D)
24. (A) (B) (C) (D)
25. (A) (B) (C) (D)
26. (A) (B) (C) (D)
27. (A) (B) (C) (D)

28. (A) (B) (C) (D)
29. (A) (B) (C) (D)
30. (A) (B) (C) (D)
31. (A) (B) (C) (D)
32. (A) (B) (C) (D)
33. (A) (B) (C) (D)
34. (A) (B) (C) (D)

35. (A) (B) (C) (D)
36. (A) (B) (C) (D)
37. (A) (B) (C) (D)
38. (A) (B) (C) (D)
39. (A) (B) (C) (D)
40. (A) (B) (C) (D)

Practice Drill 2

Coding Section

1. (A) (B) (C) (D)
2. (A) (B) (C) (D)
3. (A) (B) (C) (D)
4. (A) (B) (C) (D)
5. (A) (B) (C) (D)
6. (A) (B) (C) (D)
7. (A) (B) (C) (D)

8. (A) (B) (C) (D)
9. (A) (B) (C) (D)
10. (A) (B) (C) (D)
11. (A) (B) (C) (D)
12. (A) (B) (C) (D)
13. (A) (B) (C) (D)
14. (A) (B) (C) (D)

15. (A) (B) (C) (D)
16. (A) (B) (C) (D)
17. (A) (B) (C) (D)
18. (A) (B) (C) (D)
19. (A) (B) (C) (D)
20. (A) (B) (C) (D)

Memory Section

21. (A) (B) (C) (D)
22. (A) (B) (C) (D)
23. (A) (B) (C) (D)
24. (A) (B) (C) (D)
25. (A) (B) (C) (D)
26. (A) (B) (C) (D)
27. (A) (B) (C) (D)

28. (A) (B) (C) (D)
29. (A) (B) (C) (D)
30. (A) (B) (C) (D)
31. (A) (B) (C) (D)
32. (A) (B) (C) (D)
33. (A) (B) (C) (D)
34. (A) (B) (C) (D)

35. (A) (B) (C) (D)
36. (A) (B) (C) (D)
37. (A) (B) (C) (D)
38. (A) (B) (C) (D)
39. (A) (B) (C) (D)
40. (A) (B) (C) (D)

Practice Drill 3

Coding Section

1. Ⓐ Ⓑ Ⓒ Ⓓ
2. Ⓐ Ⓑ Ⓒ Ⓓ
3. Ⓐ Ⓑ Ⓒ Ⓓ
4. Ⓐ Ⓑ Ⓒ Ⓓ
5. Ⓐ Ⓑ Ⓒ Ⓓ
6. Ⓐ Ⓑ Ⓒ Ⓓ
7. Ⓐ Ⓑ Ⓒ Ⓓ

8. Ⓐ Ⓑ Ⓒ Ⓓ
9. Ⓐ Ⓑ Ⓒ Ⓓ
10. Ⓐ Ⓑ Ⓒ Ⓓ
11. Ⓐ Ⓑ Ⓒ Ⓓ
12. Ⓐ Ⓑ Ⓒ Ⓓ
13. Ⓐ Ⓑ Ⓒ Ⓓ
14. Ⓐ Ⓑ Ⓒ Ⓓ

15. Ⓐ Ⓑ Ⓒ Ⓓ
16. Ⓐ Ⓑ Ⓒ Ⓓ
17. Ⓐ Ⓑ Ⓒ Ⓓ
18. Ⓐ Ⓑ Ⓒ Ⓓ
19. Ⓐ Ⓑ Ⓒ Ⓓ
20. Ⓐ Ⓑ Ⓒ Ⓓ

Memory Section

21. Ⓐ Ⓑ Ⓒ Ⓓ
22. Ⓐ Ⓑ Ⓒ Ⓓ
23. Ⓐ Ⓑ Ⓒ Ⓓ
24. Ⓐ Ⓑ Ⓒ Ⓓ
25. Ⓐ Ⓑ Ⓒ Ⓓ
26. Ⓐ Ⓑ Ⓒ Ⓓ
27. Ⓐ Ⓑ Ⓒ Ⓓ

28. Ⓐ Ⓑ Ⓒ Ⓓ
29. Ⓐ Ⓑ Ⓒ Ⓓ
30. Ⓐ Ⓑ Ⓒ Ⓓ
31. Ⓐ Ⓑ Ⓒ Ⓓ
32. Ⓐ Ⓑ Ⓒ Ⓓ
33. Ⓐ Ⓑ Ⓒ Ⓓ
34. Ⓐ Ⓑ Ⓒ Ⓓ

35. Ⓐ Ⓑ Ⓒ Ⓓ
36. Ⓐ Ⓑ Ⓒ Ⓓ
37. Ⓐ Ⓑ Ⓒ Ⓓ
38. Ⓐ Ⓑ Ⓒ Ⓓ
39. Ⓐ Ⓑ Ⓒ Ⓓ
40. Ⓐ Ⓑ Ⓒ Ⓓ

Practice Drill 4

Coding Section

1. Ⓐ Ⓑ Ⓒ Ⓓ
2. Ⓐ Ⓑ Ⓒ Ⓓ
3. Ⓐ Ⓑ Ⓒ Ⓓ
4. Ⓐ Ⓑ Ⓒ Ⓓ
5. Ⓐ Ⓑ Ⓒ Ⓓ
6. Ⓐ Ⓑ Ⓒ Ⓓ
7. Ⓐ Ⓑ Ⓒ Ⓓ

8. Ⓐ Ⓑ Ⓒ Ⓓ
9. Ⓐ Ⓑ Ⓒ Ⓓ
10. Ⓐ Ⓑ Ⓒ Ⓓ
11. Ⓐ Ⓑ Ⓒ Ⓓ
12. Ⓐ Ⓑ Ⓒ Ⓓ
13. Ⓐ Ⓑ Ⓒ Ⓓ
14. Ⓐ Ⓑ Ⓒ Ⓓ

15. Ⓐ Ⓑ Ⓒ Ⓓ
16. Ⓐ Ⓑ Ⓒ Ⓓ
17. Ⓐ Ⓑ Ⓒ Ⓓ
18. Ⓐ Ⓑ Ⓒ Ⓓ
19. Ⓐ Ⓑ Ⓒ Ⓓ
20. Ⓐ Ⓑ Ⓒ Ⓓ

Memory Section

21. Ⓐ Ⓑ Ⓒ Ⓓ
22. Ⓐ Ⓑ Ⓒ Ⓓ
23. Ⓐ Ⓑ Ⓒ Ⓓ
24. Ⓐ Ⓑ Ⓒ Ⓓ
25. Ⓐ Ⓑ Ⓒ Ⓓ
26. Ⓐ Ⓑ Ⓒ Ⓓ
27. Ⓐ Ⓑ Ⓒ Ⓓ

28. Ⓐ Ⓑ Ⓒ Ⓓ
29. Ⓐ Ⓑ Ⓒ Ⓓ
30. Ⓐ Ⓑ Ⓒ Ⓓ
31. Ⓐ Ⓑ Ⓒ Ⓓ
32. Ⓐ Ⓑ Ⓒ Ⓓ
33. Ⓐ Ⓑ Ⓒ Ⓓ
34. Ⓐ Ⓑ Ⓒ Ⓓ

35. Ⓐ Ⓑ Ⓒ Ⓓ
36. Ⓐ Ⓑ Ⓒ Ⓓ
37. Ⓐ Ⓑ Ⓒ Ⓓ
38. Ⓐ Ⓑ Ⓒ Ⓓ
39. Ⓐ Ⓑ Ⓒ Ⓓ
40. Ⓐ Ⓑ Ⓒ Ⓓ

Practice Drill 5

Coding Section—Segment 1

1. Ⓐ Ⓑ Ⓒ Ⓓ
2. Ⓐ Ⓑ Ⓒ Ⓓ
3. Ⓐ Ⓑ Ⓒ Ⓓ
4. Ⓐ Ⓑ Ⓒ Ⓓ

Coding Section—Segment 2

1. Ⓐ Ⓑ Ⓒ Ⓓ
2. Ⓐ Ⓑ Ⓒ Ⓓ
3. Ⓐ Ⓑ Ⓒ Ⓓ
4. Ⓐ Ⓑ Ⓒ Ⓓ
5. Ⓐ Ⓑ Ⓒ Ⓓ
6. Ⓐ Ⓑ Ⓒ Ⓓ
7. Ⓐ Ⓑ Ⓒ Ⓓ
8. Ⓐ Ⓑ Ⓒ Ⓓ

Coding Section—Segment 3

1. Ⓐ Ⓑ Ⓒ Ⓓ
2. Ⓐ Ⓑ Ⓒ Ⓓ
3. Ⓐ Ⓑ Ⓒ Ⓓ
4. Ⓐ Ⓑ Ⓒ Ⓓ
5. Ⓐ Ⓑ Ⓒ Ⓓ
6. Ⓐ Ⓑ Ⓒ Ⓓ
7. Ⓐ Ⓑ Ⓒ Ⓓ
8. Ⓐ Ⓑ Ⓒ Ⓓ
9. Ⓐ Ⓑ Ⓒ Ⓓ
10. Ⓐ Ⓑ Ⓒ Ⓓ
11. Ⓐ Ⓑ Ⓒ Ⓓ
12. Ⓐ Ⓑ Ⓒ Ⓓ
13. Ⓐ Ⓑ Ⓒ Ⓓ
14. Ⓐ Ⓑ Ⓒ Ⓓ
15. Ⓐ Ⓑ Ⓒ Ⓓ
16. Ⓐ Ⓑ Ⓒ Ⓓ
17. Ⓐ Ⓑ Ⓒ Ⓓ
18. Ⓐ Ⓑ Ⓒ Ⓓ
19. Ⓐ Ⓑ Ⓒ Ⓓ
20. Ⓐ Ⓑ Ⓒ Ⓓ
21. Ⓐ Ⓑ Ⓒ Ⓓ
22. Ⓐ Ⓑ Ⓒ Ⓓ
23. Ⓐ Ⓑ Ⓒ Ⓓ
24. Ⓐ Ⓑ Ⓒ Ⓓ
25. Ⓐ Ⓑ Ⓒ Ⓓ
26. Ⓐ Ⓑ Ⓒ Ⓓ
27. Ⓐ Ⓑ Ⓒ Ⓓ
28. Ⓐ Ⓑ Ⓒ Ⓓ
29. Ⓐ Ⓑ Ⓒ Ⓓ
30. Ⓐ Ⓑ Ⓒ Ⓓ
31. Ⓐ Ⓑ Ⓒ Ⓓ
32. Ⓐ Ⓑ Ⓒ Ⓓ
33. Ⓐ Ⓑ Ⓒ Ⓓ
34. Ⓐ Ⓑ Ⓒ Ⓓ
35. Ⓐ Ⓑ Ⓒ Ⓓ
36. Ⓐ Ⓑ Ⓒ Ⓓ

Memory Section—Segment 2

1. Ⓐ Ⓑ Ⓒ Ⓓ
2. Ⓐ Ⓑ Ⓒ Ⓓ
3. Ⓐ Ⓑ Ⓒ Ⓓ
4. Ⓐ Ⓑ Ⓒ Ⓓ
5. Ⓐ Ⓑ Ⓒ Ⓓ
6. Ⓐ Ⓑ Ⓒ Ⓓ
7. Ⓐ Ⓑ Ⓒ Ⓓ
8. Ⓐ Ⓑ Ⓒ Ⓓ

Memory Section—Segment 4

37. Ⓐ Ⓑ Ⓒ Ⓓ
38. Ⓐ Ⓑ Ⓒ Ⓓ
39. Ⓐ Ⓑ Ⓒ Ⓓ
40. Ⓐ Ⓑ Ⓒ Ⓓ
41. Ⓐ Ⓑ Ⓒ Ⓓ
42. Ⓐ Ⓑ Ⓒ Ⓓ
43. Ⓐ Ⓑ Ⓒ Ⓓ
44. Ⓐ Ⓑ Ⓒ Ⓓ
45. Ⓐ Ⓑ Ⓒ Ⓓ
46. Ⓐ Ⓑ Ⓒ Ⓓ
47. Ⓐ Ⓑ Ⓒ Ⓓ
48. Ⓐ Ⓑ Ⓒ Ⓓ
49. Ⓐ Ⓑ Ⓒ Ⓓ
50. Ⓐ Ⓑ Ⓒ Ⓓ
51. Ⓐ Ⓑ Ⓒ Ⓓ
52. Ⓐ Ⓑ Ⓒ Ⓓ
53. Ⓐ Ⓑ Ⓒ Ⓓ
54. Ⓐ Ⓑ Ⓒ Ⓓ
55. Ⓐ Ⓑ Ⓒ Ⓓ
56. Ⓐ Ⓑ Ⓒ Ⓓ
57. Ⓐ Ⓑ Ⓒ Ⓓ
58. Ⓐ Ⓑ Ⓒ Ⓓ
59. Ⓐ Ⓑ Ⓒ Ⓓ
60. Ⓐ Ⓑ Ⓒ Ⓓ
61. Ⓐ Ⓑ Ⓒ Ⓓ
62. Ⓐ Ⓑ Ⓒ Ⓓ
63. Ⓐ Ⓑ Ⓒ Ⓓ
64. Ⓐ Ⓑ Ⓒ Ⓓ
65. Ⓐ Ⓑ Ⓒ Ⓓ
66. Ⓐ Ⓑ Ⓒ Ⓓ
67. Ⓐ Ⓑ Ⓒ Ⓓ
68. Ⓐ Ⓑ Ⓒ Ⓓ
69. Ⓐ Ⓑ Ⓒ Ⓓ
70. Ⓐ Ⓑ Ⓒ Ⓓ
71. Ⓐ Ⓑ Ⓒ Ⓓ
72. Ⓐ Ⓑ Ⓒ Ⓓ

Answer Key

Practice Drill 1

Coding Section

1. C	5. B	9. D	13. D	17. D
2. B	6. A	10. D	14. D	18. D
3. D	7. C	11. B	15. D	19. D
4. D	8. D	12. A	16. C	20. B

Memory Section

21. D	25. D	29. A	33. D	37. D
22. B	26. D	30. C	34. D	38. D
23. A	27. C	31. D	35. A	39. D
24. D	28. B	32. D	36. C	40. B

Practice Drill 2

Coding Section

1. A	5. A	9. C	13. C	17. A
2. D	6. D	10. D	14. B	18. D
3. B	7. B	11. A	15. D	19. C
4. C	8. B	12. A	16. C	20. A

Memory Section

21. C	25. D	29. C	33. C	37. A
22. A	26. B	30. D	34. D	38. C
23. C	27. A	31. B	35. B	39. B
24. B	28. D	32. A	36. A	40. D

Practice Drill 3

Coding Section

1. B	5. B	9. D	13. C	17. C
2. A	6. D	10. A	14. D	18. B
3. C	7. C	11. B	15. D	19. C
4. D	8. A	12. C	16. A	20. A

Memory Section

21. A	25. A	29. B	33. C	37. D
22. B	26. A	30. A	34. C	38. C
23. A	27. D	31. C	35. B	39. A
24. C	28. B	32. D	36. B	40. B

Practice Drill 4

Coding Section

1. B	5. C	9. A	13. D	17. D
2. D	6. A	10. B	14. B	18. A
3. A	7. C	11. D	15. A	19. A
4. C	8. D	12. C	16. C	20. B

Memory Section

21. B	25. D	29. A	33. B	37. C
22. A	26. B	30. A	34. C	38. D
23. D	27. C	31. A	35. D	39. D
24. C	28. A	32. C	36. B	40. B

Practice Drill 5

Coding Section—Segment 1

1. C	2. B	3. A	4. D

Coding Section—Segment 2

1. D	3. A	5. A	7. C
2. B	4. D	6. C	8. A

Coding Section—Segment 3

1. D	9. C	17. B	25. B	33. A
2. A	10. A	18. C	26. A	34. C
3. D	11. C	19. D	27. D	35. C
4. A	12. A	20. A	28. B	36. D
5. A	13. D	21. D	29. D	
6. C	14. C	22. D	30. C	
7. C	15. D	23. A	31. C	
8. B	16. B	24. C	32. B	

Memory Section—Segment 2

1. D	3. C	5. B	7. D
2. A	4. B	6. A	8. C

Memory Section—Segment 4

37. A	45. A	53. B	61. C	69. D
38. B	46. D	54. B	62. B	70. C
39. D	47. A	55. C	63. D	71. D
40. D	48. C	56. C	64. A	72. B
41. A	49. A	57. B	65. D	
42. D	50. B	58. D	66. C	
43. D	51. C	59. A	67. D	
44. C	52. C	60. C	68. A	

Personal Characteristics and Experience Inventory

Part D of Test 473 is called *Personal Characteristics and Experience Inventory*. In this part, you have 90 minutes to answer 236 questions. The questions in Part D are designed to assess various personal characteristics, preferences, and experiences that are relevant to working effectively as an employee of the Postal Service.

Part D consists of two sections:

- Personal Characteristics (160 questions)
- Experience (76 questions)

The directions for Part D are essentially as follows:

Directions: Read each of the following items and decide which of the alternative responses is *most true about you*. For each item, choose one and *only one response*, even if you think more than one response is true about you. Be sure to respond to each and every item, even if you are not sure which response is best.

Personal Characteristics

The Personal Characteristics section of Part D actually consists of two distinct segments:

- An *Agree/Disagree* segment, in which you decide the extent to which you agree with each of a series of statements describing you
- A *Frequency* segment, in which you decide how frequently you engage in particular actions or behaviors that are described

Agree/Disagree Questions

Here are three agree/disagree questions that are similar to the ones on Part D of the exam. Note that the four response choices for each item—strongly agree, agree, disagree, and strongly disagree—are the same ones that you'll see in each and every question of this type on the actual exam.

1. You like to complete one task before beginning another.
   A. Strongly agree
   B. Agree
   C. Disagree
   D. Strongly disagree

2. You prefer working by yourself to working with other people.
   A. Strongly agree
   B. Agree
   C. Disagree
   D. Strongly disagree

3. It is important to you that others share your opinions.
   A. Strongly agree
   B. Agree
   C. Disagree
   D. Strongly disagree

Frequency Questions

In the second segment of the Personal Characteristics section, your task is to assess how frequently you engage in the kind of actions or behavior described in each of a series of statements. Here are three frequency questions, which are similar to the ones on Part D of the exam. The four response choices for each item—very often, often, sometimes, and rarely or never—are the same ones that you'll see in each and every question of this type on the actual exam.

1. You argue with other people.
   A. Very often
   B. Often
   C. Sometimes
   D. Rarely or never

2. You repeat mistakes that you've made in the past.
   A. Very often
   B. Often
   C. Sometimes
   D. Rarely or never

3. You think about the consequences of your actions before you act.
   A. Very often
   B. Often
   C. Sometimes
   D. Rarely or never

Experience

Each item in the Experience section of Part D is designed to gauge your experience in an area that is relevant to performing effectively as a Postal Service employee. In this section, the response choices vary from one question to the next. The number of response choices varies as well, from as few as four to as many as nine lettered choices.

Here are three experience questions that are similar to the ones on Part D of the exam.

1. What type of supervisor do you like the least?
    A. Someone who corrects my job mistakes as I make them
    B. Someone who makes clear exactly how I should perform my job
    C. Someone who lets me make all my own decisions about how to do my job
    D. Someone who asks for my ideas about the best way to do my job
    E. Someone who leaves it to me to figure out how to correct my own mistakes
    F. Not sure

2. What kind of task do you enjoy the most?
    A. A task that requires a lot of walking and moving about
    B. Doing something new and different every day
    C. A repetitive task performed at a slow and steady pace
    D. A task requiring very few decisions on my part
    E. Working with other people to solve a problem
    F. Would strongly dislike all of these tasks
    G. Not sure

3. In what kind of environment do you function your best?
    A. A quiet setting in which there is very little activity
    B. A busy setting in which there is a lot of activity
    C. An organized setting in which everything is predictable
    D. Function equally well in all of these environments
    E. Not sure

Strategies for Completing the Part D Inventory

Never Choose More Than One Lettered Choice for Any Question

For some questions in the Experience section, two or more listed descriptions may seem equally correct to you. However, the instructions state explicitly that you are to select one *and only one* response choice for each question. If you have trouble narrowing down your choices to a single "best" one, be sure to check for an "all of the above" or "none of the above" choice, as well as a "not sure" choice. These choices will appear at the end of your list of choices. For example, in the three preceding examples, notice choice **F** in Question 1, choices **F** and **G** in Question 2, and choices **D** and **E** in Question 3.

Respond to the Questions in Part D Based on Your Experiences in a Job or Other Work Setting, if Possible

If you've never held a job before, or if the question at hand doesn't relate well to any job you've held, try to respond to the question based on your experiences in settings such as volunteer or school activities. For example, if a question asks about how you get along with coworkers, but you've never had coworkers in the jobs you've held, you should respond based on how you've gotten along with your peers in other settings, such as school or community activities, or even among your circle of friends and acquaintances.

Read Each Statement Very Carefully Before Responding to It

If you're not careful in reading a question, you can easily end up providing a distorted description of your preferences and experiences. Many of the statements and questions in Part D contain words such as *most* or *least*, *like* or *dislike*, and *do* or *don't*. One little word can make all the difference. Be careful not to respond to the converse of the question at hand. For example, these two statements have the opposite meaning:

It is important to you that others share your opinions.
It is not important to you whether others share your opinions.

These two questions are also opposite in meaning:

What type of supervisor do you like the least?
What type of supervisor do you like the most?

Note: The test makers try not to trick you with confusing double negatives such as "don't dislike" or confusing phrases such as "dislike the most" or "prefer the least." Nevertheless, read each statement carefully to make sure you don't get its meaning backwards.

Respond to All Questions in Part D as Honestly as Possible

The score for Part D is based largely on the consistency of your answers to all 236 questions. If you try to figure out which response to each question would make you appear to be the best possible job candidate, you'll probably end up providing a self-contradictory, distorted description of yourself. When your responses are tabulated, the computerized scoring system will detect this problem and award you a low score as a result.

Work Through Part D at a Reasonably Quick Pace

The time allowed for Part D is 90 minutes, which is more than enough time to respond to all 236 questions. Any test taker with basic English reading skills can comfortably answer at least three questions per minute (that's 20 seconds per question) on average. At this pace, you'll complete Part D in about 80 minutes.

Try not to think too much about any one item. Otherwise, you might end up overanalyzing yourself and providing responses that don't reflect your true preferences, opinions, and experiences. Your immediate, first response to any question in Part D is likely to be the most honest one—and the one the best describes you.

Mark Your Responses on the Answer Sheet in Groups

Part D consists of a total of 236 questions; that makes for a lot of bubbles to mark on your answer sheet. Just as for the other parts of the test, it's more efficient to respond to Part D questions in groups of perhaps 10 at a time. First mark your responses to a group of 10 questions directly in the test booklet. (Circle your letter choices.) Then transcribe your answers for that group of questions on your answer sheet. Repeat this procedure for each successive group of 10 questions.

> City carriers used to walk as many as 22 miles per day, delivering to residences twice each day and to businesses four times daily. Today, carriers walk far less and deliver mail only once a day except in some large cities, where business deliveries are still made twice daily. Today, the weight limit for a city carrier's load is 35 pounds, down from 50 pounds in the 1950s.

There's No Need to Practice for Part D of the Test

In fact, too much practice might be counterproductive. Why? As noted earlier, you'll be tempted to analyze the practice questions and respond in ways that do not describe your true preferences and experiences.

Note: The seven practice tests in this book do *not* include any Part D questions, for this very reason.

Practice Test 1

Part A: Address Checking

Directions: Part A of this test consists of 60 items for you to complete in 11 minutes. You will be shown a **Correct List** of addresses and ZIP codes alongside a **List to Be Checked**. The two lists should contain the same addresses and ZIP codes, except that the **List to Be Checked** may contain errors.

Each row of information consists of one item. For each item, compare the address and ZIP code in the **Correct List** with the address and ZIP code in the **List to Be Checked**. Determine whether there are **No Errors**, an error in **Address Only**, an error in **ZIP Code Only**, or an error in **Both** the address and the ZIP code. Select an answer from the following four choices:

A. No Errors	B. Address Only	C. ZIP Code Only	D. Both

Mark your answers (A, B, C, or D) on the answer sheet at the end of this chapter.

An answer key is given at the end of the chapter.

Number of Items: 60

Time: 11 minutes

A. No Errors	B. Address Only	C. ZIP Code Only	D. Both

	Correct List		**List to Be Checked**	
	Address	*ZIP Code*	*Address*	*ZIP Code*
1.	606 Reese Rd. Lincoln, NE	68503-4473	600 Reese Rd. Lincoln, NE	68503-3373
2.	1010 S. Fairmont St. Riverside, CA	92506	1010 S. Fairmount St. Riverside, CA	92506
3.	240 Forest Ave. Columbus, OH	43231	240 Forest Ave. Columbus, OH	43231
4.	3150 Darla Lane Tallahassee, FL	32308-2288	3510 Darla Lane Tallahassee, FL	32308-2288
5.	340 Hwy. 17 North State College, PA	16803	340 Hwy. 17 North State College, PA	16830
6.	2688 Willow Rd. Spartanburg, SC	29302	2688 Willow St. Spartanburg, SC	29802
7.	185 Centre Cir. Athens, GA	30607-5744	185 Center Cir. Athens, GA	30607-5744
8.	21 N. Linn St. Topeka, KS	66616-0932	21 N. Linn St. Topeka, KS	66116-0932
9.	7101 Airport Blvd. Pontiac, MI	48341	7100 Airport Blvd. Pontiac, MI	48341
10.	740 Story Rd. Montpelier, VT	05602-0001	740 Story Rd. Montpelier, VT	05602-0001
11.	7733 Jade Dr. #14 Carthage, MO	64836	7733 Jade Dr. #14 Carthage, MI	64836
12.	505 Green St. Billings, MT	59106-7266	505 Greene St. Billings, MT	59106-7262
13.	PO Box 30221 Scranton, PA	10509-0221	PO Box 30221 Scranton, PA	15090-0221
14.	1549 Pacific Drive Quinton, OK	74561	1549 Pacific Drive Quinton, OK	74561
15.	41 E. San Luis St. Austin, TX	78759	41 S. San Luis St. Austin, TX	78759

continued on next page

A. No Errors	B. Address Only	C. ZIP Code Only	D. Both

	Correct List		List to Be Checked	
	Address	**ZIP Code**	**Address**	**ZIP Code**
16.	223 Beverly Lane Los Angeles, CA	90077	233 Beverly Lane Los Angeles, CA	90077
17.	1622 Saint Olaf Ave. Bay City, MI	48708-0274	1622 Saint Olaf Ave. Bay City, MI	48768-0274
18.	5719 N. 13th Street Modesto, CA	95355-9582	5719 N. 13th Street Modesto, CA	95399-9582
19.	444 Todd Blvd. Skokie, IL	60077	44 Todd Blvd. Skokie, IL	60077
20.	1450 Superior Dr. Las Vegas, NV	89128-4392	1450 Superior St. Las Vegas, NV	89128-4932
21.	35 Pine Place, Suite 8 Mizpah, MN	56660-0937	35 Park Place, Suite 8 Mizpah, MN	56660-0937
22.	9725 State St. Dallas, TX	75232	9725 State St. Dallas, TX	75232
23.	807 Logan Circle Ogden, UT	84404	807 Logan Court Ogden, UT	84440
24.	98 Astin Dr. Arlington, VA	22204-2554	98 Austin Dr. Arlington, VA	22404-2554
25.	14783 Jeffrey Rd. Portland, ME	04103	14783 Jeffrey Rd. Portland, ME	04130
26.	PO Box 16658 Council Bluffs, IA	51503	PO Box 16658 Council Bluffs, IA	55013
27.	9400 Brighton Ct. Baltimore, MD	21202-1029	9400 Brigton Ct. Baltimore, MD	21202-1029
28.	3911 Warner Ave. Raleigh, NC	27610-2975	3911 Warner Ave. Raleigh, NC	26610-2975
29.	3301 Edith Terrace Lake City, TN	37769-5739	33011 Edith Terrace Lake City, TN	37769-5739
30.	2120 Park Lane Louisville, AL	36048	2120 Park Lane Louisville, AL	36048
31.	19900 Macy Rd., Apt. 1 Worcester, MA	01606	19900 Macy Rd., Apt. 1 Wooster, MA	01606
32.	2184 Dickson Way Saint Louis, MO	63108-2995	2184 Dickson Way Saint Louis, MS	63108-2955

continued on next page

A. No Errors	B. Address Only	C. ZIP Code Only	D. Both

	Correct List		**List to Be Checked**	
	Address	*ZIP Code*	*Address*	*ZIP Code*
33.	56 Rolling Acres Marietta, GA	30066	56 Rolling Acres Marietta, GA	63066
34.	1901 S. Alfred St. Wichita, KS	67210-0667	1901 S. Alfred St. Wichita, KS	67210-0667
35.	83 Sandusky Cir. Muskegon, MI	49441	84 Sandusky Cir. Muskegon, MI	49441
36.	2705 E. Madison Parkway Center, PA	15220	2705 N. Madison Parkway Center, PA	15220
37.	39 W. 32nd St. Groton, NY	13073-1552	39 W. 32nd St. Groton, NY	13073-1255
38.	2124 1st Ave. Troy, WV	26443-4238	2124 1st Ave. Troy, WV	26343-4238
39.	663 S. King St. New Orleans, LA	70129	633 S. King Rd. New Orleans, LA	70129
40.	5858 Boothe Rd. Youngstown, OH	44511	5858 Booth Rd. Youngstown, OH	44451
41.	8009 S. Vermont Ave. Wynne, AR	72396	9008 S. Vermont Ave. Wynne, AR	72396
42.	6211 Creek Lane #9 Great Neck, NY	11021-0078	6211 Creek Lane #9 Great Neck, NY	11021-0078
43.	3343 SE Haley Blvd. Tulsa, OK	74105-6883	4334 SE Haley Blvd. Tulsa, OK	74109-6883
44.	P.O. Box 158 Pueblo, CO	81004-0158	P.O. Box 58 Pueblo, CO	81004-0158
45.	728 Ferndale Blvd. Wilmington, DE	19801	728 Farmdale Blvd. Wilmington, DE	19181
46.	2413 Allen Road Phoenix, AZ	85040-3566	2413 Allen Road Phoenix, AZ	80540-3566
47.	36703 North L St. Peoria, IL	61602	37603 North L St. Peoria, IL	61602
48.	49 Pell Cir. Van Nuys, CA	91401-9376	49 Pell Cir. Van Nuys, CA	91401-9346
49.	1415 U.S. Highway 92 Clifton, NJ	07012	1514 U.S. Highway 92 Clifton, NJ	07022

continued on next page

A. No Errors	B. Address Only	C. ZIP Code Only	D. Both

	Correct List		List to Be Checked	
	Address	ZIP Code	Address	ZIP Code
50.	667 Zelza Ln. #9 Corpus Christi, TX	78410	667 Zelza Ln. #9 Corpus Christi, TX	78410
51.	5712 83rd Street New York, NY	10021-8368	5712 82nd Street New York, NY	10021-8368
52.	4403 Northside Pkwy. Bismarck, ND	58501-2347	4403 Northside Hwy. Bismarck, ND	58501-2347
53.	PO Box 36637 Stanleytown, VA	24168-6637	PO Box 36637 Stanleytown, VA	24168-6337
54.	3377 Middle Road La Barge, WY	83123	3377 Middle Road La Barge, WY	83123
55.	321 E. Chapman Way Klamath Falls, OR	97603	321 E. Chapman Ave. Klamath Falls, OR	97603
56.	3130 Highland St. Idaho Falls, ID	83404-1140	3131 Highland St. Idaho Falls, ID	83404-1140
57.	3900 Workman Road Minneapolis, MN	55405	3900 Workmann Road Minneapolis, MN	55400
58.	14260 Burlington Ln. Lawrence, KS	66046-3506	14260 Burlington Ln. Lawrence, KS	66056-3506
59.	323 W. Eighth Street Owensboro, KY	42301-4197	233 W. Eighth Street Owensboro, KY	42301-4197
60.	948 South Mooney Blvd. Fresno, CA	93722	948 South Money Blvd. Fresno, CA	98722

Part B: Forms Completion

Directions: Part B of this test consists of 30 questions for you to complete in 15 minutes. You will be shown a series of forms that are similar to ones used by the U.S. Postal Service. The parts of each form are labeled (for example, 3 and 4a). Each form is accompanied by several questions that test your ability to complete the form properly. For each question, choose the best answer and mark your selection (A, B, C, or D) on your answer sheet.

Go to the next page when you are ready to begin Part B under timed conditions.

An answer key is given at the end of the chapter.

Number of Questions: 30

Time: 15 minutes

Authorization to Hold Mail	
1. Hold Mail For:	2. Beginning Date
1a. Name	3. Ending Date
1b. Street Address	4a. ☐ Do NOT resume delivery until I pick up all accumulated mail.
1c. City, State, ZIP	
5. Customer Signature	4b. ☐ Resume delivery of accumulated and new mail on ending date.
POSTAL USE ONLY 6. Date Received	8. Carrier
POSTAL USE ONLY 7. Clerk	9. Route Number

1. Where should the date received be entered on this form?

    (A) Box 5

    (B) Box 4

    (C) Box 6

    (D) Box 8

2. The postal carrier is Gina Renaldi. How would you indicate this?

    (A) Enter "Gina Renaldi" in Box 9

    (B) Enter "Gina Renaldi" in Box 8

    (C) Enter Gina Renaldi's route number in Box 9

    (D) Enter Gina Renaldi's carrier number in Box 8

3. A person's name would be a correct entry for every box EXCEPT which?

    (A) Box 5

    (B) Box 7

    (C) Box 1a

    (D) Box 4

4. Which of these would be a correct entry for Box 2?

    (A) "Albany, NY"

    (B) A check mark

    (C) "10/05/07"

    (D) "418 Vista Avenue"

5. The customer wants to pick up accumulated mail upon her return. How would she indicate this?

    (A) Enter a check mark in Box 4b

    (B) Enter her signature in Box 5

    (C) Enter an ending date in Box 3

    (D) Enter a check mark in Box 4a

Bulk Mailing Certificate

Certificate Fee Schedule

1a. 1 – 1,000 pieces $ _____

1b. Each additional
    1,000 pieces (or $ _____
    fraction thereof)

                           } Use Current
                             Rate Schedule

2a. Number of Identical Pieces	2b. Mail Class	2c. Postage per Piece	2d. Total Postage
3a. Number of Pieces per Pound	3b. Total Number of Pieces		3c. Bulk Mailing Fee
4a. Mailed By	4b. Mailed For		5. Total Postage and Fees

6. Postmaster s Certificate
I hereby certify that the mailing described above has been received
and the number of pieces and the postage is correct.

X _____
                              (Postmaster)

6. Where should the number of individual pieces mailed be entered on this form?

   (A) Box 2a

   (B) Box 3b

   (C) Box 1b

   (D) Box 4b

7. Which of these is a correct entry for Box 4a?

   (A) "8/13/07"

   (B) "$14.00"

   (C) A check mark

   (D) "Frank Palmieri"

8. Where would you enter the current bulk-mailing rate for 500 total pieces?

   (A) Box 1b

   (B) Box 2d

   (C) Box 1a

   (D) Box 2a

9. A dollar amount would be a correct entry for every box EXCEPT which?

   (A) Box 5

   (B) Box 3a

   (C) Box 2c

   (D) Box 2d

10. Which of these would be an appropriate entry for Box 2b?

    (A) A check mark

    (B) "First class"

    (C) "2,700"

    (D) "$.45"

11. Which of these is a correct entry in Box 6?

    (A) A dollar amount

    (B) A weight

    (C) An address

    (D) A person's name

Customs Dispatch Order and Declaration

1. Sender Information	2. Addressee Information
1a. Name	2a. Name
1b. Street, Apt., or PO Box No.	2b. Street, Apt., or PO Box No.
1c. City, State, ZIP + 4	2c. City, State, ZIP + 4
1d. Country	2d. Country

3a. Contents (Detailed Description)	3c. Qty	3d. Weight lb. oz.	3e. Value (US $)

3b. Check One ☐ Gift ☐ Commercial Sample ☐ Document ☐ Other	3f. Restriction and Other Comments (e.g., subject to quarantine)

4. For Commercial Items Only 4a. Country of Origin _____ ☐ Unknown 4b. HS Tariff No. _____ ☐ Unknown	5. Sender's Signature and Date 6. Delivery (Check One) ☐ Priority/Air ☐ Non-Priority/Surface

12. Where should the number of delivery items be entered on this form?

    (A) Box 3d

    (B) Line 4b

    (C) Box 3c

    (D) Box 3e

13. Which of these would be a correct entry for Line 4a?

    (A) "USA"

    (B) "12"

    (C) "gift"

    (D) "Marsha Knight"

14. A person's name would be a correct entry for every line or box EXCEPT which?

    (A) Line 1a

    (B) Line 2b

    (C) Box 5

    (D) Line 2a

15. How would you indicate that an article is sent by ground transportation?

    (A) Enter "computer" in Box 3f

    (B) Put a check mark in Box 6

    (C) Enter "computer" in Box 3a

    (D) Put a check mark in Box 3b

16. Where would you enter a date on this form?

    (A) Box 6

    (B) Box 1

    (C) Box 5

    (D) Box 3

17. Which of these would be a correct entry for Line 2c?

    (A) "Paris"

    (B) "Fragile"

    (C) "England"

    (D) "328 2nd Ave."

18. The article delivered is a computer. Where would you indicate this?

    (A) Box 3c

    (B) Box 3e

    (C) Box 3b

    (D) Box 3a

Certified Mail Receipt (Domestic Mail Only)		
TO BE COMPLETED BY SENDER	**OFFICIAL USE**	
1. Sent To	Postage	4.
2. Street, Apt. No., or PO Box	Certified Fee	5.
	Return Receipt Fee	6.
3. City, State, ZIP + 4	Restricted Delivery Fee	7.
CERTIFIED MAIL NUMBER 9217 0048 5033 7002	Total Postage and Fees	8.

19. The return receipt fee is $1.25. Where would you indicate this?

    (A) Box 6
    (B) Box 8
    (C) Box 7
    (D) Box 5

20. Each of these would be an appropriate entry for Box 3 EXCEPT which?

    (A) "New York"
    (B) "PO Box 2287"
    (C) "Maryland"
    (D) "91310"

21. Which type of entry is appropriate on this form?

    (A) An article's weight
    (B) A date
    (C) A postage fee
    (D) The sender's name

22. Where should the certified fee be entered on this form?

    (A) Box 3
    (B) Box 7
    (C) Box 6
    (D) Box 5

23. A postal employee would enter each information item EXCEPT which?

    (A) The delivery address
    (B) The return receipt fee
    (C) The restricted delivery fee
    (D) The postage amount

24. Where is the fee total indicated?

    (A) Box 4
    (B) Box 8
    (C) Box 1
    (D) Box 7

Delivery Confirmation Receipt **(Do not use for insured or registered mail.)**		
1. (To Be Completed by Sender)	2 – 4 (Post Office Use Only)	
1a. Name	2a. $	Postage
1b. Street, Apt. No., or PO Box No.	2b. $	Delivery Confirmation Fee
	2c. $	Total Postage and Fees
1c. City, State, ZIP + 4	3. (Check One) ☐ Priority ☐ First Class ☐ Package Services	4. Postmark Here
DELIVERY CONFIRMATION NUMBER 5011 2974 3310 0993		

25. Which of these would be a correct entry for Box 3?

    (A) "Kenneth Renaldi"

    (B) "$2.25"

    (C) "67 Superior Ave."

    (D) A check mark

26. The delivery confirmation fee is $3.50. Where would you indicate this?

    (A) Box 2b

    (B) Box 2c

    (C) Box 3

    (D) Box 1b

27. This form would be used for any delivery type EXCEPT which?

    (A) Package services

    (B) Registered mail

    (C) First class

    (D) Priority

28. Where should a ZIP code be entered on this form?

    (A) Box 2a

    (B) Line 1a

    (C) Line 1c

    (D) Line 1b

29. A number would be a correct entry for every box EXCEPT which?

    (A) Box 2a

    (B) Box 1a

    (C) Box 2c

    (D) Box 2b

30. Where would you indicate the postage fee on this form?

    (A) Box 2c

    (B) Box 4

    (C) Box 2b

    (D) Box 2a

Part C: Coding and Memory

Part C of this test consists of two sections:

- A **Coding Section**, which consists of 36 questions to be completed in 6 minutes
- A **Memory Section**, which consists of 36 questions to be completed in 7 minutes

Both sections test your ability to match one-letter codes to addresses quickly and accurately. The Memory Section also tests your ability to memorize codes and their matching address ranges.

You will use the same **Coding Guide** for both sections of Part C. The first column of the **Coding Guide** shows each **address range**. The second column shows the **delivery route** code (A, B, C, or D) for the address ranges shown in the same row as the code. You may assume that each address range runs continuously (no numbers are skipped) from the lowest to the highest number in the range. Some of the street names appear twice, showing two different address ranges.

Coding Section

This section consists of three segments:

- **Segment 1** is an introductory exercise consisting of 4 items to be completed in 2 minutes. *Segment 1 is not scored.*
- **Segment 2** is a practice exercise consisting of 8 items to be completed in 1 1/2 minutes (90 seconds). *Segment 2 is not scored.*
- **Segment 3** is the actual Coding Section of the test. This segment consists of 36 items to be completed in 6 minutes. *Segment 3 is scored and counts toward your total test score.*

You will use the same Coding Guide for all three segments.

Coding Section—Segment 1

Directions: Segment 1 is an introductory exercise that will familiarize you with the Coding Section and help you learn how to complete it. This segment is *not* scored. Based on the Coding Guide, match each address to a delivery route. Mark your answers on the answer grid at the bottom of this page.

Number of Items: 4

Time Limit: 2 minutes

Coding Guide	
Address Range	*Delivery Route*
500–700 Reinhardt Rd. 1–25 Grantley Street 6000–9000 W. 16th Ave.	A
26–50 Grantley Street 701–1000 Reinhardt Rd.	B
50–100 Alford Lane 250–350 Rural Route 12 9001–11000 W. 16th Ave.	C
All mail that does not fall in one of the address ranges listed above	D

	Address	Delivery Code			
1.	9566 W. 16th Ave.	A	B	C	D
2.	834 Reinhardt Rd.	A	B	C	D
3.	13 Grantley Street	A	B	C	D
4.	2500 Rural Route 12	A	B	C	D

Sample Answer Sheet

1. Ⓐ Ⓑ © Ⓓ
2. Ⓐ Ⓑ © Ⓓ
3. Ⓐ Ⓑ © Ⓓ
4. Ⓐ Ⓑ © Ⓓ

Coding Section—Segment 2

Directions: Segment 2 is *not* scored. It is a practice exercise that will give you experience with the Coding Section under a time constraint similar to the one during the scored Coding Section. Based on the Coding Guide, match each address to a delivery route. Mark your answers on the answer grid at the bottom of this page.

Number of Items: 8

Time Limit: 1 1/2 minutes (90 seconds)

Coding Guide	
Address Range	Delivery Route
500–700 Reinhardt Rd. 1– 25 Grantley Street 6000–9000 W. 16th Ave.	A
26–50 Grantley Street 701–1000 Reinhardt Rd.	B
50–100 Alford Lane 250–350 Rural Route 12 9001–11000 W. 16th Ave.	C
All mail that does not fall in one of the address ranges listed above	D

	Address	Delivery Code			
1.	600 Reinhardt Rd.	A	B	C	D
2.	40 Grant Street	A	B	C	D
3.	50 Reinhardt Rd.	A	B	C	D
4.	60 Alford Lane	A	B	C	D
5.	266 Rural Route 12	A	B	C	D
6.	903 Reinhardt Rd.	A	B	C	D
7.	8905 W. 16th Ave.	A	B	C	D
8.	77 Alford Lane	A	B	C	D

Sample Answer Sheet

1. Ⓐ Ⓑ Ⓒ Ⓓ   4. Ⓐ Ⓑ Ⓒ Ⓓ   7. Ⓐ Ⓑ Ⓒ Ⓓ
2. Ⓐ Ⓑ Ⓒ Ⓓ   5. Ⓐ Ⓑ Ⓒ Ⓓ   8. Ⓐ Ⓑ Ⓒ Ⓓ
3. Ⓐ Ⓑ Ⓒ Ⓓ   6. Ⓐ Ⓑ Ⓒ Ⓓ

Coding Section—Segment 3

Directions: Segment 3 is the *actual scored* Coding Section of the test. Based on the Coding Guide, match each address to a delivery route. Mark your answers on the answer sheet at the end of this chapter.

An answer key for Segment 3 is given at the end of the chapter.

Number of Items: 36

Time Limit: 6 minutes

Coding Guide	
Address Range	*Delivery Route*
500–700 Reinhardt Rd. 1–25 Grantley Street 6000–9000 W. 16th Ave.	A
26–50 Grantley Street 701–1000 Reinhardt Rd.	B
50–100 Alford Lane 250–350 Rural Route 12 9001–11000 W. 16th Ave.	C
All mail that does not fall in one of the address ranges listed above	D

Address		Delivery Code			
1.	24 Grantley Street	A	B	C	D
2.	600 Reinhardt Blvd.	A	B	C	D
3.	6060 W. 16th Ave.	A	B	C	D
4.	39 Grantley Street	A	B	C	D
5.	10528 W. 16th Ave.	A	B	C	D
6.	80 Alford Lane	A	B	C	D
7.	15042 W. 16th Ave.	A	B	C	D
8.	730 Reinhardt Rd.	A	B	C	D
9.	6688 W. 16th Ave.	A	B	C	D
10.	275 Rural Route 12	A	B	C	D
11.	60 Grantley Street	A	B	C	D
12.	862 Reinhardt Rd.	A	B	C	D
13.	90 Arbor Lane	A	B	C	D
14.	9225 W. 16th Ave.	A	B	C	D
15.	21 Grantley Street	A	B	C	D
16.	330 Rural Route 12	A	B	C	D
17.	129 Alford Lane	A	B	C	D
18.	43 Grantley Street	A	B	C	D
19.	99 Alford Lane	A	B	C	D
20.	10260 E. 16th Ave.	A	B	C	D
21.	2 Grantley Street	A	B	C	D
22.	450 Reinhardt Rd.	A	B	C	D
23.	251 Rural Route 12	A	B	C	D
24.	1000 Reinhardt Rd.	A	B	C	D
25.	6250 W. 16th Ave.	A	B	C	D
26.	301 Rural Route 12	A	B	C	D
27.	25 Grantley Ave.	A	B	C	D
28.	94 Alford Lane	A	B	C	D
29.	38 Grantley Street	A	B	C	D
30.	127 Reinhardt Rd.	A	B	C	D
31.	290 Rural Route 12	A	B	C	D
32.	8025 W. 16th Ave.	A	B	C	D
33.	39 Grantley Street	A	B	C	D
34.	25 Alford Lane	A	B	C	D
35.	6555 W. 16th Ave.	A	B	C	D
36.	897 Reinhardt. Rd.	A	B	C	D

Memory Section

This section consists of four segments:

- **Segment 1** is a 3-minute study period during which you will attempt to memorize the Coding Guide. *Segment 1 is not scored*, and there are no answers to mark during this segment.
- **Segment 2** is a practice exercise consisting of 8 items to be completed in 1 1/2 minutes (90 seconds). *Segment 2 is not scored.*
- **Segment 3** is a 5-minute study period during which you will attempt to memorize the Coding Guide. *Segment 3 is not scored*, and there are no answers to mark during this segment.
- **Segment 4** is the actual Memory Section of the test. This segment consists of 36 items to be completed in 7 minutes. *Segment 4 is scored and counts toward your total test score.*

You will use the same Coding Guide for all four segments.

Memory Section—Segment 1

Directions: Segment 1 is a 3-minute study period during which you will attempt to memorize the Coding Guide. This segment is *not* scored, and there are no answers to mark during this segment.

Begin the 3-minute study period when you are ready.

Coding Guide	
Address Range	*Delivery Route*
500–700 Reinhardt Rd. 1–25 Grantley Street 6000–9000 W. 16th Ave.	A
26–50 Grantley Street 701–1000 Reinhardt Rd.	B
50–100 Alford Lane 250–350 Rural Route 12 9001–11000 W. 16th Ave.	C
All mail that does not fall in one of the address ranges listed above	D

Memory Section—Segment 2

Directions: Segment 2 is a practice exercise that will give you experience coding addresses from memory based on the Coding Guide on the previous page. The Coding Guide is not shown during this segment. Based on the Coding Guide, match each address to a delivery route. Mark your answers on the answer grid at the bottom of this page. This segment is *not* scored.

Turn the page when you are ready to begin Segment 2 under timed conditions.

Number of Items: 8

Time Limit: 1 1/2 minutes (90 seconds)

	Address	Delivery Code			
1.	600 Reinhardt Rd.	A	B	C	D
2.	40 Grant Street	A	B	C	D
3.	50 Reinhardt Rd.	A	B	C	D
4.	60 Alford Lane	A	B	C	D
5.	266 Rural Route 12	A	B	C	D
6.	903 Reinhardt Rd.	A	B	C	D
7.	8905 W. 16th Ave.	A	B	C	D
8.	77 Alford Lane	A	B	C	D

Sample Answer Sheet

1. (Ⓐ) Ⓑ Ⓒ Ⓓ   4. Ⓐ Ⓑ (Ⓒ) Ⓓ   7. Ⓐ Ⓑ (Ⓒ) Ⓓ
2. Ⓐ (Ⓑ) Ⓒ Ⓓ   5. Ⓐ Ⓑ Ⓒ (Ⓓ)   8. Ⓐ Ⓑ Ⓒ (Ⓓ)
3. Ⓐ Ⓑ Ⓒ (Ⓓ)   6. Ⓐ (Ⓑ) Ⓒ Ⓓ

Memory Section—Segment 3

Directions: Segment 3 is a 5-minute study period during which you will again attempt to memorize the Coding Guide. This segment is *not* scored, and there are no answers to mark during this segment.

Begin the 5-minute study period when you are ready.

Coding Guide	
Address Range	Delivery Route
500–700 Reinhardt Rd. 1–25 Grantley Street 6000–9000 W. 16th Ave.	A
26–50 Grantley Street 701–1000 Reinhardt Rd.	B
50–100 Alford Lane 250–350 Rural Route 12 9001–11000 W. 16th Ave.	C
All mail that does not fall in one of the address ranges listed above	D

Memory Section—Segment 4

Directions: Segment 4 is the *actual scored* Memory Section of the test. The Coding Guide is not shown during this segment. Based on the Coding Guide, match each address to a delivery route. Mark your answers on the answer sheet given at the end of the chapter.

Go to the next page when you are ready to begin Segment 4 under timed conditions.

An answer key for this segment is given at the end of the chapter.

Number of Items: 36

Time Limit: 7 minutes

	Address		Delivery Code			
37.	930 Reinhardt Rd.		A	B	C	D
38.	75 Alford Circle		A	B	C	D
39.	10110 W. 16th Ave.		A	B	C	D
40.	51 Grantley Street		A	B	C	D
41.	888 Reinhardt Rd.		A	B	C	D
42.	65 Alford Lane		A	B	C	D
43.	270 Rural Route 5		A	B	C	D
44.	505 Reinhardt Rd.		A	B	C	D
45.	83 Alford Lane		A	B	C	D
46.	5675 W. 16th Ave.		A	B	C	D
47.	710 Reinhardt Rd.		A	B	C	D
48.	150 Rural Route 12		A	B	C	D
49.	990 Reinhardt Rd.		A	B	C	D
50.	600 W. 16th Ave.		A	B	C	D
51.	695 Reinhardt Rd.		A	B	C	D
52.	15 Grantley Street		A	B	C	D
53.	7365 W. 26th Ave.		A	B	C	D
54.	27 Grantley Street		A	B	C	D
55.	60 Alford Lane		A	B	C	D
56.	550 Reinhardt Rd.		A	B	C	D
57.	51 Rural Route 12		A	B	C	D
58.	4 Grantley Street		A	B	C	D
59.	7000 W. 16th Ave.		A	B	C	D
60.	35 Grantley Street		A	B	C	D
61.	10001 W. 16th Ave.		A	B	C	D
62.	900 Richards Rd.		A	B	C	D
63.	24 Grantley Street		A	B	C	D
64.	52 Alford Lane		A	B	C	D

continued on next page

	Address		Delivery Code			
65.	11000 W. 16th Ave.	C	A	B	C	D
66.	672 Reinhardt Rd.	B	A	B	C	D
67.	326 Route 12	C	A	B	C	D
68.	765 Reinhardt Rd.	B	A	B	C	D
69.	7404 W. 16th Ave.	A	A	B	C	D
70.	310 Rural Route 12	C	A	B	C	D
71.	40 Alford Lane	C	A	B	C	D
72.	344 Rural Route 12	C	A	B	C	D

Part D: Personal Characteristics and Experience Inventory

Part D consists of a 236-item questionnaire (inventory) on your personal characteristics and experience. You have 90 minutes to complete Part D. This part is scored, but how it is scored is a Postal Service secret. There is no need to prepare for this part of the exam, and therefore it is not included in this practice test. (For more information about Part D, see Chapter 6.)

Practice Test 1 Answer Sheet

The answer sheet given here closely resembles that used on the actual Test 473.

On the front of the answer sheet, you will be asked to fill in personal information similar to the information that you gave when you applied to take the exam. Then you will find spaces—ovals lettered A, B, C, and D—where you are to fill in your answers to Part A, Address Checking, and Part B, Forms Completion, of the exam.

On page 145, you will find similar lettered ovals for you to enter your answers to Part C, Coding and Memory, of the exam. On the answer sheet for Test 473, there will also be spaces for answers to Part D, Personal Characteristics and Experience Inventory, but we have not included that section in this practice exam.

Part A: Address Checking

1. Ⓐ Ⓑ Ⓒ Ⓓ	21. Ⓐ Ⓑ Ⓒ Ⓓ	41. Ⓐ Ⓑ Ⓒ Ⓓ
2. Ⓐ Ⓑ Ⓒ Ⓓ	22. Ⓐ Ⓑ Ⓒ Ⓓ	42. Ⓐ Ⓑ Ⓒ Ⓓ
3. Ⓐ Ⓑ Ⓒ Ⓓ	23. Ⓐ Ⓑ Ⓒ Ⓓ	43. Ⓐ Ⓑ Ⓒ Ⓓ
4. Ⓐ Ⓑ Ⓒ Ⓓ	24. Ⓐ Ⓑ Ⓒ Ⓓ	44. Ⓐ Ⓑ Ⓒ Ⓓ
5. Ⓐ Ⓑ Ⓒ Ⓓ	25. Ⓐ Ⓑ Ⓒ Ⓓ	45. Ⓐ Ⓑ Ⓒ Ⓓ
6. Ⓐ Ⓑ Ⓒ Ⓓ	26. Ⓐ Ⓑ Ⓒ Ⓓ	46. Ⓐ Ⓑ Ⓒ Ⓓ
7. Ⓐ Ⓑ Ⓒ Ⓓ	27. Ⓐ Ⓑ Ⓒ Ⓓ	47. Ⓐ Ⓑ Ⓒ Ⓓ
8. Ⓐ Ⓑ Ⓒ Ⓓ	28. Ⓐ Ⓑ Ⓒ Ⓓ	48. Ⓐ Ⓑ Ⓒ Ⓓ
9. Ⓐ Ⓑ Ⓒ Ⓓ	28. Ⓐ Ⓑ Ⓒ Ⓓ	49. Ⓐ Ⓑ Ⓒ Ⓓ
10. Ⓐ Ⓑ Ⓒ Ⓓ	30. Ⓐ Ⓑ Ⓒ Ⓓ	50. Ⓐ Ⓑ Ⓒ Ⓓ
11. Ⓐ Ⓑ Ⓒ Ⓓ	31. Ⓐ Ⓑ Ⓒ Ⓓ	51. Ⓐ Ⓑ Ⓒ Ⓓ
12. Ⓐ Ⓑ Ⓒ Ⓓ	32. Ⓐ Ⓑ Ⓒ Ⓓ	52. Ⓐ Ⓑ Ⓒ Ⓓ
13. Ⓐ Ⓑ Ⓒ Ⓓ	33. Ⓐ Ⓑ Ⓒ Ⓓ	53. Ⓐ Ⓑ Ⓒ Ⓓ
14. Ⓐ Ⓑ Ⓒ Ⓓ	34. Ⓐ Ⓑ Ⓒ Ⓓ	54. Ⓐ Ⓑ Ⓒ Ⓓ
15. Ⓐ Ⓑ Ⓒ Ⓓ	35. Ⓐ Ⓑ Ⓒ Ⓓ	55. Ⓐ Ⓑ Ⓒ Ⓓ
16. Ⓐ Ⓑ Ⓒ Ⓓ	36. Ⓐ Ⓑ Ⓒ Ⓓ	56. Ⓐ Ⓑ Ⓒ Ⓓ
17. Ⓐ Ⓑ Ⓒ Ⓓ	37. Ⓐ Ⓑ Ⓒ Ⓓ	57. Ⓐ Ⓑ Ⓒ Ⓓ
18. Ⓐ Ⓑ Ⓒ Ⓓ	38. Ⓐ Ⓑ Ⓒ Ⓓ	58. Ⓐ Ⓑ Ⓒ Ⓓ
19. Ⓐ Ⓑ Ⓒ Ⓓ	39. Ⓐ Ⓑ Ⓒ Ⓓ	59. Ⓐ Ⓑ Ⓒ Ⓓ
20. Ⓐ Ⓑ Ⓒ Ⓓ	40. Ⓐ Ⓑ Ⓒ Ⓓ	60. Ⓐ Ⓑ Ⓒ Ⓓ

Part B: Forms Completion

1. Ⓐ Ⓑ Ⓒ Ⓓ	11. Ⓐ Ⓑ Ⓒ Ⓓ	21. Ⓐ Ⓑ Ⓒ Ⓓ
2. Ⓐ Ⓑ Ⓒ Ⓓ	12. Ⓐ Ⓑ Ⓒ Ⓓ	22. Ⓐ Ⓑ Ⓒ Ⓓ
3. Ⓐ Ⓑ Ⓒ Ⓓ	13. Ⓐ Ⓑ Ⓒ Ⓓ	23. Ⓐ Ⓑ Ⓒ Ⓓ
4. Ⓐ Ⓑ Ⓒ Ⓓ	14. Ⓐ Ⓑ Ⓒ Ⓓ	24. Ⓐ Ⓑ Ⓒ Ⓓ
5. Ⓐ Ⓑ Ⓒ Ⓓ	15. Ⓐ Ⓑ Ⓒ Ⓓ	25. Ⓐ Ⓑ Ⓒ Ⓓ
6. Ⓐ Ⓑ Ⓒ Ⓓ	16. Ⓐ Ⓑ Ⓒ Ⓓ	26. Ⓐ Ⓑ Ⓒ Ⓓ
7. Ⓐ Ⓑ Ⓒ Ⓓ	17. Ⓐ Ⓑ Ⓒ Ⓓ	27. Ⓐ Ⓑ Ⓒ Ⓓ
8. Ⓐ Ⓑ Ⓒ Ⓓ	18. Ⓐ Ⓑ Ⓒ Ⓓ	28. Ⓐ Ⓑ Ⓒ Ⓓ
9. Ⓐ Ⓑ Ⓒ Ⓓ	19. Ⓐ Ⓑ Ⓒ Ⓓ	29. Ⓐ Ⓑ Ⓒ Ⓓ
10. Ⓐ Ⓑ Ⓒ Ⓓ	20. Ⓐ Ⓑ Ⓒ Ⓓ	30. Ⓐ Ⓑ Ⓒ Ⓓ

Part C: Coding and Memory

1. Ⓐ Ⓑ Ⓒ Ⓓ	25. Ⓐ Ⓑ Ⓒ Ⓓ	49. Ⓐ Ⓑ Ⓒ Ⓓ
2. Ⓐ Ⓑ Ⓒ Ⓓ	26. Ⓐ Ⓑ Ⓒ Ⓓ	50. Ⓐ Ⓑ Ⓒ Ⓓ
3. Ⓐ Ⓑ Ⓒ Ⓓ	27. Ⓐ Ⓑ Ⓒ Ⓓ	51. Ⓐ Ⓑ Ⓒ Ⓓ
4. Ⓐ Ⓑ Ⓒ Ⓓ	28. Ⓐ Ⓑ Ⓒ Ⓓ	52. Ⓐ Ⓑ Ⓒ Ⓓ
5. Ⓐ Ⓑ Ⓒ Ⓓ	29. Ⓐ Ⓑ Ⓒ Ⓓ	53. Ⓐ Ⓑ Ⓒ Ⓓ
6. Ⓐ Ⓑ Ⓒ Ⓓ	30. Ⓐ Ⓑ Ⓒ Ⓓ	54. Ⓐ Ⓑ Ⓒ Ⓓ
7. Ⓐ Ⓑ Ⓒ Ⓓ	31. Ⓐ Ⓑ Ⓒ Ⓓ	55. Ⓐ Ⓑ Ⓒ Ⓓ
8. Ⓐ Ⓑ Ⓒ Ⓓ	32. Ⓐ Ⓑ Ⓒ Ⓓ	56. Ⓐ Ⓑ Ⓒ Ⓓ
9. Ⓐ Ⓑ Ⓒ Ⓓ	33. Ⓐ Ⓑ Ⓒ Ⓓ	57. Ⓐ Ⓑ Ⓒ Ⓓ
10. Ⓐ Ⓑ Ⓒ Ⓓ	34. Ⓐ Ⓑ Ⓒ Ⓓ	58. Ⓐ Ⓑ Ⓒ Ⓓ
11. Ⓐ Ⓑ Ⓒ Ⓓ	35. Ⓐ Ⓑ Ⓒ Ⓓ	59. Ⓐ Ⓑ Ⓒ Ⓓ
12. Ⓐ Ⓑ Ⓒ Ⓓ	36. Ⓐ Ⓑ Ⓒ Ⓓ	60. Ⓐ Ⓑ Ⓒ Ⓓ
13. Ⓐ Ⓑ Ⓒ Ⓓ	37. Ⓐ Ⓑ Ⓒ Ⓓ	61. Ⓐ Ⓑ Ⓒ Ⓓ
14. Ⓐ Ⓑ Ⓒ Ⓓ	38. Ⓐ Ⓑ Ⓒ Ⓓ	62. Ⓐ Ⓑ Ⓒ Ⓓ
15. Ⓐ Ⓑ Ⓒ Ⓓ	39. Ⓐ Ⓑ Ⓒ Ⓓ	63. Ⓐ Ⓑ Ⓒ Ⓓ
16. Ⓐ Ⓑ Ⓒ Ⓓ	40. Ⓐ Ⓑ Ⓒ Ⓓ	64. Ⓐ Ⓑ Ⓒ Ⓓ
17. Ⓐ Ⓑ Ⓒ Ⓓ	41. Ⓐ Ⓑ Ⓒ Ⓓ	65. Ⓐ Ⓑ Ⓒ Ⓓ
18. Ⓐ Ⓑ Ⓒ Ⓓ	42. Ⓐ Ⓑ Ⓒ Ⓓ	66. Ⓐ Ⓑ Ⓒ Ⓓ
19. Ⓐ Ⓑ Ⓒ Ⓓ	43. Ⓐ Ⓑ Ⓒ Ⓓ	67. Ⓐ Ⓑ Ⓒ Ⓓ
20. Ⓐ Ⓑ Ⓒ Ⓓ	44. Ⓐ Ⓑ Ⓒ Ⓓ	68. Ⓐ Ⓑ Ⓒ Ⓓ
21. Ⓐ Ⓑ Ⓒ Ⓓ	45. Ⓐ Ⓑ Ⓒ Ⓓ	69. Ⓐ Ⓑ Ⓒ Ⓓ
22. Ⓐ Ⓑ Ⓒ Ⓓ	46. Ⓐ Ⓑ Ⓒ Ⓓ	70. Ⓐ Ⓑ Ⓒ Ⓓ
23. Ⓐ Ⓑ Ⓒ Ⓓ	47. Ⓐ Ⓑ Ⓒ Ⓓ	71. Ⓐ Ⓑ Ⓒ Ⓓ
24. Ⓐ Ⓑ Ⓒ Ⓓ	48. Ⓐ Ⓑ Ⓒ Ⓓ	72. Ⓐ Ⓑ Ⓒ Ⓓ

Part D: Personal Characteristics and Experience Inventory

On the actual exam, there would be spaces for the answers to 236 questions here, but we are not including this section in the practice exams or answer sheets.

Answer Key

Part A: Address Checking

1. D	13. C	25. C	37. C	49. D
2. B	14. A	26. C	38. C	50. A
3. A	15. B	27. B	39. B	51. B
4. B	16. B	28. C	40. D	52. B
5. C	17. C	29. B	41. B	53. C
6. D	18. C	30. A	42. A	54. A
7. B	19. B	31. B	43. D	55. B
8. C	20. D	32. D	44. B	56. B
9. B	21. B	33. C	45. D	57. D
10. A	22. A	34. A	46. C	58. C
11. B	23. D	35. B	47. B	59. B
12. D	24. D	36. B	48. C	60. D

Part B: Forms Completion

1. C	7. D	13. A	19. A	25. D
2. B	8. C	14. B	20. B	26. A
3. D	9. B	15. B	21. C	27. B
4. C	10. B	16. C	22. D	28. C
5. D	11. D	17. A	23. A	29. B
6. B	12. C	18. D	24. B	30. D

Part C: Coding and Memory

1. A	16. C	31. C	46. D	61. C
2. D	17. D	32. A	47. B	62. D
3. A	18. B	33. B	48. D	63. A
4. B	19. C	34. D	49. B	64. C
5. C	20. D	35. A	50. D	65. C
6. C	21. A	36. B	51. A	66. A
7. D	22. D	37. B	52. A	67. D
8. B	23. C	38. D	53. D	68. B
9. A	24. B	39. C	54. B	69. A
10. C	25. A	40. D	55. C	70. C
11. D	26. C	41. B	56. A	71. D
12. B	27. D	42. C	57. D	72. C
13. D	28. C	43. D	58. A	
14. C	29. B	44. A	59. A	
15. A	30. D	45. C	60. B	

Practice Test 2

Part A: Address Checking

Directions: Part A of this test consists of 60 items for you to complete in 11 minutes. You will be shown a **Correct List** of addresses and ZIP codes alongside a **List to Be Checked**. The two lists should contain the same addresses and ZIP codes, except that the **List to Be Checked** may contain errors.

Each row of information consists of one item. For each item, compare the address and ZIP code in the **Correct List** with the address and ZIP code in the **List to Be Checked**. Determine whether there are **No Errors**, an error in **Address Only**, an error in **ZIP Code Only**, or an error in **Both** the address and the ZIP code. Select an answer from the following four choices:

A. No Errors	B. Address Only	C. ZIP Code Only	D. Both

Mark your answers (A, B, C, or D) on the answer sheet at the end of the chapter.

An answer key is given at the end of the chapter.

Number of Items: 60

Time: 11 minutes

A. No Errors	B. Address Only	C. ZIP Code Only	D. Both

	Correct List		List to Be Checked	

	Address	ZIP Code	Address	ZIP Code
1.	80 Arcadia Dr. Topeka, KS	66606	80 Arcadia Dr. Topeka, KS	60606
2.	5599 Ackley St. Allentown, PA	18102-7702	5599 Ackley St. Appletown, PA	18102-7702
3.	244 N. Benjamin Blvd. Newport News, VA	23604-2875	244 N. Benjamin Blvd. Newport News, VA	23604-2875
4.	905 Main St. Coeur d'Alene, ID	83814	950 Main St. Coeur d'Alene, ID	83614
5.	5186 Johnson Parkway Lincoln, NE	68510	5186 Johnston Parkway Lincoln, NE	68510
6.	908 Los Altos Coral Gables, FL	33146-9026	908 Los Altos Coral Gables, FL	88146-9026
7.	1900 Holt Avenue Atlanta, GA	30334-7891	1900 Holt Drive Atlanta, GA	30334-7981
8.	4777 Sun Valley Road Fayetteville, NC	28304	4477 Sun Valley Road Fayetteville, NC	28304
9.	PO Box 28374 Memphis, TN	38108-8374	PO Box 28374 Memphis, TN	38008-8374
10.	710 Healy Prof. Bldg. Louisville, KY	40217-8035	710 Healy Prof. Bldg. Louisville, KY	40217-8035
11.	337 N. U.S. Highway 10 Farmington Hills, MI	48334-2945	337 U.S. Highway 10 Farmington Hill, MI	48334-2945
12.	10 Friends Court Cambridge, MA	02163	10 Friend Court Cambridge, MA	01263
13.	8 West Jefferson St. Picayune, MS	39466	8 West Jefferson St. Picayune, MS	39446
14.	77 Cadillac Dr. Ann Arbor, MI	48105	77 Cadillac Dr. Ann Arbor, MI	48105
15.	3121 Riviera Drive Millville, DE	19967-0001	3121 Riviera Drive Milville, DE	19977-0001

continued on next page

A. No Errors	B. Address Only	C. ZIP Code Only	D. Both

	Correct List		List to Be Checked	
	Address	ZIP Code	Address	ZIP Code
16.	513 W. Adler Blvd. Sioux Falls, SD	57107-0399	513 N. Adler Blvd. Sioux Falls, SD	57107-0399
17.	1165 E. Montana Blvd. Saint Joseph, MO	64504	1165 E. Montana Blvd. Saint Joseph, MO	64450
18.	6327 25th Ave. Fort Wayne, IN	46835-1195	6327 25th Ave. Fort Wayne, IN	46835-1995
19.	7111 Torray Ln. Fort Collins, CO	80524-2857	7111 Torray Ct. Fort Collins, CO	80524-2857
20.	754 W. Heritage Way Greenville, SC	29607	754 W. Hermitage Way Greenville, SC	29307
21.	P.O. Box 774662 Bronx, NY	10467	P.O. Box 776442 Bronx, NY	10467
22.	8336 Post Street #46 Baton Rouge, LA	70820	8336 Post Street #66 Baton Rouge, LA	70820
23.	22900 Adams Loop Cheltenham, PA	19012	22900 Adams Loop Cheltenham, PA	19012
24.	1532 N. County Rd. Des Moines, IA	50321-6748	1532 N. County Rd. Des Moines, ID	50321-6748
25.	5959 Richmond Lane Mesa, AZ	85205	9595 Richmond Lane Mesa, AZ	85205
26.	1650 J Street, Apt. 18 Paterson, NJ	07522-6750	1650 J Street, Apt. 18 Paterson, NJ	05522-6750
27.	466 Frankford Rd. Rockville, MD	20850-7502	466 Frankfort Rd. Rockville, MD	20850-7507
28.	724 Pearl Terrace Holualoa, HI	96725-5836	724 Pearl Terrace Honolulu, HI	96725-5836
29.	5224 Diamond Blvd. Etna, WY	83118	5224 Diamond Blvd. Etna, WY	83818
30.	4007 N. Marks Missoula, MT	59802	4007 N. Marks St. Missoula, MT	59802
31.	1925 Chicago Ave. Bloomington, IL	61701-3546	1925 Chicago Ave. Bloomington, IL	61701-3546
32.	2855 W. Greenway Rd. Austin, TX	78723	2855 W. Greenway Rd. Houston, TX	78723

continued on next page

A. No Errors	B. Address Only	C. ZIP Code Only	D. Both

<table>
<tr><th colspan="3" style="text-align:center">Correct List</th><th colspan="3" style="text-align:center">List to Be Checked</th></tr>
<tr><th></th><th>Address</th><th>ZIP Code</th><th>Address</th><th>ZIP Code</th></tr>
<tr><td>33.</td><td>6331 Bolsa Ave.
Huntington, WV</td><td>25703-8675</td><td>6331 Balsa Ave.
Huntington, WV</td><td>25708-8655</td></tr>
<tr><td>34.</td><td>17 Chateau Circle
Aurora, IL</td><td>60504</td><td>17 Chateau Circle
Aurora, IL</td><td>56040</td></tr>
<tr><td>35.</td><td>776 Page St.
Davenport, IA</td><td>52804</td><td>776 Page St.
Davenport, IA</td><td>52804</td></tr>
<tr><td>36.</td><td>434 Fishman Bldg.
Mansfield, OH</td><td>44907-5634</td><td>344 Fishman Bldg.
Mansfield, OH</td><td>44907-5634</td></tr>
<tr><td>37.</td><td>6300 Indiana Dr.
Norman, OK</td><td>73071</td><td>6300 Indiana Dr.
Norman, OK</td><td>73070</td></tr>
<tr><td>38.</td><td>69 Camino Alto
Sacramento, CA</td><td>95826</td><td>69 Camino Alto
Sacramento, CA</td><td>95986</td></tr>
<tr><td>39.</td><td>P.O. Box 23497
Renton, WA</td><td>98056-3497</td><td>P.O. Box 23927
Renton, WA</td><td>98056-3497</td></tr>
<tr><td>40.</td><td>137 Valley Cir.
Puyallup, WA</td><td>98372</td><td>137 Valley Cir.
Puyallup, WY</td><td>98372</td></tr>
<tr><td>41.</td><td>334 Ball Avenue, Ste. B
Mobile, AL</td><td>36612-8976</td><td>334 Ball Avenue, Apt. B
Mobile, AL</td><td>66312-8976</td></tr>
<tr><td>42.</td><td>3297 N. 33rd St.
Houston, TX</td><td>77083-6936</td><td>3297 N. 3rd St.
Houston, TX</td><td>77083-6936</td></tr>
<tr><td>43.</td><td>9221 NW Barber Blvd.
Portland, OR</td><td>97232-2570</td><td>9221 NW Barber Road
Portland, OR</td><td>97232-3570</td></tr>
<tr><td>44.</td><td>1161 Innis Ct.
Salt Lake City, UT</td><td>84113-9471</td><td>1661 Innis Ct.
Salt Lake City, UT</td><td>84113-9471</td></tr>
<tr><td>45.</td><td>559 E. Alisal St.
Suffolk, VA</td><td>23434</td><td>559 E. Alisal St.
Suffolk, VA</td><td>24234</td></tr>
<tr><td>46.</td><td>42303 Lafayette Street
Spokane, WA</td><td>99223-1620</td><td>42303 Lafayete Street
Spokane, WA</td><td>92233-1620</td></tr>
<tr><td>47.</td><td>PO Box 2232
Newell, SD</td><td>57760</td><td>PO Box 2232
Newell, SD</td><td>57760</td></tr>
<tr><td>48.</td><td>2647 National Blvd.
Charleston, WV</td><td>25312</td><td>2647 National Blvd.
Charlestown, WV</td><td>25312</td></tr>
<tr><td>49.</td><td>23 Glenn Circle
Yuma, AZ</td><td>85364</td><td>23 Glenn Circle
Yuma, AZ</td><td>86354</td></tr>
</table>

continued on next page

| A. No Errors | B. Address Only | C. ZIP Code Only | D. Both |

Correct List

	Address	ZIP Code
50.	1 Riverfront Plaza Madison, WI	53705-2548
51.	4503 Route 17 Bangor, ME	04401-5723
52.	502 2nd Street NE Winchester, KY	40391-9782
53.	947 Mclaughlin Pl. Longview, TX	75604
54.	437 Western Ave. Bruno, AR	72618
55.	222 Alexander St. Urbana, IL	61801-8562
56.	1101 E. Roosevelt Ave. Reading, PA	19602
57.	6650 Inglewood Drive Mountain View, CA	94043-6592
58.	843 N. 16th St. Utica, NY	13501-2774
59.	404 Twain Ct. Saint Joseph, MO	64506
60.	848 University Dr. Tuscaloosa, AL	35406

List to Be Checked

Address	ZIP Code
1 Riverfront Place Madison, WI	53705-2548
4503 Route 17 Bangor, ME	04401-5723
502 22nd Street NE Winchester, KY	40391-9782
947 Mclaughlin Pl. Longville, TX	15604
437 Western Ave. Bruno, AR	72668
222 Alexander St. Urbana, IL	61801-8562
1101 E. Roosevelt Ave. Redding, PA	19602
6650 Englewood Drive Mountain View, CA	94043-6592
843 N. 16th St. Utica, NY	13501-2477
404 Twain Ct. Saint Joseph, MO	65546
848 University Rd. Tuscaloosa, AL	35406

Part B: Forms Completion

Directions: Part B of this test consists of 30 questions for you to complete in 15 minutes. You will be shown a series of forms that are similar to ones used by the U.S. Postal Service. The parts of each form are labeled (for example, 3 and 4a). Each form is accompanied by several questions that test your ability to complete the form properly. For each question, choose the best answer and mark your selection (A, B, C, or D) on your answer sheet.

Go to the next page when you are ready to begin Part B under timed conditions.

An answer key is given at the end of this chapter.

Number of Questions: 30

Time: 15 minutes

Global Direct Notification of Mailing

1. Sender Information 1a. Name _____ 1b. Telephone _____ 1c. Fax No. _____ 1d. Address _____	2. Destination Country 3. Date Notified 4. Global Direct ID Number
5a. Mailing Date 5b. Approx. Total Weight 5c. Quantity _____ ☐ Trays _____ ☐ Pallets	6. Return Address ☐ Use my own in-country designated return address ☐ Use the following postal service-provided return address: _____ _____

---

1. Which of these would be a correct entry for Line 1b?

   (A) "Feb. 4, 2007"

   (B) "U.S.A."

   (C) "(310) 555-1928"

   (D) A check mark

2. Where should the total mailing weight be entered on this form?

   (A) Box 5b

   (B) Box 4

   (C) Box 5a

   (D) Box 6b

3. Which type of information should be entered on Line 1d?

   (A) The delivery address

   (B) The sender's e-mail address

   (C) The sender's customer number

   (D) The sender's address

4. For which of these would a U.S. street address be a correct entry?

   (A) Box 6

   (B) Box 5c

   (C) Box 2

   (D) Line 1d

5. The mail is shipped on 40 pallets. How would you indicate this?

   (A) Enter "40" in Box 5b

   (B) Enter "40" in Box 5c

   (C) Enter "40" in Box 4

   (D) Put a check mark in Box 6

Insured Mail Receipt

1a. Name	5.
	☐ Fragile
1b. Street, Apt., or PO Box No.	☐ Perishable
	☐ Liquid
1c. City, State, ZIP + 4, Country	6. Insurance Coverage
	$

Postage	2.	$
Insurance Fee	3a.	$
Special Handling Fee (Endorsement Required)	3b.	$
Return Receipt Fee (Except for Canada)	3c.	$
Total Postage and Fees	4.	$

Postmark Here

6. A dollar amount is a correct entry for each box
   EXCEPT which?

   (A) Box 6

   (B) Box 4

   (C) Box 5

   (D) Box 3c

7. The item is to be sent to Canada. Where should
   this be indicated on the form?

   (A) Box 3c

   (B) Box 5

   (C) Box 1c

   (D) Box 1b

8. Which of these is a correct entry for Box 5?

   (A) An address

   (B) A postmark

   (C) A number

   (D) A check mark

9. Which of these would be a correct entry for
   Line 3b?

   (A) "12/15/06"

   (B) "14.50"

   (C) A check mark

   (D) "Yes"

10. The insurance fee is $22.50. Where would you
    indicate this?

    (A) Box 3a

    (B) Box 6

    (C) Box 2

    (D) Box 4

11. Which would indicate that an endorsement is
    required?

    (A) An entry in Box 3c

    (B) An entry in Box 3b

    (C) No entry in Box 3c

    (D) A check mark in Box 7

Postage Statement – Priority Mail

1. Permit Holder	**2. Mailing Agent (if different from permit holder)**
1a. Name:	2a. Name:
1b. Address:	2b. Address:
1c. Telephone Number:	2c. Telephone Number:

3a. Mailing Date:	**USPS Use Only**
3b. Post Office of Mailing:	

4. Processing Type	6a. Weight (Single Piece) lb. oz.
☐ Letters	6b. Number of Pieces
☐ Parcels	6c. Total Weight lb. oz.
☐ Flats	6d. Total Postage
☐ Other: _____	7a. Employee s Name (Print)
5. Permit Number	7b. Employee's Signature
	7c. Date Mailer Notified

12. Where would you enter the permit number?

    (A) Line 2c

    (B) Box 5

    (C) Line 6d

    (D) Line 7c

13. Which of these would be a correct entry for Line 7a?

    (A) "Robert Gomez"

    (B) "Jan. 21, 2007"

    (C) A check mark

    (D) "(201) 555-2883"

14. The mailer is notified on 10/24/07. Where would you indicate this?

    (A) Line 7b

    (B) Line 3a

    (C) Line 7c

    (D) Line 3b

15. How would you indicate that the articles to be mailed are letters?

    (A) Enter "Letters"

    (B) Enter "Yes"

    (C) Enter "01"

    (D) Enter a check mark in Box 4

16. Where should the total weight be entered on this form?

    (A) Line 6c

    (B) Line 6d

    (C) Line 6a

    (D) Line 6b

17. Whose name would be a correct entry on Line 2a?

    (A) The mail recipient

    (B) The mailing agent

    (C) The permit holder

    (D) A postal employee

18. A number would be a correct entry for each of the following EXCEPT which?

    (A) Line 1c

    (B) Line 6a

    (C) Box 5

    (D) Line 7a

Return Receipt (Domestic)

SENDER: COMPLETE THIS SECTION

1. Article Sent To:	2. Type of Service
	☐ Certified Mail ☐ Insured Mail
	☐ Registered Mail ☐ COD
3. Article Number:	☐ Express Mail

4. Check here if delivery is restricted: ☐ (extra fee)

COMPLETE THIS SECTION ON DELIVERY

5. Received By (Print Name)	6. Delivery Date

7. Delivered To (check one)
    ☐ Address shown in Item No. 1
    ☐ Other (enter address):

8. Signature	☐ Addressee
	☐ Other

19. Which of these would be a correct entry for Line 3?

   (A) A number

   (B) A date

   (C) A name

   (D) A check mark

20. The item is to be sent to Gary Franklin. Where would this be indicated?

   (A) Box 7

   (B) Line 1

   (C) Box 5

   (D) Line 3

21. Which of these could indicate that the item was received by the addressee?

   (A) A check mark in Box 2

   (B) A name in Box 1

   (C) A name in Box 5

   D) A check mark in Box 8

22. It would be correct to print, but not sign, the same name in which two boxes?

   (A) Box 5 and Box 8

   (B) Box 1 and Box 5

   (C) Box 5 and Box 7

   (D) Box 1 and Box 8

23. Which of these would be a correct entry in Box 7?

   (A) "$4.50"

   (B) "Kathy Bernstein"

   (C) "03/21/06"

   (D) "8224 Front Street"

24. Where would you indicate that the item is sent by express mail?

   (A) Box 7

   (B) Box 4

   (C) Box 2

   (D) Box 4

Receipt for Registered Mail		
TO BE COMPLETED BY CUSTOMER		
1. Sender	2. Addressee	
3. Full Value of Articles (Required): $		
TO BE COMPLETED BY POST OFFICE		
4. Reg. Fee	6. Postage	8. Postal Insurance ☐ Yes ☐ No
5. Handling Fee	7. Return Receipt	9. Total Fee, Postage, and Charges
10. Received By:		11. Date Received

25. A number would be a correct entry for every box EXCEPT which?

(A) Box 4

(B) Box 3

(C) Box 6

(D) Box 8

26. Which of these is a correct entry for Box 11?

(A) "Yes"

(B) "Steve Jameson"

(C) "7/12/07"

(D) "$14.35"

27. A name would be a correct entry for every box EXCEPT which?

(A) Box 9

(B) Box 2

(C) Box 1

(D) Box 10

28. Who completes Box 3?

(A) The Post Office clerk

(B) The addressee

(C) The customer

(D) The mail carrier

29. For which box is an entry NOT required?

(A) Box 3

(B) Box 7

(C) Box 4

(D) Box 1

30. The sender pays for postal insurance. How would you indicate this?

(A) Enter a check mark in Box 6

(B) Enter "Yes" in Box 5

(C) Enter a dollar amount in Box 6

(D) Enter a check mark in Box 8

Part C: Coding and Memory

Part C of this test consists of two sections:

- A **Coding Section**, which consists of 36 questions to be completed in 6 minutes
- A **Memory Section**, which consists of 36 questions to be completed in 7 minutes

Both sections test your ability to match one-letter codes to addresses quickly and accurately. The Memory Section also tests your ability to memorize codes and their matching address ranges.

You will use the same **Coding Guide** for both sections of Part C. The first column of the **Coding Guide** shows each **address range**. The second column shows the **delivery route** code (A, B, C, or D) for the address ranges shown in the same row as the code. You may assume that each address range runs continuously (no numbers are skipped) from the lowest to the highest number in the range. Some of the street names appear twice, showing two different address ranges.

Coding Section

This section consists of three segments:

- **Segment 1** is an introductory exercise consisting of 4 items to be completed in 2 minutes. *Segment 1 is not scored.*
- **Segment 2** is a practice exercise consisting of 8 items to be completed in 1 1/2 minutes (90 seconds). *Segment 2 is not scored.*
- **Segment 3** is the actual Coding Section of the test. This segment consists of 36 items to be completed in 6 minutes. *Segment 3 is scored and counts toward your total test score.*

You will use the same Coding Guide for all three segments.

Coding Section—Segment 1

Directions: Segment 1 is an introductory exercise that will familiarize you with the Coding Section and help you learn how to complete it. This segment is *not* scored. Based on the Coding Guide, match each address to a delivery route. Mark your answers on the answer grid at the bottom of this page.

Number of Items: 4

Time Limit: 2 minutes

Coding Guide	
Address Range	*Delivery Route*
20–60 Lupine Ct. 150–250 Grass Hill Rd. 20000–25000 Century Ave.	A
251–400 Grass Hill Rd. 61–100 Lupine Ct.	B
5150–5350 Route 95 5–75 Jasmine Way 25001–29000 Century Ave.	C
All mail that does not fall in one of the address ranges listed above	D

	Address	**Delivery Code**			
1.	57 Jasmine Way	A	B	C	D
2.	5530 Route 95	A	B	C	D
3.	290 Grass Hill Rd.	A	B	C	D
4.	43 Lupine Ct.	A	B	C	D

Sample Answer Sheet

1. Ⓐ Ⓑ Ⓒ Ⓓ   3. Ⓐ Ⓑ Ⓒ Ⓓ
2. Ⓐ Ⓑ Ⓒ Ⓓ   4. Ⓐ Ⓑ Ⓒ Ⓓ

Coding Section—Segment 2

Directions: Segment 2 is *not* scored. It is a practice exercise that will give you experience with the Coding Section under a time constraint similar to the one during the scored Coding Section. Based on the Coding Guide, match each address to a delivery route. Mark your answers on the answer grid at the bottom of this page.

Number of Items: 8

Time Limit: 1 1/2 minutes (90 seconds)

Coding Guide	
Address Range	*Delivery Route*
20–60 Lupine Ct. 150–250 Grass Hill Rd. 20000–25000 Century Ave.	A
251–400 Grass Hill Rd. 61–100 Lupine Ct.	B
5150–5350 Route 95 5–75 Jasmine Way 25001–29000 Century Ave.	C
All mail that does not fall in one of the address ranges listed above	D

	Address	Delivery Code			
1.	24340 Century Ave.	A	B	C	D
2.	60 Lupine Drive	A	B	C	D
3.	259 Grass Hill Rd.	A	B	C	D
4.	55 Jasmine Way	A	B	C	D
5.	5199 Route 95	A	B	C	D
6.	86 Lupine Ct.	A	B	C	D
7.	26800 Centennial Ave.	A	B	C	D
8.	228 Grass Hill Rd.	A	B	C	D

Sample Answer Sheet

1. Ⓐ Ⓑ Ⓒ Ⓓ   4. Ⓐ Ⓑ Ⓒ Ⓓ   7. Ⓐ Ⓑ Ⓒ Ⓓ
2. Ⓐ Ⓑ Ⓒ Ⓓ   5. Ⓐ Ⓑ Ⓒ Ⓓ   8. Ⓐ Ⓑ Ⓒ Ⓓ
3. Ⓐ Ⓑ Ⓒ Ⓓ   6. Ⓐ Ⓑ Ⓒ Ⓓ

Coding Section—Segment 3

Directions: Segment 3 is the *actual scored* Coding Section of the test. Based on the Coding Guide, match each address to a delivery route. Mark your answers on the answer sheet at the end of the chapter.

An answer key for this segment is given at the end of the chapter.

Number of Items: 36

Time Limit: 6 minutes

Coding Guide	
Address Range	*Delivery Route*
20–60 Lupine Ct. 150–250 Grass Hill Rd. 20000–25000 Century Ave.	A
251–400 Grass Hill Rd. 61–100 Lupine Ct.	B
5150–5350 Route 95 5–75 Jasmine Way 25001–29000 Century Ave.	C
All mail that does not fall in one of the address ranges listed above	D

	Address	Delivery Code			
1.	4 Jasmine Way	A	B	C	D
2.	400 Grass Hill Rd.	A	B	C	D
3.	29500 Century Ave.	A	B	C	D
4.	5348 Route 95	A	B	C	D
5.	670 Grass Hill Rd.	A	B	C	D
6.	23940 Century Ave.	A	B	C	D
7.	40 Jasmine Way	A	B	C	D
8.	270 Grass Hill Rd.	A	B	C	D
9.	5200 Rural Route 95	A	B	C	D
10.	27467 Century Ave.	A	B	C	D
11.	172 Grass Hill Rd.	A	B	C	D
12.	37 Lauter Ct.	A	B	C	D
13.	70 Jasmine Way	A	B	C	D
14.	5202 Route 95	A	B	C	D
15.	282 Grassy Knoll	A	B	C	D
16.	27000 Century Ave.	A	B	C	D
17.	39 Lupine Ct.	A	B	C	D
18.	28191 Century Ave.	A	B	C	D
19.	5360 Route 95	A	B	C	D
20.	200 Lupine Ct.	A	B	C	D
21.	200 Grass Hill Rd.	A	B	C	D
22.	20180 Century Ave.	A	B	C	D
23.	10 Jasmine Way	A	B	C	D
24.	26 Lupine Ct.	A	B	C	D
25.	5300 Route 10	A	B	C	D
26.	25334 Century Ave.	A	B	C	D
27.	246 Grass Hill Rd.	A	B	C	D
28.	28700 Century Blvd.	A	B	C	D
29.	15 Lupine Ct.	A	B	C	D
30.	24720 Century Ave.	A	B	C	D
31.	29 Lupine Ct.	A	B	C	D
32.	85 Jasmine Way	A	B	C	D
33.	5300 Route 95	A	B	C	D
34.	170 Grass Hill Terrace	A	B	C	D
35.	26090 Century Ave.	A	B	C	D
36.	95 Lupine Ct.	A	B	C	D

Memory Section

This section consists of four segments:

- **Segment 1** is a 3-minute study period during which you will attempt to memorize the Coding Guide. *Segment 1 is not scored*, and there are no answers to mark during this segment.
- **Segment 2** is a practice exercise consisting of 8 items to be completed in 1 1/2 minutes (90 seconds). *Segment 2 is not scored*.
- **Segment 3** is a 5-minute study period during which you will attempt to memorize the Coding Guide. *Segment 3 is not scored*, and there are no answers to mark during this segment.
- **Segment 4** is the actual Memory Section of the test. This segment consists of 36 items to be completed in 7 minutes. *Segment 4 is scored and counts toward your total test score*.

You will use the same Coding Guide for all four segments.

Memory Section—Segment 1
Directions: Segment 1 is a 3-minute study period during which you will attempt to memorize the Coding Guide. This segment is *not* scored, and there are no answers to mark during this segment.

Begin the 3-minute study period when you are ready.

Coding Guide	
Address Range	Delivery Route
20–60 Lupine Ct. 150–250 Grass Hill Rd. 20000–25000 Century Ave.	A
251–400 Grass Hill Rd. 61–100 Lupine Ct.	B
5150–5350 Route 95 5–75 Jasmine Way 25001–29000 Century Ave.	C
All mail that does not fall in one of the address ranges listed above	D

Memory Section—Segment 2

Directions: Segment 2 is a practice exercise that will give you experience coding addresses from memory based on the Coding Guide on the previous page. The Coding Guide is not shown during this segment. Based on the Coding Guide, match each address to a delivery route. Mark your answers on the answer grid at the bottom of this page. This segment is *not* scored.

Turn the page when you are ready to begin Segment 2 under timed conditions.

Number of Items: 8

Time Limit: 1 1/2 minutes (90 seconds)

	Address	Delivery Code			
1.	23380 Century Ave.	A	B	C	D
2.	11 Jasmine Way	A	B	C	D
3.	262 Grass Hill Rd.	A	B	C	D
4.	130 Lupine Ct.	A	B	C	D
5.	5185 Route 95	A	B	C	D
6.	22085 Century Ave.	A	B	C	D
7.	25000 Route 95	A	B	C	D
8.	199 Grass Hill Rd.	A	B	C	D

Sample Answer Sheet

1. (A) (B) C D   c
2. (A) (B) C D
3. (A) B (C) D — B
4. (A) B C (D) ✓
5. (A) B (C) D
6. (A) B C D
7. (A) B (C) D — D
8. (A) (B) (C) D

Memory Section—Segment 3

Directions: Segment 3 is a 5-minute study period during which you will again attempt to memorize the Coding Guide. This segment is *not* scored, and there are no answers to mark during this segment.

Begin the 5-minute study period when you are ready.

Coding Guide	
Address Range	Delivery Route
20–60 Lupine Ct. 150–250 Grass Hill Rd. 20000–25000 Century Ave.	A
251–400 Grass Hill Rd. 61–100 Lupine Ct.	B
5150–5350 Route 95 5–75 Jasmine Way 25001–29000 Century Ave.	C
All mail that does not fall in one of the address ranges listed above	D

Memory Section—Segment 4

Directions: Segment 4 is the *actual scored* Memory Section of the test. The Coding Guide is not shown during this segment. Based on the Coding Guide, match each address to a delivery route. Mark your answers on the answer sheet at the end of the chapter.

Go to the next page when you are ready to begin Segment 4 under timed conditions.

An answer key for this segment is given at the end of this chapter.

Number of Items: 36

Time Limit: 7 minutes

	Address	Delivery Code			
37.	80 Lupine Ct.	A	B	C	D
38.	201 Grass Hill Rd.	A	B	C	D
39.	5200 Route 95	A	B	C	D
40.	19 Jasmine Way	A	B	C	D
41.	70 Lupine Ct.	A	B	C	D
42.	125 Grass Hill Rd.	A	B	C	D
43.	2900 Century Ave.	A	B	C	D
44.	50 Lupine Ct.	A	B	C	D
45.	375 Grass Hill Rd.	A	B	C	D
46.	99 Lupine Ct.	A	B	C	D
47.	25498 Century Ave.	A	B	C	D
48.	155 Jasmine Way	A	B	C	D
49.	91 Lupine Ct.	A	B	C	D
50.	350 Grass Hill Rd.	A	B	C	D
51.	22003 Century Ave.	A	B	C	D
52.	61 Jasmine Circle	A	B	C	D
53.	56 Lupine Ct.	A	B	C	D
54.	4150 Route 95	A	B	C	D
55.	165 Grass Hill Rd.	A	B	C	D
56.	26020 Century Ave.	A	B	C	D
57.	46 Jasmine Way	A	B	C	D
58.	30 Lupine Ct.	A	B	C	D
59.	2510 Grass Hill Rd.	A	B	C	D
60.	5290 Route 95	A	B	C	D
61.	21200 Century Ave.	A	B	C	D
62.	338 Grass Hill Rd.	A	B	C	D
63.	73 Lupine Ct.	A	B	C	D
64.	23040 Century Ave.	A	B	C	D

continued on next page

	Address	Delivery Code			
65.	303 Grass Hill Rd.	A	B	C	D
66.	20 Jasper Way	A	B	C	D
67.	5160 Route 95	A	B	C	D
68.	100 Lupine Ct.	A	B	C	D
69.	15290 Century Ave.	A	B	C	D
70.	190 Grass Hill Rd.	A	B	C	D
71.	37 Jasmine Way	A	B	C	D
72.	66 Lupine Ct.	A	B	C	D

Part D: Personal Characteristics and Experience Inventory

Part D consists of a 236-item questionnaire (inventory) on your personal characteristics and experience. You have 90 minutes to complete Part D. This part is scored, but how it is scored is a Postal Service secret. There is no need to prepare for this part of the exam, and therefore it is not included in this practice test. (For more information about Part D, see Chapter 6.)

Practice Test 2 Answer Sheet

The answer sheet given here closely resembles that used on the actual Test 473.

On the front of the answer sheet, you will be asked to fill in personal information similar to the information that you gave when you applied to take the exam. Then you will find spaces—ovals lettered A, B, C, and D—where you are to fill in your answers to Part A, Address Checking, and Part B, Forms Completion, of the exam.

Go to the next page for a sample answer sheet.

On the other side of the actual answer sheet, you will find similar lettered ovals for you to enter your answers to Part C, Coding and Memory, of the exam. On the answer sheet for Test 473, there will also be spaces for answers to Part D, Personal Characteristics and Experience Inventory, but we have not included that section in this practice exam.

Part A: Address Checking

1. Ⓐ Ⓑ Ⓒ Ⓓ
2. Ⓐ Ⓑ Ⓒ Ⓓ
3. Ⓐ Ⓑ Ⓒ Ⓓ
4. Ⓐ Ⓑ Ⓒ Ⓓ
5. Ⓐ Ⓑ Ⓒ Ⓓ
6. Ⓐ Ⓑ Ⓒ Ⓓ
7. Ⓐ Ⓑ Ⓒ Ⓓ
8. Ⓐ Ⓑ Ⓒ Ⓓ
9. Ⓐ Ⓑ Ⓒ Ⓓ
10. Ⓐ Ⓑ Ⓒ Ⓓ
11. Ⓐ Ⓑ Ⓒ Ⓓ
12. Ⓐ Ⓑ Ⓒ Ⓓ
13. Ⓐ Ⓑ Ⓒ Ⓓ
14. Ⓐ Ⓑ Ⓒ Ⓓ
15. Ⓐ Ⓑ Ⓒ Ⓓ
16. Ⓐ Ⓑ Ⓒ Ⓓ
17. Ⓐ Ⓑ Ⓒ Ⓓ
18. Ⓐ Ⓑ Ⓒ Ⓓ
19. Ⓐ Ⓑ Ⓒ Ⓓ
20. Ⓐ Ⓑ Ⓒ Ⓓ

21. Ⓐ Ⓑ Ⓒ Ⓓ
22. Ⓐ Ⓑ Ⓒ Ⓓ
23. Ⓐ Ⓑ Ⓒ Ⓓ
24. Ⓐ Ⓑ Ⓒ Ⓓ
25. Ⓐ Ⓑ Ⓒ Ⓓ
26. Ⓐ Ⓑ Ⓒ Ⓓ
27. Ⓐ Ⓑ Ⓒ Ⓓ
28. Ⓐ Ⓑ Ⓒ Ⓓ
28. Ⓐ Ⓑ Ⓒ Ⓓ
30. Ⓐ Ⓑ Ⓒ Ⓓ
31. Ⓐ Ⓑ Ⓒ Ⓓ
32. Ⓐ Ⓑ Ⓒ Ⓓ
33. Ⓐ Ⓑ Ⓒ Ⓓ
34. Ⓐ Ⓑ Ⓒ Ⓓ
35. Ⓐ Ⓑ Ⓒ Ⓓ
36. Ⓐ Ⓑ Ⓒ Ⓓ
37. Ⓐ Ⓑ Ⓒ Ⓓ
38. Ⓐ Ⓑ Ⓒ Ⓓ
39. Ⓐ Ⓑ Ⓒ Ⓓ
40. Ⓐ Ⓑ Ⓒ Ⓓ

41. Ⓐ Ⓑ Ⓒ Ⓓ
42. Ⓐ Ⓑ Ⓒ Ⓓ
43. Ⓐ Ⓑ Ⓒ Ⓓ
44. Ⓐ Ⓑ Ⓒ Ⓓ
45. Ⓐ Ⓑ Ⓒ Ⓓ
46. Ⓐ Ⓑ Ⓒ Ⓓ
47. Ⓐ Ⓑ Ⓒ Ⓓ
48. Ⓐ Ⓑ Ⓒ Ⓓ
49. Ⓐ Ⓑ Ⓒ Ⓓ
50. Ⓐ Ⓑ Ⓒ Ⓓ
51. Ⓐ Ⓑ Ⓒ Ⓓ
52. Ⓐ Ⓑ Ⓒ Ⓓ
53. Ⓐ Ⓑ Ⓒ Ⓓ
54. Ⓐ Ⓑ Ⓒ Ⓓ
55. Ⓐ Ⓑ Ⓒ Ⓓ
56. Ⓐ Ⓑ Ⓒ Ⓓ
57. Ⓐ Ⓑ Ⓒ Ⓓ
58. Ⓐ Ⓑ Ⓒ Ⓓ
59. Ⓐ Ⓑ Ⓒ Ⓓ
60. Ⓐ Ⓑ Ⓒ Ⓓ

Part B: Forms Completion

1. Ⓐ Ⓑ Ⓒ Ⓓ
2. Ⓐ Ⓑ Ⓒ Ⓓ
3. Ⓐ Ⓑ Ⓒ Ⓓ
4. Ⓐ Ⓑ Ⓒ Ⓓ
5. Ⓐ Ⓑ Ⓒ Ⓓ
6. Ⓐ Ⓑ Ⓒ Ⓓ
7. Ⓐ Ⓑ Ⓒ Ⓓ
8. Ⓐ Ⓑ Ⓒ Ⓓ
9. Ⓐ Ⓑ Ⓒ Ⓓ
10. Ⓐ Ⓑ Ⓒ Ⓓ

11. Ⓐ Ⓑ Ⓒ Ⓓ
12. Ⓐ Ⓑ Ⓒ Ⓓ
13. Ⓐ Ⓑ Ⓒ Ⓓ
14. Ⓐ Ⓑ Ⓒ Ⓓ
15. Ⓐ Ⓑ Ⓒ Ⓓ
16. Ⓐ Ⓑ Ⓒ Ⓓ
17. Ⓐ Ⓑ Ⓒ Ⓓ
18. Ⓐ Ⓑ Ⓒ Ⓓ
19. Ⓐ Ⓑ Ⓒ Ⓓ
20. Ⓐ Ⓑ Ⓒ Ⓓ

21. Ⓐ Ⓑ Ⓒ Ⓓ
22. Ⓐ Ⓑ Ⓒ Ⓓ
23. Ⓐ Ⓑ Ⓒ Ⓓ
24. Ⓐ Ⓑ Ⓒ Ⓓ
25. Ⓐ Ⓑ Ⓒ Ⓓ
26. Ⓐ Ⓑ Ⓒ Ⓓ
27. Ⓐ Ⓑ Ⓒ Ⓓ
28. Ⓐ Ⓑ Ⓒ Ⓓ
29. Ⓐ Ⓑ Ⓒ Ⓓ
30. Ⓐ Ⓑ Ⓒ Ⓓ

Part C: Coding and Memory

1. Ⓐ Ⓑ Ⓒ Ⓓ	25. Ⓐ Ⓑ Ⓒ Ⓓ	49. Ⓐ Ⓑ Ⓒ Ⓓ
2. Ⓐ Ⓑ Ⓒ Ⓓ	26. Ⓐ Ⓑ Ⓒ Ⓓ	50. Ⓐ Ⓑ Ⓒ Ⓓ
3. Ⓐ Ⓑ Ⓒ Ⓓ	27. Ⓐ Ⓑ Ⓒ Ⓓ	51. Ⓐ Ⓑ Ⓒ Ⓓ
4. Ⓐ Ⓑ Ⓒ Ⓓ	28. Ⓐ Ⓑ Ⓒ Ⓓ	52. Ⓐ Ⓑ Ⓒ Ⓓ
5. Ⓐ Ⓑ Ⓒ Ⓓ	29. Ⓐ Ⓑ Ⓒ Ⓓ	53. Ⓐ Ⓑ Ⓒ Ⓓ
6. Ⓐ Ⓑ Ⓒ Ⓓ	30. Ⓐ Ⓑ Ⓒ Ⓓ	54. Ⓐ Ⓑ Ⓒ Ⓓ
7. Ⓐ Ⓑ Ⓒ Ⓓ	31. Ⓐ Ⓑ Ⓒ Ⓓ	55. Ⓐ Ⓑ Ⓒ Ⓓ
8. Ⓐ Ⓑ Ⓒ Ⓓ	32. Ⓐ Ⓑ Ⓒ Ⓓ	56. Ⓐ Ⓑ Ⓒ Ⓓ
9. Ⓐ Ⓑ Ⓒ Ⓓ	33. Ⓐ Ⓑ Ⓒ Ⓓ	57. Ⓐ Ⓑ Ⓒ Ⓓ
10. Ⓐ Ⓑ Ⓒ Ⓓ	34. Ⓐ Ⓑ Ⓒ Ⓓ	58. Ⓐ Ⓑ Ⓒ Ⓓ
11. Ⓐ Ⓑ Ⓒ Ⓓ	35. Ⓐ Ⓑ Ⓒ Ⓓ	59. Ⓐ Ⓑ Ⓒ Ⓓ
12. Ⓐ Ⓑ Ⓒ Ⓓ	36. Ⓐ Ⓑ Ⓒ Ⓓ	60. Ⓐ Ⓑ Ⓒ Ⓓ
13. Ⓐ Ⓑ Ⓒ Ⓓ	37. Ⓐ Ⓑ Ⓒ Ⓓ	61. Ⓐ Ⓑ Ⓒ Ⓓ
14. Ⓐ Ⓑ Ⓒ Ⓓ	38. Ⓐ Ⓑ Ⓒ Ⓓ	62. Ⓐ Ⓑ Ⓒ Ⓓ
15. Ⓐ Ⓑ Ⓒ Ⓓ	39. Ⓐ Ⓑ Ⓒ Ⓓ	63. Ⓐ Ⓑ Ⓒ Ⓓ
16. Ⓐ Ⓑ Ⓒ Ⓓ	40. Ⓐ Ⓑ Ⓒ Ⓓ	64. Ⓐ Ⓑ Ⓒ Ⓓ
17. Ⓐ Ⓑ Ⓒ Ⓓ	41. Ⓐ Ⓑ Ⓒ Ⓓ	65. Ⓐ Ⓑ Ⓒ Ⓓ
18. Ⓐ Ⓑ Ⓒ Ⓓ	42. Ⓐ Ⓑ Ⓒ Ⓓ	66. Ⓐ Ⓑ Ⓒ Ⓓ
19. Ⓐ Ⓑ Ⓒ Ⓓ	43. Ⓐ Ⓑ Ⓒ Ⓓ	67. Ⓐ Ⓑ Ⓒ Ⓓ
20. Ⓐ Ⓑ Ⓒ Ⓓ	44. Ⓐ Ⓑ Ⓒ Ⓓ	68. Ⓐ Ⓑ Ⓒ Ⓓ
21. Ⓐ Ⓑ Ⓒ Ⓓ	45. Ⓐ Ⓑ Ⓒ Ⓓ	69. Ⓐ Ⓑ Ⓒ Ⓓ
22. Ⓐ Ⓑ Ⓒ Ⓓ	46. Ⓐ Ⓑ Ⓒ Ⓓ	70. Ⓐ Ⓑ Ⓒ Ⓓ
23. Ⓐ Ⓑ Ⓒ Ⓓ	47. Ⓐ Ⓑ Ⓒ Ⓓ	71. Ⓐ Ⓑ Ⓒ Ⓓ
24. Ⓐ Ⓑ Ⓒ Ⓓ	48. Ⓐ Ⓑ Ⓒ Ⓓ	72. Ⓐ Ⓑ Ⓒ Ⓓ

Part D: Personal Characteristics and Experience Inventory

On the actual exam, there would be spaces for the answers to 236 questions here, but we are not including this section in the practice exams or answer sheets.

Answer Key

Part A: Address Checking

1. C	13. C	25. B	37. C	49. C
2. B	14. A	26. C	38. C	50. B
3. A	15. D	27. D	39. B	51. A
4. D	16. B	28. B	40. B	52. B
5. B	17. C	29. C	41. D	53. D
6. C	18. C	30. B	42. B	54. C
7. D	19. B	31. A	43. D	55. A
8. B	20. D	32. B	44. B	56. B
9. C	21. B	33. D	45. C	57. B
10. A	22. B	34. C	46. D	58. C
11. B	23. A	35. A	47. A	59. C
12. D	24. B	36. B	48. B	60. B

Part B: Forms Completion

1. C	7. C	13. A	19. A	25. D
2. A	8. D	14. C	20. B	26. C
3. D	9. B	15. D	21. D	27. A
4. D	10. A	16. A	22. B	28. C
5. B	11. B	17. B	23. D	29. B
6. C	12. B	18. D	24. C	30. D

Part C: Coding and Memory

1. D	16. C	31. A	46. B	61. A
2. B	17. A	32. D	47. C	62. B
3. D	18. C	33. C	48. D	63. B
4. C	19. D	34. D	49. B	64. A
5. D	20. D	35. C	50. B	65. B
6. A	21. A	36. B	51. A	66. D
7. C	22. A	37. B	52. D	67. C
8. B	23. C	38. A	53. A	68. B
9. D	24. A	39. C	54. D	69. D
10. C	25. D	40. C	55. A	70. A
11. A	26. C	41. B	56. C	71. C
12. D	27. A	42. D	57. C	72. B
13. C	28. D	43. D	58. A	
14. C	29. D	44. A	59. D	
15. D	30. A	45. B	60. C	

Practice Test 3

Part A: Address Checking

Directions: Part A of this test consists of 60 items for you to complete in 11 minutes. You will be shown a **Correct List** of addresses and ZIP codes alongside a **List to Be Checked**. The two lists should contain the same addresses and ZIP codes, except that the **List to Be Checked** may contain errors.

Each row of information consists of one item. For each item, compare the address and ZIP code in the **Correct List** with the address and ZIP code in the **List to Be Checked**. Determine whether there are **No Errors**, an error in **Address Only**, an error in **ZIP Code Only**, or an error in **Both** the address and the ZIP code. Select an answer from the following four choices:

A. No Errors	B. Address Only	C. ZIP Code Only	D. Both

Mark your answers (A, B, C, or D) on the answer sheet at the end of the chapter.

An answer key is given at the end of the chapter.

Number of Items: 60

Time: 11 minutes

A. No Errors	B. Address Only	C. ZIP Code Only	D. Both

	Correct List		List to Be Checked	
	Address	*ZIP Code*	*Address*	*ZIP Code*
1.	135 Woodlawn Circle Garrett, PA	15542	135 Woodlawn Circle Garrett, PA	14542
2.	70 Barker Ter. Miami, FL	33172-4289	70 Parker Ter. Miami, FL	33172-4829
3.	1174 Lincoln Ave. Torrance, CA	90504	1174 Lincoln Blvd. Torrance, CA	90504
4.	2806 Route 2 Lubbock, TX	79407-2499	2806 Route 2 Lubbock, TX	79407-2499
5.	137 Central Pl. Columbia, SC	29209-7741	137 Central Pl. Columbia, SC	29209-4741
6.	711 W. School Ave. Boise, ID	83704	7111 W. School Ave. Boise, ID	83742
7.	95 S. Market St. West Saint Paul, MN	55107	95 S. Market St. West Saint Paul, MN	55170
8.	101 River Walk Greenville, NY	12083-0922	101 River Walk Greenwich, NY	12083-0933
9.	755 Spring St. Kirksville, MO	63501	557 Spring St. Kirksville, MO	63501
10.	1720 East End Dr. Great Falls, MT	59404-1964	1720 East End Dr. Great Falls, MT	59444-1964
11.	P.O. Box 23493 Lincoln, NE	68508	P.O. Box 23493 Lincoln, NE	68508
12.	2701 SW College Rd. Little Rock, AR	72202	2701 SW College Rd. Little Rock, AR	72202
13.	1221 S. Grand Blvd. Everett, WA	98204-1745	1221 Grand Blvd. Everett, WA	98204-1745
14.	80 Phelps Avenue Waterloo, IA	50702-3569	80 Philips Avenue Waterloo, IA	57072-3569
15.	2404 White Ave. Marbleton, WY	83113	2404 White Ave. Marbleton, WY	81133

continued on next page

A. No Errors	B. Address Only	C. ZIP Code Only	D. Both

	Correct List		**List to Be Checked**	
	Address	ZIP Code	Address	ZIP Code
16.	81 H Street, Suite 10 Detroit, MI	48207	81 H Street, Suite 10 Detroit, MI	48207
17.	3522 Granger Rd. Nashville, TN	37208-0562	3522 Granger Dr. Nashville, TN	37208-0562
18.	92 E. 25th St. Manchester, NH	03103-1246	92 E. 26th St. Manchester, NH	03103-1246
19.	996 Strawberry Ct. Tyler, TX	75704	996 Strawberry Ct. Tyler, TX	70754
20.	811 Aspen Glen Brigham City, UT	84302	811 Aspen Glen Brigham City, UT	83302
21.	1330 Shattuck Dr. Decatur, IL	62522-9175	1330 Shattuck Dr. Decater, IL	62522-9175
22.	313 Reef Rd. Unionville, VA	22567-5729	313 Reed Rd. Unionville, VA	22567-5229
23.	2433 W. Shaw Ave. Hallowell, ME	04347	2433 W. Shaw Ave. Halowell, ME	04347
24.	8926 Gary Pl. #33 Jackson, PA	18825-7510	8926 Gary Pl. #33 Jackson, PA	18825-7510
25.	P.O. Box 43366 Des Moines, IA	50315-3366	P.O. Box 43663 Des Moines, IA	50315-6366
26.	303 E. Baseline Rd. Tuscaloosa, AL	35405	303 E. Baseline Rd. Tuskaloosa, AL	35405
27.	116 Briar Circle Charlotte, NC	28202	116 Briar Circle Charlotte, NC	22802
28.	77556 Industry Park Elkhart, IN	46514	77556 Industry Park Elkart, IN	46914
29.	440 Cambria Way, Apt. 9 Phoenix, AZ	85033-5510	440 Cambria Way, Apt. 3 Phoenix, AZ	85033-5510
30.	1441 N. Kolb Rd. Syracuse, NY	13204-9446	1441 N. Kolb Rd. Syracuse, NY	13205-9446
31.	3900 12th St. Odessa, TX	79765	3900 12th Ave. Odessa, TX	79755
32.	2719 W. Arnsby Mansfield, MA	02048-2683	2719 W. Arnsby Mansfield, MA	02048-2683

continued on next page

A. No Errors	B. Address Only	C. ZIP Code Only	D. Both

	Correct List		List to Be Checked	
	Address	ZIP Code	Address	ZIP Code
33.	7725 Harper Place Saint Louis, MO	63110	7725 Harbor Place Saint Louis, MO	63110
34.	12 Glade Cir. Gainesville, GA	30504-6629	12 Glade Ct. Gainesville, GA	30504-6229
35.	1544 Shaefer Ter. Dayton, OH	45407-0228	1544 Shaefer Ter. Dayton, OH	45507-0228
36.	5151 F St. Kalamazoo, MI	49008	5151 F St. Kalamazoo, MI	49008
37.	9450 SW Barnes Rd. Grand Forks, ND	58203	9450 SW Barnes Rd. Grand Forks, SD	58203
38.	401 Saddle Way Austin, TX	78748-1388	4010 Saddle Way Austin, TX	78748-1388
39.	P.O. Box 93883 Howards Grove, WI	53083-3883	P.O. Box 93883 Howards Grove, WI	53033-8833
40.	19335 U.S. 98 North Eagan, MN	55123	19335 U.S. 98 North Eagan, MN	53123
41.	63032 E. Garfield Blvd. Rockford, IL	61104-0943	6303 E. Garfield Blvd. Rockford, IL	61104-0943
42.	1003 South B Street Bakersfield, CA	93308	1003 South Street Bakersfield, CA	93008
43.	1436 Dixie Highway New Orleans, LA	70131	1436 Dixie Parkway New Orleans, LA	70131
44.	1277 W. Commercial Blvd. Henderson, NV	89014-1289	1277 W. Commercial Blvd. Henderson, NV	89014-1289
45.	90 Public Square Cincinnati, OH	45225	99 Public Square Cincinnati, OH	42552
46.	846 South Union Avenue Alva, OK	73717-6822	846 South Union Avenue Alva, OH	73717-6822
47.	500 Brookside Little Rock, AR	72206	500 Brookside Little Rock, AR	76606
48.	PO Box 301 Cedar Grove, TN	38321-0301	PO Box 311 Cedar Grove, TN	38321-0310
49.	41 Walnut Lane Claremont, NH	03743-7784	41 Walnut Lane Clairmont, NH	03743-7784

continued on next page

| | A. No Errors | B. Address Only | C. ZIP Code Only | D. Both |

Correct List | **List to Be Checked**

	Address	ZIP Code	Address	ZIP Code
50.	1570 E. Idaho Blvd. Uniontown, MD	21158	1570 E. Idaho Blvd. Uniontown, MD	12158
51.	195 S. Harley Street Roscoe, SD	57471	195 S. Haley Street Roscoe, SD	57471
52.	6300 Central Avenue Wooster, OH	44691-6711	6300 Central Avenue Wooster, OH	44691-6711
53.	2621 K Street West Covina, CA	91790	2621 K Street East Covina, CA	91790
54.	28000 Ontario Pkwy. Erie, PA	16507-1322	2800 Ontario Pkwy. Erie, PA	16077-1322
55.	16007 Shaker Blvd. Houston, TX	77021	16007 Shaker Blvd. Houston, TX	72021
56.	721 Lake View #2 Minneapolis, MN	55406-5770	721 Lake View #2 Minneapolis, MN	55406-5770
57.	2505 N. 54th St. Milwaukee, WI	53208-3286	2505 N. 54th Ave. Milwaukee, WI	53208-2286
58.	460 Willow Circle Columbus, GA	31907-3573	460 Willow Circle Columbus, OH	31907-3573
59.	8488 Van Buren Blvd. Oak Grove, OR	97267	8488 Van Buren Blvd. Oak Grove, OR	97276
60.	9593 McGeorge Avenue West Sacramento, CA	95691	9593 McGeorge Avenue West Sacramento, CA	99691

Part B: Forms Completion

Directions: Part B of this test consists of 30 questions for you to complete in 15 minutes. You will be shown a series of forms that are similar to ones used by the U.S. Postal Service. The parts of each form are labeled (for example, 3 and 4a). Each form is accompanied by several questions that test your ability to complete the form properly. For each question, choose the best answer and mark your selection (A, B, C, or D) on your answer sheet.

Turn the page when you are ready to begin Part B under timed conditions.

An answer key is provided at the end of this chapter.

Number of Questions: 30

Time: 15 minutes

Sender's Application for Mail Recall		
1. Description of Mailed Item (Check all that apply) ☐ Letter ☐ Express Mail ☐ Approx. Size: _____ x _____ ☐ Package ☐ Special Delivery ☐ Color: _____	3a. Date Mailed	
	3b. Time Mailed A.M. P.M.	
2. Identifying Number (Check and complete all that apply) ☐ Certified No. _____ ☐ Registered No. _____ ☐ Insured No. _____ ☐ COD No. _____	4a. Date Appl. Filed	
	4b. Time Appl. Filed A.M. P.M.	
5. Return Address on Mail	7a. Delivery Address on Mail	
6. Check One: ☐ Postage Stamp ☐ Postage Meter Stamp ☐ Other	7b. Check One: ☐ Typewritten ☐ Handwritten ☐ Other	
8a. Applicant s Name _____		
8b. Applicant's Address _____		
8c. Applicant's Telephone Number _____		
8d. Signature of Applicant _____		
POSTAL USE ONLY	9a. Date Received 9b. Time Received A.M. P.M.	9c. Received by (employee name)

1. Where should the sender applicant's name be entered on this form?

   (A) Box 9c

   (B) Line 8a

   (C) Box 5

   (D) Box 2

2. Which of these would be a correct entry for Box 3b?

   (A) "04/13/06"

   (B) A check mark

   (C) "10:45 A.M."

   (D) "Jason Haley"

3. Where would you enter the date received on this form?

   (A) Box 4a

   (B) Box 3a

   (C) Line 9a

   (D) Box 9b

4. How would you indicate that the article was sent by C.O.D. mail?

   (A) Enter a check mark and a number in Box 2

   (B) Enter a number only in Box 2

   (C) Enter a check mark only in Box 2

   (D) Put a check mark in Box 6

5. Entering a person's name might be appropriate in every box EXCEPT which?

   (A) Box 5

   (B) Box 7a

   (C) Box 8d

   (D) Box 1

6. All of these could be correct entries in Box 1 EXCEPT which?

   (A) "Yellow"

   (B) "4772"

   (C) "8 in. x 8 in."

   (D) Three check marks

7. Which of these does a check mark next to "Other" in Box 7b indicate?

   (A) The delivery address is outside the U.S.

   (B) The delivery address was handwritten

   (C) The delivery address was incorrect

   (D) The delivery address was not typewritten

	Signature Confirmation and Receipt	
SIGNATURE CONFIRMATION RECEIPT	TO BE COMPLETED BY SENDER	POST OFFICE USE ONLY
	1a. Sent To (Name): _____ 1b. Address: _____ _____ Signature Confirmation Number 4258 0092 1773 8108	2a. Check One: ☐ Priority ☐ Package Service 2b. Waiver of Signature? ☐ Yes ☐ No 2c. Postmark Here
SIGNATURE CONFIRMATION	3. WAIVER OF SIGNATURE. I authorize that the postal delivery employee's signature suffices as proof of delivery if the item is left in a secure location.	
	4. Customer Signature	Signature Confirmation Number 4258 0092 1173 8108

8. Which of these would be a correct entry in Line 3?

(A) A check mark

(B) A post office employee's name

(C) The signature confirmation number

(D) None of the above

9. The post office employee should enter information in every line EXCEPT which?

(A) Line 2b

(B) Line 1b

(C) Line 2c

(D) Line 2a

10. Which of the following would be a correct pair of entries on this form?

(A) A check mark in Line 2b and in Line 3

(B) A check mark in Line 2a and in Line 2c

(C) A name in Line 4 and in Line 1a

(D) A check mark in Line 3 and in Line 2a

11. How would you indicate that the item is to be sent by priority mail?

(A) Enter "Priority" on Line 2c

(B) Enter the signature confirmation number on Line 4

(C) Detach the Signature Confirmation

(D) Enter a check mark on Line 2a

12. Where would you enter the type of delivery service?

(A) Line 2d

(B) Line 2b

(C) Line 2a

(D) Line 2c

Authorization to Hold Mail	
1. Hold Mail For:	2. Beginning Date
1a. Name	3. Ending Date
1b. Street Address	4a. ☐ Do NOT resume delivery until I pick up all accumulated mail.
1c. City, State, ZIP	
5. Customer Signature	4b. ☐ Resume delivery of accumulated and new mail on ending date.
POSTAL USE ONLY 6. Date Received	8. Carrier
7. Clerk	9. Route Number

13. Where would the customer's ZIP code be entered on this form?

(A) Line 1c

(B) Box 9

(C) Line 1b

(D) Box 3

14. Where should the carrier's route number be entered on this form?

(A) Box 8

(B) Box 9

(C) Box 4

(D) Box 7

15. The postal clerk is James Friedman. How would you indicate this?

(A) Enter "James Friedman" in Box 8

(B) Enter James Friedman's post office number in Box 9

(C) Enter "James Friedman" in Box 5

(D) Enter "James Friedman" in Box 7

16. A date would be a correct entry for each box EXCEPT which?

(A) Box 3

(B) Box 6

(C) Box 2

(D) Box 9

17. Which of these would be a correct entry for Line 1b?

(A) "Madison, WI"

(B) A check mark

(C) "80 Alta Dr., Suite B"

(D) "Stephanie Beale"

Bulk Mailing Certificate

Certificate Fee Schedule

1a. 1 – 1,000 pieces $ _____

1b. Each additional
    1,000 pieces (or $ _____
    fraction thereof)

} Use Current
Rate Schedule

2a. Number of Identical Pieces	2b. Mail Class	2c. Postage per Piece	2d. Total Postage
3a. Number of Pieces per Pound	3b. Total Number of Pieces		3c. Bulk Mailing Fee
4a. Mailed By	4b. Mailed For		5. Total Postage and Fees

6. Postmaster's Certificate
I hereby certify that the mailing described above has been received
and the number of pieces and the postage is correct.

X _____

(Postmaster)

18. Where would you indicate the bulk mailing fee on this form?

(A) Box 3c

(B) Box 2d

(C) Box 2c

(D) Box 5

19. Which of these is a correct entry for Box 3b?

(A) "$160.00"

(B) "01/23/08"

(C) A check mark

(D) "380"

20. Where would you enter the total postage on this form?

(A) Box 5

(B) Box 3c

(C) Box 2d

(D) Box 2a

21. Which of these would be an appropriate entry for Box 1a?

(A) A check mark

(B) "125.40"

(C) "02/17/07"

(D) "Jason Flynn"

22. A person's name would be an appropriate entry for each box EXCEPT which?

(A) Box 6

(B) Box 1b

(C) Box 4a

(D) Box 4b

23. Which of these is an appropriate entry in Box 2b?

(A) "$14.30"

(B) "638 lbs."

(C) "3rd"

(D) "380"

Customs Dispatch Order and Declaration

1. Sender Information	2. Addressee Information
1a. Name	2a. Name
1b. Street, Apt., or PO Box No.	2b. Street, Apt., or PO Box No.
1c. City, State, ZIP + 4	2c. City, State, ZIP + 4
1d. Country	2d. Country

3a. Contents (Detailed Description)	3c. Qty	3d. Weight lb. / oz.	3e. Value (US $)

3b. Check One	3f. Restriction and Other Comments
☐ Gift ☐ Commercial Sample ☐ Document ☐ Other	(e.g., subject to quarantine)

4. For Commercial Items Only	5. Sender's Signature and Date
4a. Country of Origin _____ ☐ Unknown 4b. HS Tariff No. _____ ☐ Unknown	6. Delivery (Check One) ☐ Priority/Air ☐ Non-Priority/Surface

24. Which of these would be a correct entry for Box 3e?

(A) "77339"

(B) "Priority"

(C) "06/27/07"

(D) "$350.00"

25. The item delivered is a document. Where would you indicate this?

(A) Box 3c

(B) Box 3e

(C) Box 3b

(D) Box 1d

26. Which of these would be a correct entry for Line 4b?

(A) A check mark

(B) "$2.80"

(C) Unknown

(D) "England"

27. Where should the weight of the delivery items be entered on this form?

(A) Box 3d

(B) Box 4b

(C) Box 3c

(D) Box 3a

28. How would you indicate that the article is sent from the U.S.?

(A) Enter "U.S." in Line 2d

(B) Enter a check mark in Line 1d

(C) Enter a check mark in Box 6

(D) Enter "U.S." in Line 4a

29. Where does the sender sign this form?

(A) Box 1

(B) Box 3a

(C) Box 5

(D) Box 3f

30. A check mark would be a correct entry for every box EXCEPT which?

(A) Box 6

(B) Box 3f

(C) Box 3b

(D) Box 4

Part C: Coding and Memory

Part C of this test consists of two sections:

- A **Coding Section**, which consists of 36 questions to be completed in 6 minutes
- A **Memory Section**, which consists of 36 questions to be completed in 7 minutes

Both sections test your ability to match one-letter codes to addresses quickly and accurately. The Memory Section also tests your ability to memorize codes and their matching address ranges.

You will use the same **Coding Guide** for both sections of Part C. The first column of the **Coding Guide** shows each **address range**. The second column shows the **delivery route** code (A, B, C, or D) for the address ranges shown in the same row as the code. You may assume that each address range runs continuously (no numbers are skipped) from the lowest to the highest number in the range. Some of the street names appear twice, showing two different address ranges.

Coding Section

This section consists of three segments:

- **Segment 1** is an introductory exercise consisting of 4 items to be completed in 2 minutes. *Segment 1 is not scored.*
- **Segment 2** is a practice exercise consisting of 8 items to be completed in 1 1/2 minutes (90 seconds). *Segment 2 is not scored.*
- **Segment 3** is the actual Coding Section of the test. This segment consists of 36 items to be completed in 6 minutes. *Segment 3 is scored and counts toward your total test score.*

You will use the same Coding Guide for all three segments.

Coding Section—Segment 1

Directions: Segment 1 is an introductory exercise that will familiarize you with the Coding Section and help you learn how to complete it. This segment is *not* scored. Based on the Coding Guide, match each address to a delivery route. Mark your answers on the answer grid at the bottom of this page.

Number of Items: 4

Time Limit: 2 minutes

Coding Guide	
Address Range	*Delivery Route*
1200–1700 Haley St. 950–1050 53rd Ave. 8000–12000 West Lake Blvd.	A
1701–2000 Haley St. 1051–1150 53rd Ave.	B
1–30 Chavez Terrace 75–125 Windy Shores 12001–15000 West Lake Blvd.	C
All mail that does not fall in one of the address ranges listed above	D

	Address	Delivery Code			
1.	13015 West Lake Blvd.	A	B	C	D
2.	1755 Haley St.	A	B	C	D
3.	33 Chavez Terrace	A	B	C	D
4.	1030 53rd Ave.	A	B	C	D

Sample Answer Sheet

1. Ⓐ Ⓑ Ⓒ Ⓓ   3. Ⓐ Ⓑ Ⓒ Ⓓ
2. Ⓐ Ⓑ Ⓒ Ⓓ   4. Ⓐ Ⓑ Ⓒ Ⓓ

Coding Section—Segment 2

Directions: Segment 2 is *not* scored. It is a practice exercise that will give you experience with the Coding Section under a time constraint similar to the one during the scored Coding Section. Based on the Coding Guide, match each address to a delivery route. Mark your answers on the answer grid at the bottom of this page.

Number of Items: 8

Time Limit: 1 1/2 minutes (90 seconds)

Coding Guide	
Address Range	*Delivery Route*
1200–1700 Haley St. 950–1050 53rd Ave. 8000–12000 West Lake Blvd.	A
1701–2000 Haley St. 1051–1150 53rd Ave.	B
1–30 Chavez Terrace 75–125 Windy Shores 12001–15000 West Lake Blvd.	C
All mail that does not fall in one of the address ranges listed above	D

	Address	Delivery Code			
1.	8030 West Lake Blvd.	A	B	C	D
2.	1758 Haley St.	A	B	C	D
3.	995 53rd Ave.	A	B	C	D
4.	82 Windy Shores	A	B	C	D
5.	11182 West Lake Blvd.	A	B	C	D
6.	6 Chavez Terrace	A	B	C	D
7.	1052 53rd Ave.	A	B	C	D
8.	79 Windy Shores	A	B	C	D

Sample Answer Sheet

1. Ⓐ Ⓑ Ⓒ Ⓓ   4. Ⓐ Ⓑ Ⓒ Ⓓ   7. Ⓐ Ⓑ Ⓒ Ⓓ
2. Ⓐ Ⓑ Ⓒ Ⓓ   5. Ⓐ Ⓑ Ⓒ Ⓓ   8. Ⓐ Ⓑ Ⓒ Ⓓ
3. Ⓐ Ⓑ Ⓒ Ⓓ   6. Ⓐ Ⓑ Ⓒ Ⓓ

Coding Section—Segment 3

Directions: Segment 3 is the *actual scored* Coding Section of the test. Based on the Coding Guide, match each address to a delivery route. Mark your answers on the answer sheet at the end of the chapter.

An answer key for this segment is given at the end of the chapter.

Number of Items: 36

Time Limit: 6 minutes

Coding Guide	
Address Range	*Delivery Route*
1200–1700 Haley St. 950–1050 53rd Ave. 8000–12000 West Lake Blvd.	A
1701–2000 Haley St. 1051–1150 53rd Ave.	B
1–30 Chavez Terrace 75–125 Windy Shores 12001–15000 West Lake Blvd.	C
All mail that does not fall in one of the address ranges listed above	D

#	Address	Delivery Code			
1.	20 Chavez Terrace	A	B	C	D
2.	1100 53rd Ave.	A	B	C	D
3.	8 Windy Shores	A	B	C	D
4.	1404 Haley St.	A	B	C	D
5.	7150 53rd Ave.	A	B	C	D
6.	13374 West Lake Blvd.	A	B	C	D
7.	81 Windy Lane	A	B	C	D
8.	1 Chavez Terrace	A	B	C	D
9.	1970 Haley St.	A	B	C	D
10.	967 53rd Ave.	A	B	C	D
11.	15 Chavez Drive	A	B	C	D
12.	92 Windy Shores	A	B	C	D
13.	965 53rd Ave.	A	B	C	D
14.	5200 Haley St.	A	B	C	D
15.	9116 West Lake Blvd.	A	B	C	D
16.	970 53rd Ave.	A	B	C	D
17.	83 Windy Shores	A	B	C	D
18.	5 Chavez Terrace	A	B	C	D
19.	1127 53rd Ave.	A	B	C	D
20.	1801 Haley St.	A	B	C	D
21.	9501 West Lake Blvd.	A	B	C	D
22.	1111 53rd Ave.	A	B	C	D
23.	21 Chelham Terrace	A	B	C	D
24.	8394 West Lake Blvd.	A	B	C	D
25.	120 Windy Shores	A	B	C	D
26.	995 53rd St.	A	B	C	D
27.	12060 West Lake Blvd.	A	B	C	D
28.	101 Windy Shores	A	B	C	D
29.	23 Chavez Terrace	A	B	C	D
30.	5800 West Lake Blvd.	A	B	C	D
31.	1094 53rd Ave.	A	B	C	D
32.	1680 Haley St.	A	B	C	D
33.	1200 West Lake Blvd.	A	B	C	D
34.	28 Chavez Terrace	A	B	C	D
35.	1058 53rd Ave.	A	B	C	D
36.	1999 Haley St.	A	B	C	D

Memory Section

This section consists of four segments:

- **Segment 1** is a 3-minute study period during which you will attempt to memorize the Coding Guide. *Segment 1 is not scored*, and there are no answers to mark during this segment.
- **Segment 2** is a practice exercise consisting of 8 items to be completed in 1 1/2 minutes (90 seconds). *Segment 2 is not scored*.
- **Segment 3** is a 5-minute study period during which you will attempt to memorize the Coding Guide. *Segment 3 is not scored*, and there are no answers to mark during this segment.
- **Segment 4** is the actual Memory Section of the test. This segment consists of 36 items to be completed in 7 minutes. *Segment 4 is scored and counts toward your total test score.*

You will use the same Coding Guide for all four segments.

Memory Section—Segment 1

Directions: Segment 1 is a 3-minute study period during which you will attempt to memorize the Coding Guide. This segment is *not* scored, and there are no answers to mark during this segment.

Begin the 3-minute study period when you are ready.

Coding Guide	
Address Range	*Delivery Route*
1200–1700 Haley St. 950–1050 53rd Ave. 8000–12000 West Lake Blvd.	A
1701–2000 Haley St. 1051–1150 53rd Ave.	B
1–30 Chavez Terrace 75–125 Windy Shores 12001–15000 West Lake Blvd.	C
All mail that does not fall in one of the address ranges listed above	D

Memory Section—Segment 2

Directions: Segment 2 is a practice exercise that will give you experience coding addresses from memory based on the Coding Guide on the previous page. The Coding Guide is not shown during this segment. Based on the Coding Guide, match each address to a delivery route. Mark your answers on the answer grid at the bottom of the next page. This segment is *not* scored.

Turn the page when you are ready to begin Segment 2 under timed conditions.

Number of Items: 8

Time Limit: 1 1/2 minutes (90 seconds)

	Address	Delivery Code			
1.	77 Windy Shores	A	B	C	D
2.	13350 East Lake Blvd.	A	B	C	D
3.	1301 Haley St.	A	B	C	D
4.	24 Chavez Terrace	A	B	C	D
5.	961 53rd Ave.	A	B	C	D
6.	2000 Haley St.	A	B	C	D
7.	13488 West Lake Blvd.	A	B	C	D
8.	1775 Haley Blvd.	A	B	C	D

Sample Answer Sheet

1. Ⓐ Ⓑ Ⓒ Ⓓ   4. Ⓐ Ⓑ Ⓒ Ⓓ   7. Ⓐ Ⓑ Ⓒ Ⓓ
2. Ⓐ Ⓑ Ⓒ Ⓓ   5. Ⓐ Ⓑ Ⓒ Ⓓ   8. Ⓐ Ⓑ Ⓒ Ⓓ
3. Ⓐ Ⓑ Ⓒ Ⓓ   6. Ⓐ Ⓑ Ⓒ Ⓓ

Memory Section—Segment 3

Directions: Segment 3 is a 5-minute study period during which you will again attempt to memorize the Coding Guide. This segment is *not* scored, and there are no answers to mark during this segment.

Begin the 5-minute study period when you are ready.

Coding Guide	
Address Range	*Delivery Route*
1200–1700 Haley St. 950–1050 53rd Ave. 8000–12000 West Lake Blvd.	A
1701–2000 Haley St. 1051–1150 53rd Ave.	B
1–30 Chavez Terrace 75–125 Windy Shores 12001–15000 West Lake Blvd.	C
All mail that does not fall in one of the address ranges listed above	D

Memory Section—Segment 4

Directions: Segment 4 is the *actual scored* Memory Section of the test. The Coding Guide is not shown during this segment. Based on the Coding Guide, match each address to a delivery route. Mark your answers on the answer sheet at the end of the chapter.

Go to the next page when you are ready to begin Segment 4 under timed conditions.

An answer key for this segment is provided at the end of the chapter.

Number of Items: 36

Time Limit: 7 minutes

	Address	Delivery Code			
37.	80 Windy Shores	A	B	C	D
38.	1946 Haley St.	A	B	C	D
39.	982 53rd Ave.	A	B	C	D
40.	99 Windy Shores	A	B	C	D
41.	12550 West Lake Blvd.	A	B	C	D
42.	1345 Haley St.	A	B	C	D
43.	76 Chavez Terrace	A	B	C	D
44.	1597 Haley St.	A	B	C	D
45.	105 West Shores	A	B	C	D
46.	1045 53rd Ave.	A	B	C	D
47.	9275 West Lake Blvd.	A	B	C	D
48.	1730 Haley St.	A	B	C	D
49.	39 Chavez Terrace	A	B	C	D
50.	1520 Haley St.	A	B	C	D
51.	1072 53rd Ave.	A	B	C	D
52.	52050 West Lake Blvd.	A	B	C	D
53.	68 Chavez Terrace	A	B	C	D
54.	80 Windy Shores	A	B	C	D
55.	14937 West Lake Blvd.	A	B	C	D
56.	1285 Harper St.	A	B	C	D
57.	990 53rd Ave.	A	B	C	D
58.	1883 Haley St.	A	B	C	D
59.	10800 West Lake Blvd.	A	B	C	D
60.	30 Windy Shores	A	B	C	D
61.	7 Chavez Terrace	A	B	C	D
62.	1090 Haley St.	A	B	C	D
63.	1126 53rd Ave.	A	B	C	D
64.	995 3rd Ave.	A	B	C	D

continued on next page

	Address	Delivery Code			
65.	14802 West Lake Blvd.	A	B	C	D
66.	1081 53rd Ave.	A	B	C	D
67.	30 Chavez Terrace	A	B	C	D
68.	1220 Haley St.	A	B	C	D
69.	8002 West Lake Blvd.	A	B	C	D
70.	1144 53rd Ave.	A	B	C	D
71.	29 Chavez Terrace	A	B	C	D
72.	12168 West Lake Blvd.	A	B	C	D

Part D: Personal Characteristics and Experience Inventory

Part D consists of a 236-item questionnaire (inventory) on your personal characteristics and experience. You have 90 minutes to complete Part D. This part is scored, but how it is scored is a Postal Service secret. There is no need to prepare for this part of the exam, and therefore it is not included in this practice test. (For more information about Part D, see Chapter 6.)

Practice Test 3 Answer Sheet

The answer sheet given here closely resembles that used on the actual Test 473.

On the front of the answer sheet, you will be asked to fill in personal information similar to the information that you gave when you applied to take the exam. Then you will find spaces—ovals lettered A, B, C, and D—where you are to fill in your answers to Part A, Address Checking, and Part B, Forms Completion, of the exam.

On the other side of the actual answer sheet, you will find similar lettered ovals for you to enter your answers to Part C, Coding and Memory, of the exam. On the answer sheet for Test 473, there will also be spaces for answers to Part D, Personal Characteristics and Experience Inventory, but we have not included that section in this practice exam.

Part A: Address Checking

1. Ⓐ Ⓑ Ⓒ Ⓓ
2. Ⓐ Ⓑ Ⓒ Ⓓ
3. Ⓐ Ⓑ Ⓒ Ⓓ
4. Ⓐ Ⓑ Ⓒ Ⓓ
5. Ⓐ Ⓑ Ⓒ Ⓓ
6. Ⓐ Ⓑ Ⓒ Ⓓ
7. Ⓐ Ⓑ Ⓒ Ⓓ
8. Ⓐ Ⓑ Ⓒ Ⓓ
9. Ⓐ Ⓑ Ⓒ Ⓓ
10. Ⓐ Ⓑ Ⓒ Ⓓ
11. Ⓐ Ⓑ Ⓒ Ⓓ
12. Ⓐ Ⓑ Ⓒ Ⓓ
13. Ⓐ Ⓑ Ⓒ Ⓓ
14. Ⓐ Ⓑ Ⓒ Ⓓ
15. Ⓐ Ⓑ Ⓒ Ⓓ
16. Ⓐ Ⓑ Ⓒ Ⓓ
17. Ⓐ Ⓑ Ⓒ Ⓓ
18. Ⓐ Ⓑ Ⓒ Ⓓ
19. Ⓐ Ⓑ Ⓒ Ⓓ
20. Ⓐ Ⓑ Ⓒ Ⓓ

21. Ⓐ Ⓑ Ⓒ Ⓓ
22. Ⓐ Ⓑ Ⓒ Ⓓ
23. Ⓐ Ⓑ Ⓒ Ⓓ
24. Ⓐ Ⓑ Ⓒ Ⓓ
25. Ⓐ Ⓑ Ⓒ Ⓓ
26. Ⓐ Ⓑ Ⓒ Ⓓ
27. Ⓐ Ⓑ Ⓒ Ⓓ
28. Ⓐ Ⓑ Ⓒ Ⓓ
28. Ⓐ Ⓑ Ⓒ Ⓓ
30. Ⓐ Ⓑ Ⓒ Ⓓ
31. Ⓐ Ⓑ Ⓒ Ⓓ
32. Ⓐ Ⓑ Ⓒ Ⓓ
33. Ⓐ Ⓑ Ⓒ Ⓓ
34. Ⓐ Ⓑ Ⓒ Ⓓ
35. Ⓐ Ⓑ Ⓒ Ⓓ
36. Ⓐ Ⓑ Ⓒ Ⓓ
37. Ⓐ Ⓑ Ⓒ Ⓓ
38. Ⓐ Ⓑ Ⓒ Ⓓ
39. Ⓐ Ⓑ Ⓒ Ⓓ
40. Ⓐ Ⓑ Ⓒ Ⓓ

41. Ⓐ Ⓑ Ⓒ Ⓓ
42. Ⓐ Ⓑ Ⓒ Ⓓ
43. Ⓐ Ⓑ Ⓒ Ⓓ
44. Ⓐ Ⓑ Ⓒ Ⓓ
45. Ⓐ Ⓑ Ⓒ Ⓓ
46. Ⓐ Ⓑ Ⓒ Ⓓ
47. Ⓐ Ⓑ Ⓒ Ⓓ
48. Ⓐ Ⓑ Ⓒ Ⓓ
49. Ⓐ Ⓑ Ⓒ Ⓓ
50. Ⓐ Ⓑ Ⓒ Ⓓ
51. Ⓐ Ⓑ Ⓒ Ⓓ
52. Ⓐ Ⓑ Ⓒ Ⓓ
53. Ⓐ Ⓑ Ⓒ Ⓓ
54. Ⓐ Ⓑ Ⓒ Ⓓ
55. Ⓐ Ⓑ Ⓒ Ⓓ
56. Ⓐ Ⓑ Ⓒ Ⓓ
57. Ⓐ Ⓑ Ⓒ Ⓓ
58. Ⓐ Ⓑ Ⓒ Ⓓ
59. Ⓐ Ⓑ Ⓒ Ⓓ
60. Ⓐ Ⓑ Ⓒ Ⓓ

Part B: Forms Completion

1. Ⓐ Ⓑ Ⓒ Ⓓ
2. Ⓐ Ⓑ Ⓒ Ⓓ
3. Ⓐ Ⓑ Ⓒ Ⓓ
4. Ⓐ Ⓑ Ⓒ Ⓓ
5. Ⓐ Ⓑ Ⓒ Ⓓ
6. Ⓐ Ⓑ Ⓒ Ⓓ
7. Ⓐ Ⓑ Ⓒ Ⓓ
8. Ⓐ Ⓑ Ⓒ Ⓓ
9. Ⓐ Ⓑ Ⓒ Ⓓ
10. Ⓐ Ⓑ Ⓒ Ⓓ

11. Ⓐ Ⓑ Ⓒ Ⓓ
12. Ⓐ Ⓑ Ⓒ Ⓓ
13. Ⓐ Ⓑ Ⓒ Ⓓ
14. Ⓐ Ⓑ Ⓒ Ⓓ
15. Ⓐ Ⓑ Ⓒ Ⓓ
16. Ⓐ Ⓑ Ⓒ Ⓓ
17. Ⓐ Ⓑ Ⓒ Ⓓ
18. Ⓐ Ⓑ Ⓒ Ⓓ
19. Ⓐ Ⓑ Ⓒ Ⓓ
20. Ⓐ Ⓑ Ⓒ Ⓓ

21. Ⓐ Ⓑ Ⓒ Ⓓ
22. Ⓐ Ⓑ Ⓒ Ⓓ
23. Ⓐ Ⓑ Ⓒ Ⓓ
24. Ⓐ Ⓑ Ⓒ Ⓓ
25. Ⓐ Ⓑ Ⓒ Ⓓ
26. Ⓐ Ⓑ Ⓒ Ⓓ
27. Ⓐ Ⓑ Ⓒ Ⓓ
28. Ⓐ Ⓑ Ⓒ Ⓓ
29. Ⓐ Ⓑ Ⓒ Ⓓ
30. Ⓐ Ⓑ Ⓒ Ⓓ

Part C: Coding and Memory

1. (A) (B) (C) (D)		25. (A) (B) (C) (D)		49. (A) (B) (C) (D)
2. (A) (B) (C) (D)		26. (A) (B) (C) (D)		50. (A) (B) (C) (D)
3. (A) (B) (C) (D)		27. (A) (B) (C) (D)		51. (A) (B) (C) (D)
4. (A) (B) (C) (D)		28. (A) (B) (C) (D)		52. (A) (B) (C) (D)
5. (A) (B) (C) (D)		29. (A) (B) (C) (D)		53. (A) (B) (C) (D)
6. (A) (B) (C) (D)		30. (A) (B) (C) (D)		54. (A) (B) (C) (D)
7. (A) (B) (C) (D)		31. (A) (B) (C) (D)		55. (A) (B) (C) (D)
8. (A) (B) (C) (D)		32. (A) (B) (C) (D)		56. (A) (B) (C) (D)
9. (A) (B) (C) (D)		33. (A) (B) (C) (D)		57. (A) (B) (C) (D)
10. (A) (B) (C) (D)		34. (A) (B) (C) (D)		58. (A) (B) (C) (D)
11. (A) (B) (C) (D)		35. (A) (B) (C) (D)		59. (A) (B) (C) (D)
12. (A) (B) (C) (D)		36. (A) (B) (C) (D)		60. (A) (B) (C) (D)
13. (A) (B) (C) (D)		37. (A) (B) (C) (D)		61. (A) (B) (C) (D)
14. (A) (B) (C) (D)		38. (A) (B) (C) (D)		62. (A) (B) (C) (D)
15. (A) (B) (C) (D)		39. (A) (B) (C) (D)		63. (A) (B) (C) (D)
16. (A) (B) (C) (D)		40. (A) (B) (C) (D)		64. (A) (B) (C) (D)
17. (A) (B) (C) (D)		41. (A) (B) (C) (D)		65. (A) (B) (C) (D)
18. (A) (B) (C) (D)		42. (A) (B) (C) (D)		66. (A) (B) (C) (D)
19. (A) (B) (C) (D)		43. (A) (B) (C) (D)		67. (A) (B) (C) (D)
20. (A) (B) (C) (D)		44. (A) (B) (C) (D)		68. (A) (B) (C) (D)
21. (A) (B) (C) (D)		45. (A) (B) (C) (D)		69. (A) (B) (C) (D)
22. (A) (B) (C) (D)		46. (A) (B) (C) (D)		70. (A) (B) (C) (D)
23. (A) (B) (C) (D)		47. (A) (B) (C) (D)		71. (A) (B) (C) (D)
24. (A) (B) (C) (D)		48. (A) (B) (C) (D)		72. (A) (B) (C) (D)

Part D: Personal Characteristics and Experience Inventory

On the actual exam, there would be spaces for the answers to 236 questions here, but we are not including this section in the practice exams or answer sheets.

Answer Key

Part A: Address Checking

1. C	13. B	25. D	37. B	49. B
2. D	14. D	26. B	38. B	50. C
3. B	15. C	27. C	39. C	51. B
4. A	16. A	28. D	40. C	52. A
5. C	17. B	29. B	41. B	53. B
6. D	18. B	30. C	42. D	54. D
7. C	19. C	31. D	43. B	55. C
8. D	20. C	32. A	44. A	56. A
9. B	21. B	33. B	45. D	57. D
10. C	22. D	34. D	46. B	58. B
11. A	23. B	35. C	47. C	59. C
12. A	24. A	36. A	48. D	60. C

Part B: Forms Completion

1. B	7. D	13. A	19. D	25. C
2. C	8. D	14. B	20. C	26. A
3. C	9. B	15. D	21. B	27. A
4. A	10. A	16. D	22. B	28. D
5. D	11. D	17. C	23. C	29. C
6. B	12. C	18. A	24. D	30. B

Part C: Coding and Memory

1. C	16. A	31. B	46. A	61. C
2. B	17. C	32. A	47. A	62. D
3. D	18. C	33. D	48. B	63. B
4. A	19. B	34. C	49. D	64. D
5. D	20. B	35. B	50. A	65. C
6. C	21. A	36. B	51. B	66. B
7. D	22. B	37. C	52. D	67. C
8. C	23. D	38. B	53. D	68. A
9. B	24. A	39. A	54. C	69. A
10. A	25. C	40. C	55. C	70. B
11. D	26. D	41. C	56. D	71. C
12. C	27. C	42. A	57. A	72. C
13. A	28. C	43. D	58. B	
14. D	29. C	44. A	59. A	
15. A	30. D	45. D	60. D	

Practice Test 4

Part A: Address Checking

Directions: Part A of this test consists of 60 items for you to complete in 11 minutes. You will be shown a **Correct List** of addresses and ZIP codes alongside a **List to Be Checked**. The two lists should contain the same addresses and ZIP codes, except that the **List to Be Checked** may contain errors.

Each row of information consists of one item. For each item, compare the address and ZIP code in the **Correct List** with the address and ZIP code in the **List to Be Checked**. Determine whether there are **No Errors**, an error in **Address Only**, an error in **ZIP Code Only**, or an error in **Both** the address and the ZIP code. Select an answer from the following four choices:

A. No Errors	B. Address Only	C. ZIP Code Only	D. Both

Mark your answers (A, B, C, or D) on the answer sheet at the end of the chapter.

An answer key is given at the end of the chapter.

Number of Items: 60

Time: 11 minutes

A. No Errors	B. Address Only	C. ZIP Code Only	D. Both

	Correct List			List to Be Checked	
	Address	*ZIP Code*		*Address*	*ZIP Code*
1.	273 High St. Stamford, CT	06906-2299		273 High St. Stanford, CT	06960-2299
2.	46 Quail Ct. Wilkes Barre, PA	18701		46 Quail Ct. Wilkes Barre, PA	81701
3.	4522 N. Deering Way Freeport, MN	56331-8362		4566 N. Deering Way Freeport, MN	56331-8362
4.	33722 Route 20 Joliet, IL	60432		33722 Rte. 20 Joliet, IL	60432
5.	1532 Hamilton St. Providence, RI	02903		1532 Hamilton St. Providence, RI	02903
6.	8270 Navidad Brookings, SD	57006-9783		8270 Navidad Rd. Brookings, SD	57066-9783
7.	30 Oxbow Rd. Waco, TX	76708-0003		33 Oxbow Rd. Waco, TX	76708-0003
8.	300 W. Noble Pl. Orlando, FL	32835		300 W. Noble Pl. Orlando, FL	32825
9.	1656 4th St. Greenville, NC	27834-2945		1565 4th St. Greenville, NC	27384-2945
10.	PO Box 80370 Kansas City, MO	64105		PO Box 8370 Kansas City, MO	64105
11.	1406 Esplanade North Platte, NE	69101-4176		1406 Esplanade North Platte, NE	69101-4776
12.	329 Archer Rd. Somersworth, NH	03878-8432		329 Archer Rd. Summersworth, NH	03878-8432
13.	1840 Church St. Burlington, VT	05401		1840 Church St. Burlington, VT	05401
14.	15 Bickford St. Niagara Falls, NY	14305		15 Bickford Rd. Niagara Falls, NY	14305
15.	450 S. Bristol Court Twin Falls, ID	83301		450 S. Bristle Court Twin Falls, ID	81310

continued on next page

A. No Errors	B. Address Only	C. ZIP Code Only	D. Both

	Correct List		List to Be Checked	
	Address	ZIP Code	Address	ZIP Code
16.	183 Vale Rd., Suite 11 Eagan, MN	55121-3589	183 Vale Rd., Suite 11 Eagan, MN	51221-3589
17.	5352 Cochran St. Reno, NV	89509-8240	5352 Cochran St. Reno, NV	89509-8240
18.	14130 Culver Dr. Sioux Falls, SD	57105	14030 Culver Dr. Sioux Falls, SD	57105
19.	P.O. Box 85641 Toledo, IL	62468-5641	P.O. Box 85641 Toledo, IL	62468-5641
20.	639 1st Ave. #22 Fredericksburg, VA	22407	639 1st Ave. #22 Fredericksburg, VA	22409
21.	3533 Roosevelt Blvd. SW Seattle, WA	98102-7721	3533 Roosevelt Blvd. SW Seattle, WA	98102-7221
22.	63 Town Square Bridgton, ME	04009	63 Town Square Bridgeton, ME	04409
23.	925 S. 9th St. Oklahoma City, OK	73128-0288	925 E. 9th St. Oklahoma City, OK	73228-0288
24.	9510 Lange Point Easton, MD	21601	9510 Lang Point Easton, MD	21601
25.	290 13th Avenue, Apt. 2C East Pittsburgh, PA	15112	290 13th Avenue, Apt. 2C East Pittsburgh, PA	15112
26.	3322 Piedmont Rd. Monroe, LA	71203-4775	3322 Peidmont Rd. Monroe, LA	71203-4575
27.	4158 Fairmount Way Knoxville, TN	37917-5016	4158 Fairmount Way Nashville, TN	37917-5016
28.	49 Treeline Cir. #48 Colorado Springs, CO	80907-0137	49 Treeline Cir. #48 Colorado Springs, CO	80901-0137
29.	899 N. Wilma Southbridge, MA	01550	898 N. Wilma Southbridge, MA	01505
30.	210 S. End Ave. Bethlehem, PA	18015	210 S. Elm Ave. Bethlehem, PA	18015
31.	8622 35th Ave. Detroit, MI	48223-2753	8622 35th Ave. Detroit, MI	45223-2753
32.	89 Pleasant Shores Gulfport, MS	39503	89 Pleasant Shore Gulfport, MS	39503

continued on next page

A. No Errors	B. Address Only	C. ZIP Code Only	D. Both

	Correct List		List to Be Checked	
	Address	*ZIP Code*	*Address*	*ZIP Code*
33.	1310 Pecan Terrace Savannah, GA	31411-8377	1310 Pecan Terrace Savannah, GA	31411-8377
34.	105 Cyclone St. Helena, MO	64459	105 Cyclone St. Helena, MT	64459
35.	P.O. Box 14445 Cincinnati, OH	45232	P.O. Box 14445 Cincinati, OH	42232
36.	24103 Allen Road Kansas City, KS	66118	24103 Allen Road Kansas City, KS	16118
37.	3232 W. 8th St. White Plains, NY	10606-9257	3232 W. 8th St. White Plains, NY	10606-9257
38.	1200 Central Avenue Kennewick, WA	99337-2498	1200 Center Avenue Kennewick, WA	99337-2498
39.	1600 Old Imperial Hwy. Lexington, KY	40503	1680 Old Imperial Hwy. Lexington, KY	40503
40.	2428 Clearlake Rd. Tulsa, OK	74146	2428 Clearlake Rd. Tulsa, OK	74164
41.	998 East Grant Huntington, WV	25704-8923	998 East Grant Huntington, WV	25774-8923
42.	52544 West Lambert Road Asheville, NC	28804-4582	52544 West Lambert Road Ashville, NC	28804-4582
43.	16 Gage Tower New Haven, CT	06511-0027	19 Gage Tower New Haven, CT	06511-0097
44.	103 South DeSoto Avenue Chicago, IL	60641	103 South De Soto Avenue Chicago, IL	60641
45.	1216 E. Hunt Ave. Trenton, NJ	08618-3051	1216 E. Hunt Ave. Trenton, NJ	08618-3051
46.	507 El Carrillo Blvd. La Luz, NM	88337	507 El Carrillo Blvd. Las Luz, NM	88387
47.	7500 Culver Parkway Sioux City, IA	51106-0035	7500 Culver Highway Sioux City, IA	51106-0052
48.	4300 Central Avenue El Paso, TX	79915	4300 Central Avenue El Paso, TX	79515
49.	1930 Canter Street Minot, ND	58701-2004	1930 Carter Street Minot, ND	58701-2204

continued on next page

A. No Errors	B. Address Only	C. ZIP Code Only	D. Both

	Correct List		List to Be Checked	
	Address	ZIP Code	Address	ZIP Code
50.	77 Pine Bluff Racine, WI	53404	11 Pine Bluff Racine, WI	53404
51.	PO Box 475562 Virginia Beach, VA	23455-5562	PO Box 475562 Virginia Beach, VA	23554-5562
52.	46640 Anda Blvd. Fort Wayne, IN	46815-2478	46640 Ande Blvd. Fort Wayne, IN	46815-2478
53.	6025 Camino Del Rio Altadena, CA	91001	6025 Camino Del Rio Altadena, CA	91001
54.	9700 Oak Drive Kent, MN	56553-1367	9700 Oak Road Kent, MN	56553-1367
55.	11 Holt Cir. Lancaster, PA	17602	11 Holden Cir. Lancaster, PA	17620
56.	1771 Buckeye Terrace Canton, OH	44705	1771 Buckeye Terrace Canton, OH	44775
57.	421 Ranch Road Denver, CO	80204-5720	421 Ranch Road Denver, CO	80204-5720
58.	145 Rita Way Bowling Green, KY	42104-2173	145 Rita Road Bowling Green, KY	42014-2173
59.	5520 Balboa Blvd. Tampa, FL	33604	5520 Balboa Blvd. Tampa Bay, FL	33604
60.	671 Burrows Ct. Auburn, IL	62615	671 Burrows Ct. Auburn, IL	26615

Part B: Forms Completion

Directions: Part B of this test consists of 30 questions for you to complete in 15 minutes. You will be shown a series of forms that are similar to ones used by the U.S. Postal Service. The parts of each form are labeled (for example, 3 and 4a). Each form is accompanied by several questions that test your ability to complete the form properly. For each question, choose the best answer and mark your selection (A, B, C, or D) on your answer sheet.

Go to the next page when you are ready to begin Part B under timed conditions.

An answer key is provided at the end of the chapter.

Number of Questions: 30

Time: 15 minutes

Certified Mail Receipt (Domestic Mail Only)			
TO BE COMPLETED BY SENDER		**OFFICIAL USE**	
1. Sent To		Postage	4.
2. Street, Apt. No., or PO Box		Certified Fee	5.
		Return Receipt Fee	6.
3. City, State, ZIP + 4		Restricted Delivery Fee	7.
CERTIFIED MAIL NUMBER 9217 0048 5033 7002		Total Postage and Fees	8.

1. Where should the total postage and fees be entered on this form?

   (A) Box 4

   (B) Box 7

   (C) Box 6

   (D) Box 8

2. Each type of entry is appropriate on this form EXCEPT which?

   (A) The addressee's name

   (B) The sender's name

   (C) The delivery street address

   (D) The addressee's ZIP code

3. The certified fee is $4.50. Where would you indicate this?

   (A) Box 6

   (B) Box 8

   (C) Box 7

   (D) Box 5

4. Which of these would be an appropriate entry for Line 1?

   (A) "Texas"

   (B) "San Antonio"

   (C) "Carla Sanchez"

   (D) "U.S."

5. Where is the return receipt fee indicated on this form?

   (A) Box 5

   (B) Box 8

   (C) Box 6

   (D) Box 4

6. Each of these entries is appropriate on this form EXCEPT which?

   (A) A check mark

   (B) "$3.65"

   (C) "PO Box 38887"

   (D) "Seattle, WA 98115"

Delivery Confirmation Receipt **(Do not use for insured or registered mail.)**		
1. (To Be Completed by Sender)	2 – 4 (Post Office Use Only)	
1a. Name	2a. $	Postage
1b. Street, Apt. No., or PO Box No.	2b. $	Delivery Confirmation Fee
1c. City, State, ZIP + 4	2c. $	Total Postage and Fees
	3. (Check One) ☐ Priority ☐ First Class ☐ Package Services	4. Postmark Here
DELIVERY CONFIRMATION NUMBER 5011 2974 3310 0993		

7. The total postage and fees is $4.50. Where would you indicate this?

(A) Box 2b

(B) Box 2c

(C) Box 3

(D) Box 1b

8. Which type of delivery service can you indicate on this form?

(A) Insured mail

(B) Restricted delivery

(C) Priority mail

(D) Express mail

9. The sender completes each of these portions of the form EXCEPT which?

(A) Box 3

(B) Line 1a

(C) Line 1c

(D) Line 1b

10. Which of these would be a correct entry for Box 2a?

(A) "Gladstone, OR 97027"

(B) "2.55"

(C) "7009 Faulkner Blvd. #5"

(D) A check mark

11. Which of these entries does a postal employee make on this form?

(A) The delivery confirmation number

(B) The sender's name

(C) The weight of the article

(D) The type of mailing service

12. Where should the delivery address be entered on this form?

(A) Line 1b

(B) Box 2a

(C) Line 1a

(D) Line 1c

Global Direct Notification of Mailing

1. Sender Information 1a. Name _____ 1b. Telephone _____ 1c. Fax No. _____ 1d. Address _____	2. Destination Country
	3. Date Notified
	4. Global Direct ID Number

5a. Mailing Date
 	
5b. Approx. Total Weight
 	
5c. Quantity _____ ☐ Trays
 	
_____ ☐ Pallets
	6. Return Address
	☐ Use my own in-country
	  designated return address
	
	☐ Use the following postal
	  service-provided return
	  address: _____
	  _____

---

13. Which type of information should be entered in Box 5a?

    (A) A description of the items shipped
    (B) The shipping fee
    (C) The destination city
    (D) The mailing date

14. Which of these would be a correct entry for Box 3?

    (A) "05/04/07"
    (B) A check mark
    (C) "Sanjay Kapoor"
    (D) "(216) 555-9483"

15. Where should the destination country be entered on this form?

    (A) Box 5b
    (B) Box 4
    (C) Box 2
    (D) Box 6

16. The shipment weighs 4.3 tons. How would you indicate this?

    (A) Enter "4.3 tons" in Box 5b
    (B) Enter "4.3" in Box 5b
    (C) Enter "4.3 tons" in Box 5c
    (D) Enter "4.3" in Box 5c

17. In which of these boxes would a number be a correct entry?

    (A) Box 6
    (B) Box 1a
    (C) Box 2
    (D) Box 4

Insured Mail Receipt

1a. Name	5. ☐ Fragile ☐ Perishable ☐ Liquid
1b. Street, Apt., or PO Box No.	
1c. City, State, ZIP + 4, Country	6. Insurance Coverage $

Postage	2.	$
Insurance Fee	3a.	$
Special Handling Fee *(Endorsement Required)*	3b.	$
Return Receipt Fee *(Except for Canada)*	3c.	$
Total Postage and Fees	4.	$

Postmark Here

18. Where is the customer's name entered on this form?

   (A) Box 1a
   (B) Box 2a
   (C) Box 3a
   (D) The customer's name is not entered on this form

19. Which type of information is a correct entry for Box 4?

   (A) An address
   (B) A check mark
   (C) A postmark
   (D) A dollar amount

20. The item mailed is fragile. Where should this be indicated on the form?

   (A) Box 3c
   (B) Box 5
   (C) Box 1c
   (D) Box 1b

21. Which of these would an entry in Box 3b indicate?

   (A) Insurance coverage is provided
   (B) An endorsement is required
   (C) Postage is not required
   (D) The article is perishable

22. For which of the following would "Apt. C" be a correct entry?

   (A) Box 1c
   (B) Box 4
   (C) Box 1b
   (D) Box 3c

23. Which of these would be a correct entry for Box 3c?

   (A) "Sarah Cutter"
   (B) "3.50"
   (C) "45 Palm St., San Diego, CA"
   (D) "33820-5527"

Postage Statement – Priority Mail

1. Permit Holder	2. Mailing Agent (if different from permit holder)
1a. Name:	2a. Name:
1b. Address:	2b. Address:
1c. Telephone Number:	2c. Telephone Number:

3a. Mailing Date:	**USPS Use Only**
3b. Post Office of Mailing:	

4. Processing Type	6a. Weight (Single Piece)	lb.	oz.
☐ Letters	6b. Number of Pieces		
☐ Parcels	6c. Total Weight	lb.	oz.
☐ Flats	6d. Total Postage		
☐ Other: _____			
	7a. Employees Name (Print)		
5. Permit Number	7b. Employee's Signature		
	7c. Date Mailer Notified		

24. Where would you indicate the permit holder's permit number?

(A) Box 5

(B) Box 4

(C) Box 6d

(D) Line 1c

25. Which of these would be a correct entry in Box 4?

(A) "89442-0990"

(B) A check mark

(C) "Other"

(D) "Laura Denke"

26. Where would you enter the total postage?

(A) Box 5

(B) Line 6d

(C) Line 7a

(D) Line 2c

27. Which of these would be a correct entry for Line 3a?

(A) A check mark

(B) "88-902"

(C) "April 2, 2007"

(D) "$1.75"

28. The mailing agent's telephone number is (760) 555-0922. Where would you indicate this?

(A) Line 1c

(B) Line 3a

(C) Line 3b

(D) Line 2c

29. Which of these entries would you need to print to indicate the processing type?

(A) "Flat"

(B) "Parcel"

(C) "Pallet"

(D) "Letter"

30. Where should the permit holder's name be entered on this form?

(A) Line 1a

(B) Line 2a

(C) Line 7a

(D) Line 7b

Part C: Coding and Memory

Part C of this test consists of two sections:

- A **Coding Section**, which consists of 36 questions to be completed in 6 minutes
- A **Memory Section**, which consists of 36 questions to be completed in 7 minutes

Both sections test your ability to match one-letter codes to addresses quickly and accurately. The Memory Section also tests your ability to memorize codes and their matching address ranges.

You will use the same **Coding Guide** for both sections of Part C. The first column of the **Coding Guide** shows each **address range**. The second column shows the **delivery route** code (A, B, C, or D) for the address ranges shown in the same row as the code. You may assume that each address range runs continuously (no numbers are skipped) from the lowest to the highest number in the range. Some of the street names appear twice, showing two different address ranges.

Coding Section

This section consists of three segments:

- **Segment 1** is an introductory exercise consisting of 4 items to be completed in 2 minutes. *Segment 1 is not scored.*
- **Segment 2** is a practice exercise consisting of 8 items to be completed in 1 1/2 minutes (90 seconds). *Segment 2 is not scored.*
- **Segment 3** is the actual Coding Section of the test. This segment consists of 36 items to be completed in 6 minutes. *Segment 3 is scored and counts toward your total test score.*

You will use the same Coding Guide for all three segments.

Coding Section—Segment 1

Directions: Segment 1 is an introductory exercise that will familiarize you with the Coding Section and help you learn how to complete it. This segment is *not* scored. Based on the Coding Guide, match each address to a delivery route. Mark your answers on the answer grid at the bottom of this page.

Number of Items: 4

Time Limit: 2 minutes

Coding Guide	
Address Range	Delivery Route
15–65 Pepper Ln. 19500–20500 Barranca Blvd. 175–225 Foothill Road	A
66–100 Pepper Ln. 226–500 Foothill Road	B
20501–22000 Barranca Blvd. 4000–11000 E. 25th St. 900–1300 Magellan Parkway	C
All mail that does not fall in one of the address ranges listed above	D

	Address	Delivery Code			
1.	70 Pepper Ln.	A	B	C	D
2.	220 Foothill Road	A	B	C	D
3.	21926 Barranca Blvd.	A	B	C	D
4.	460 E. 25th St.	A	B	C	D

Sample Answer Sheet

1. Ⓐ Ⓑ Ⓒ Ⓓ
2. Ⓐ Ⓑ Ⓒ Ⓓ
3. Ⓐ Ⓑ Ⓒ Ⓓ
4. Ⓐ Ⓑ Ⓒ Ⓓ

Coding Section—Segment 2

Directions: Segment 2 is *not* scored. It is a practice exercise that will give you experience with the Coding Section under a time constraint similar to the one during the scored Coding Section. Based on the Coding Guide, match each address to a delivery route. Mark your answers on the answer grid at the bottom of this page.

Number of Items: 8

Time Limit: 1 1/2 minutes (90 seconds)

Coding Guide	
Address Range	*Delivery Route*
15–65 Pepper Ln. 19500–20500 Barranca Blvd. 175–225 Foothill Road	A
66–100 Pepper Ln. 226–500 Foothill Road	B
20501–22000 Barranca Blvd. 4000–11000 E. 25th St. 900–1300 Magellan Parkway	C
All mail that does not fall in one of the address ranges listed above	D

	Address	Delivery Code			
1.	255 Foothill Road	A	B	C	D
2.	47 Pepper Ln.	A	B	C	D
3.	4444 E. 25th St.	A	B	C	D
4.	12550 Magellan Parkway	A	B	C	D
5.	21022 Barranca Blvd.	A	B	C	D
6.	69 Pepper Ln.	A	B	C	D
7.	225 Foothill Road	A	B	C	D
8.	1000 E. 25th St.	A	B	C	D

Sample Answer Sheet

1. Ⓐ Ⓑ Ⓒ Ⓓ   4. Ⓐ Ⓑ Ⓒ Ⓓ   7. Ⓐ Ⓑ Ⓒ Ⓓ
2. Ⓐ Ⓑ Ⓒ Ⓓ   5. Ⓐ Ⓑ Ⓒ Ⓓ   8. Ⓐ Ⓑ Ⓒ Ⓓ
3. Ⓐ Ⓑ Ⓒ Ⓓ   6. Ⓐ Ⓑ Ⓒ Ⓓ

Coding Section—Segment 3

Directions: Segment 3 is the *actual scored* Coding Section of the test. Based on the Coding Guide, match each address to a delivery route. Mark your answers on the answer sheet at the end of the chapter.

An answer key for this segment is given at the end of the chapter.

Number of Items: 36

Time Limit: 6 minutes

Coding Guide	
Address Range	Delivery Route
15–65 Pepper Ln. 19500–20500 Barranca Blvd. 175–225 Foothill Road	A
66–100 Pepper Ln. 226–500 Foothill Road	B
20501–22000 Barranca Blvd. 4000–11000 E. 25th St. 900–1300 Magellan Parkway	C
All mail that does not fall in one of the address ranges listed above	D

	Address			**Delivery Code**		
1.	432 Foothill Road		A	B	C	D
2.	20620 Barranca Blvd.		A	B	C	D
3.	1176 Magellan Parkway		A	B	C	D
4.	61 Pepper Ln.		A	B	C	D
5.	20000 Barranca Blvd.		A	B	C	D
6.	12500 E. 25th St.		A	B	C	D
7.	222 Foothill Road		A	B	C	D
8.	39 Pepper Ln.		A	B	C	D
9.	4088 E. 25th St.		A	B	C	D
10.	990 Magellan Parkway		A	B	C	D
11.	228 Foothill Road		A	B	C	D
12.	21001 Barranca Blvd.		A	B	C	D
13.	1245 Magellan Parkway		A	B	C	D
14.	84 Pepper Place		A	B	C	D
15.	190 Foothill Road		A	B	C	D
16.	2380 Magellan Parkway		A	B	C	D
17.	460 Foothill Road		A	B	C	D
18.	20 Pepper Ln.		A	B	C	D
19.	19995 Barranca Blvd.		A	B	C	D
20.	10100 52nd St.		A	B	C	D
21.	449 Foothill Road		A	B	C	D
22.	976 Magellan Parkway		A	B	C	D
23.	30 Poppy Ln.		A	B	C	D
24.	9375 E. 25th St.		A	B	C	D
25.	1098 Magellan Way		A	B	C	D
26.	83 Pepper Ln.		A	B	C	D
27.	2250 Foothill Road		A	B	C	D
28.	15900 Barranca Blvd.		A	B	C	D
29.	5500 E. 25th St.		A	B	C	D
30.	21500 Barranca Blvd.		A	B	C	D
31.	740 Foothill Road		A	B	C	D
32.	100 Pepper Ln.		A	B	C	D
33.	19501 Barranca Blvd.		A	B	C	D
34.	228 Foothill Road		A	B	C	D
35.	20400 Barranca Blvd.		A	B	C	D
36.	91 Pepper Ln.		A	B	C	D

Memory Section

This section consists of four segments:

- **Segment 1** is a 3-minute study period during which you will attempt to memorize the Coding Guide. *Segment 1 is not scored*, and there are no answers to mark during this segment.
- **Segment 2** is a practice exercise consisting of 8 items to be completed in 1 1/2 minutes (90 seconds). *Segment 2 is not scored.*
- **Segment 3** is a 5-minute study period during which you will attempt to memorize the Coding Guide. *Segment 3 is not scored*, and there are no answers to mark during this segment.
- **Segment 4** is the actual Memory Section of the test. This segment consists of 36 items to be completed in 7 minutes. *Segment 4 is scored and counts toward your total test score.*

You will use the same Coding Guide for all four segments.

Memory Section—Segment 1

Directions: Segment 1 is a 3-minute study period during which you will attempt to memorize the Coding Guide. This segment is *not* scored, and there are no answers to mark during this segment.

Begin the 3-minute study period when you are ready.

Coding Guide	
Address Range	*Delivery Route*
15–65 Pepper Ln. 19500–20500 Barranca Blvd. 175–225 Foothill Road	A
66–100 Pepper Ln. 226–500 Foothill Road	B
20501–22000 Barranca Blvd. 4000–11000 E. 25th St. 900–1300 Magellan Parkway	C
All mail that does not fall in one of the address ranges listed above	D

Memory Section—Segment 2

Directions: Segment 2 is a practice exercise that will give you experience coding addresses from memory based on the Coding Guide on the previous page. The Coding Guide is not shown during this segment. Based on the Coding Guide, match each address to a delivery route. Mark your answers on the answer grid at the bottom of this page. This segment is *not* scored.

Turn the page when you are ready to begin Segment 2 under timed conditions.

Number of Items: 8

Time Limit: 1 1/2 minutes (90 seconds)

	Address	Delivery Code			
1.	201 Foothill Road	A	B	C	D
2.	1460 Magellan Parkway	A	B	C	D
3.	6290 E. 25th St.	A	B	C	D
4.	79 Pepper Ln.	A	B	C	D
5.	19702 Barranca Blvd.	A	B	C	D
6.	1010 Magellan Parkway	A	B	C	D
7.	404 Foothill Road	A	B	C	D
8.	6308 S. 26th St.	A	B	C	D

Sample Answer Sheet

1. Ⓐ Ⓑ Ⓒ Ⓓ   4. Ⓐ Ⓑ Ⓒ Ⓓ   7. Ⓐ Ⓑ Ⓒ Ⓓ
2. Ⓐ Ⓑ Ⓒ Ⓓ   5. Ⓐ Ⓑ Ⓒ Ⓓ   8. Ⓐ Ⓑ Ⓒ Ⓓ
3. Ⓐ Ⓑ Ⓒ Ⓓ   6. Ⓐ Ⓑ Ⓒ Ⓓ

Memory Section—Segment 3

Directions: Segment 3 is a 5-minute study period during which you will again attempt to memorize the Coding Guide. This segment is *not* scored, and there are no answers to mark during this segment.

Begin the 5-minute study period when you are ready.

Coding Guide	
Address Range	*Delivery Route*
15–65 Pepper Ln. 19500–20500 Barranca Blvd. 175–225 Foothill Road	A
66–100 Pepper Ln. 226–500 Foothill Road	B
20501–22000 Barranca Blvd. 4000–11000 E. 25th St. 900–1300 Magellan Parkway	C
All mail that does not fall in one of the address ranges listed above	D

Memory Section—Segment 4

Directions: Segment 4 is the *actual scored* Memory Section of the test. The Coding Guide is not shown during this segment. Based on the Coding Guide, match each address to a delivery route. Mark your answers on the answer sheet at the end of the chapter.

Go to the next page when you are ready to begin Segment 4 under timed conditions.

An answer key for this segment is given at the end of the chapter.

Number of Items: 36

Time Limit: 7 minutes

	Address		Delivery Code			
37.	150 Pepper Ln.	*B*	A	B	C	D
38.	900 Magellan Parkway	*C*	A	B	C	D
39.	177 Foothill Road	*B*	A	B	C	D
40.	73 Pepper Ln.	*A*	A	B	C	D
41.	21482 Barranca Drive		A	B	C	D
42.	7381 E. 25th St.	*C*	A	B	C	D
43.	209 Foothill Dr.	*B*	A	B	C	D
44.	19650 Barranca Blvd.		A	B	C	D
45.	68 Pepper Ln.	*a*	A	B	C	D
46.	2400 E. 25th St.	*C*	A	B	C	D
47.	185 Foothill Road	*B*	A	B	C	D
48.	20300 Barranca Blvd.		A	B	C	D
49.	11000 E. 25th St.	*C*	A	B	C	D
50.	209 Footbridge Road	*D*	A	B	C	D
51.	1200 Magellan Parkway	*C*	A	B	C	D
52.	88 Pepper Ln.	*a*	A	B	C	D
53.	20750 Barranca Blvd.		A	B	C	D
54.	4600 E. 2nd St.	*D*	A	B	C	D
55.	76 Pepper Ln.	*A D*	A	B	C	D
56.	208 Foothill Road	*B*	A	B	C	D
57.	21020 Barranca Blvd.		A	B	C	D
58.	1290 Magellan Terrace	*D*	A	B	C	D
59.	8032 E. 25th St.	*C*	A	B	C	D
60.	22 Pepper Ln.	*a*	A	B	C	D
61.	917 Magellan Parkway	*C*	A	B	C	D
62.	330 Foothill Road	*B*	A	B	C	D
63.	21800 Barista Blvd.		A	B	C	D
64.	22 Pepper Ln.	*A*	A	B	C	D

continued on next page

	Address		Delivery Code			
65.	1150 Magellan Parkway	*C*	A	B	C	D
66.	390 Foothill Road	*B*	A	B	C	D
67.	6044 E. 25th St.	*C*	A	B	C	D
68.	1100 Magellan Parkway		A	B	C	D
69.	21470 Barranca Blvd.		A	B	C	D
70.	74 Pepper Ln.	*a*	A	B	C	D
71.	215 Foothill Road	*B*	A	B	C	D
72.	3600 E. 25th St.	*C*	A	B	C	D

Part D: Personal Characteristics and Experience Inventory

Part D consists of a 236-item questionnaire (inventory) on your personal characteristics and experience. You have 90 minutes to complete Part D. This part is scored, but how it is scored is a Postal Service secret. There is no need to prepare for this part of the exam, and therefore it is not included in this practice test. (For more information about Part D, see Chapter 6.)

Practice Test 4 Answer Sheet

The answer sheet given here closely resembles that used on the actual Test 473.

On the front of the answer sheet, you will be asked to fill in personal information similar to the information that you gave when you applied to take the exam. Then you will find spaces—ovals lettered A, B, C, and D—where you are to fill in your answers to Part A, Address Checking, and Part B, Forms Completion, of the exam.

On the other side of the actual answer sheet, you will find similar lettered ovals for you to enter your answers to Part C, Coding and Memory, of the exam. On the answer sheet for Test 473, there will also be spaces for answers to Part D, Personal Characteristics and Experience Inventory, but we have not included that section in this practice exam.

Part A: Address Checking

1. Ⓐ Ⓑ Ⓒ Ⓓ
2. Ⓐ Ⓑ Ⓒ Ⓓ
3. Ⓐ Ⓑ Ⓒ Ⓓ
4. Ⓐ Ⓑ Ⓒ Ⓓ
5. Ⓐ Ⓑ Ⓒ Ⓓ
6. Ⓐ Ⓑ Ⓒ Ⓓ
7. Ⓐ Ⓑ Ⓒ Ⓓ
8. Ⓐ Ⓑ Ⓒ Ⓓ
9. Ⓐ Ⓑ Ⓒ Ⓓ
10. Ⓐ Ⓑ Ⓒ Ⓓ
11. Ⓐ Ⓑ Ⓒ Ⓓ
12. Ⓐ Ⓑ Ⓒ Ⓓ
13. Ⓐ Ⓑ Ⓒ Ⓓ
14. Ⓐ Ⓑ Ⓒ Ⓓ
15. Ⓐ Ⓑ Ⓒ Ⓓ
16. Ⓐ Ⓑ Ⓒ Ⓓ
17. Ⓐ Ⓑ Ⓒ Ⓓ
18. Ⓐ Ⓑ Ⓒ Ⓓ
19. Ⓐ Ⓑ Ⓒ Ⓓ
20. Ⓐ Ⓑ Ⓒ Ⓓ

21. Ⓐ Ⓑ Ⓒ Ⓓ
22. Ⓐ Ⓑ Ⓒ Ⓓ
23. Ⓐ Ⓑ Ⓒ Ⓓ
24. Ⓐ Ⓑ Ⓒ Ⓓ
25. Ⓐ Ⓑ Ⓒ Ⓓ
26. Ⓐ Ⓑ Ⓒ Ⓓ
27. Ⓐ Ⓑ Ⓒ Ⓓ
28. Ⓐ Ⓑ Ⓒ Ⓓ
28. Ⓐ Ⓑ Ⓒ Ⓓ
30. Ⓐ Ⓑ Ⓒ Ⓓ
31. Ⓐ Ⓑ Ⓒ Ⓓ
32. Ⓐ Ⓑ Ⓒ Ⓓ
33. Ⓐ Ⓑ Ⓒ Ⓓ
34. Ⓐ Ⓑ Ⓒ Ⓓ
35. Ⓐ Ⓑ Ⓒ Ⓓ
36. Ⓐ Ⓑ Ⓒ Ⓓ
37. Ⓐ Ⓑ Ⓒ Ⓓ
38. Ⓐ Ⓑ Ⓒ Ⓓ
39. Ⓐ Ⓑ Ⓒ Ⓓ
40. Ⓐ Ⓑ Ⓒ Ⓓ

41. Ⓐ Ⓑ Ⓒ Ⓓ
42. Ⓐ Ⓑ Ⓒ Ⓓ
43. Ⓐ Ⓑ Ⓒ Ⓓ
44. Ⓐ Ⓑ Ⓒ Ⓓ
45. Ⓐ Ⓑ Ⓒ Ⓓ
46. Ⓐ Ⓑ Ⓒ Ⓓ
47. Ⓐ Ⓑ Ⓒ Ⓓ
48. Ⓐ Ⓑ Ⓒ Ⓓ
49. Ⓐ Ⓑ Ⓒ Ⓓ
50. Ⓐ Ⓑ Ⓒ Ⓓ
51. Ⓐ Ⓑ Ⓒ Ⓓ
52. Ⓐ Ⓑ Ⓒ Ⓓ
53. Ⓐ Ⓑ Ⓒ Ⓓ
54. Ⓐ Ⓑ Ⓒ Ⓓ
55. Ⓐ Ⓑ Ⓒ Ⓓ
56. Ⓐ Ⓑ Ⓒ Ⓓ
57. Ⓐ Ⓑ Ⓒ Ⓓ
58. Ⓐ Ⓑ Ⓒ Ⓓ
59. Ⓐ Ⓑ Ⓒ Ⓓ
60. Ⓐ Ⓑ Ⓒ Ⓓ

Part B: Forms Completion

1. Ⓐ Ⓑ Ⓒ Ⓓ
2. Ⓐ Ⓑ Ⓒ Ⓓ
3. Ⓐ Ⓑ Ⓒ Ⓓ
4. Ⓐ Ⓑ Ⓒ Ⓓ
5. Ⓐ Ⓑ Ⓒ Ⓓ
6. Ⓐ Ⓑ Ⓒ Ⓓ
7. Ⓐ Ⓑ Ⓒ Ⓓ
8. Ⓐ Ⓑ Ⓒ Ⓓ
9. Ⓐ Ⓑ Ⓒ Ⓓ
10. Ⓐ Ⓑ Ⓒ Ⓓ

11. Ⓐ Ⓑ Ⓒ Ⓓ
12. Ⓐ Ⓑ Ⓒ Ⓓ
13. Ⓐ Ⓑ Ⓒ Ⓓ
14. Ⓐ Ⓑ Ⓒ Ⓓ
15. Ⓐ Ⓑ Ⓒ Ⓓ
16. Ⓐ Ⓑ Ⓒ Ⓓ
17. Ⓐ Ⓑ Ⓒ Ⓓ
18. Ⓐ Ⓑ Ⓒ Ⓓ
19. Ⓐ Ⓑ Ⓒ Ⓓ
20. Ⓐ Ⓑ Ⓒ Ⓓ

21. Ⓐ Ⓑ Ⓒ Ⓓ
22. Ⓐ Ⓑ Ⓒ Ⓓ
23. Ⓐ Ⓑ Ⓒ Ⓓ
24. Ⓐ Ⓑ Ⓒ Ⓓ
25. Ⓐ Ⓑ Ⓒ Ⓓ
26. Ⓐ Ⓑ Ⓒ Ⓓ
27. Ⓐ Ⓑ Ⓒ Ⓓ
28. Ⓐ Ⓑ Ⓒ Ⓓ
29. Ⓐ Ⓑ Ⓒ Ⓓ
30. Ⓐ Ⓑ Ⓒ Ⓓ

Part C: Coding and Memory

1. Ⓐ Ⓑ Ⓒ Ⓓ	25. Ⓐ Ⓑ Ⓒ Ⓓ	49. Ⓐ Ⓑ Ⓒ Ⓓ		
2. Ⓐ Ⓑ Ⓒ Ⓓ	26. Ⓐ Ⓑ Ⓒ Ⓓ	50. Ⓐ Ⓑ Ⓒ Ⓓ		
3. Ⓐ Ⓑ Ⓒ Ⓓ	27. Ⓐ Ⓑ Ⓒ Ⓓ	51. Ⓐ Ⓑ Ⓒ Ⓓ		
4. Ⓐ Ⓑ Ⓒ Ⓓ	28. Ⓐ Ⓑ Ⓒ Ⓓ	52. Ⓐ Ⓑ Ⓒ Ⓓ		
5. Ⓐ Ⓑ Ⓒ Ⓓ	29. Ⓐ Ⓑ Ⓒ Ⓓ	53. Ⓐ Ⓑ Ⓒ Ⓓ		
6. Ⓐ Ⓑ Ⓒ Ⓓ	30. Ⓐ Ⓑ Ⓒ Ⓓ	54. Ⓐ Ⓑ Ⓒ Ⓓ		
7. Ⓐ Ⓑ Ⓒ Ⓓ	31. Ⓐ Ⓑ Ⓒ Ⓓ	55. Ⓐ Ⓑ Ⓒ Ⓓ		
8. Ⓐ Ⓑ Ⓒ Ⓓ	32. Ⓐ Ⓑ Ⓒ Ⓓ	56. Ⓐ Ⓑ Ⓒ Ⓓ		
9. Ⓐ Ⓑ Ⓒ Ⓓ	33. Ⓐ Ⓑ Ⓒ Ⓓ	57. Ⓐ Ⓑ Ⓒ Ⓓ		
10. Ⓐ Ⓑ Ⓒ Ⓓ	34. Ⓐ Ⓑ Ⓒ Ⓓ	58. Ⓐ Ⓑ Ⓒ Ⓓ		
11. Ⓐ Ⓑ Ⓒ Ⓓ	35. Ⓐ Ⓑ Ⓒ Ⓓ	59. Ⓐ Ⓑ Ⓒ Ⓓ		
12. Ⓐ Ⓑ Ⓒ Ⓓ	36. Ⓐ Ⓑ Ⓒ Ⓓ	60. Ⓐ Ⓑ Ⓒ Ⓓ		
13. Ⓐ Ⓑ Ⓒ Ⓓ	37. Ⓐ Ⓑ Ⓒ Ⓓ	61. Ⓐ Ⓑ Ⓒ Ⓓ		
14. Ⓐ Ⓑ Ⓒ Ⓓ	38. Ⓐ Ⓑ Ⓒ Ⓓ	62. Ⓐ Ⓑ Ⓒ Ⓓ		
15. Ⓐ Ⓑ Ⓒ Ⓓ	39. Ⓐ Ⓑ Ⓒ Ⓓ	63. Ⓐ Ⓑ Ⓒ Ⓓ		
16. Ⓐ Ⓑ Ⓒ Ⓓ	40. Ⓐ Ⓑ Ⓒ Ⓓ	64. Ⓐ Ⓑ Ⓒ Ⓓ		
17. Ⓐ Ⓑ Ⓒ Ⓓ	41. Ⓐ Ⓑ Ⓒ Ⓓ	65. Ⓐ Ⓑ Ⓒ Ⓓ		
18. Ⓐ Ⓑ Ⓒ Ⓓ	42. Ⓐ Ⓑ Ⓒ Ⓓ	66. Ⓐ Ⓑ Ⓒ Ⓓ		
19. Ⓐ Ⓑ Ⓒ Ⓓ	43. Ⓐ Ⓑ Ⓒ Ⓓ	67. Ⓐ Ⓑ Ⓒ Ⓓ		
20. Ⓐ Ⓑ Ⓒ Ⓓ	44. Ⓐ Ⓑ Ⓒ Ⓓ	68. Ⓐ Ⓑ Ⓒ Ⓓ		
21. Ⓐ Ⓑ Ⓒ Ⓓ	45. Ⓐ Ⓑ Ⓒ Ⓓ	69. Ⓐ Ⓑ Ⓒ Ⓓ		
22. Ⓐ Ⓑ Ⓒ Ⓓ	46. Ⓐ Ⓑ Ⓒ Ⓓ	70. Ⓐ Ⓑ Ⓒ Ⓓ		
23. Ⓐ Ⓑ Ⓒ Ⓓ	47. Ⓐ Ⓑ Ⓒ Ⓓ	71. Ⓐ Ⓑ Ⓒ Ⓓ		
24. Ⓐ Ⓑ Ⓒ Ⓓ	48. Ⓐ Ⓑ Ⓒ Ⓓ	72. Ⓐ Ⓑ Ⓒ Ⓓ		

Part D: Personal Characteristics and Experience Inventory

On the actual exam, there would be spaces for the answers to 236 questions here, but we are not including this section in the practice exams or answer sheets.

Answer Key

Part A: Address Checking

1. D	13. A	25. A	37. A	49. D
2. C	14. B	26. D	38. B	50. B
3. B	15. D	27. B	39. B	51. C
4. B	16. C	28. C	40. C	52. B
5. A	17. A	29. D	41. C	53. A
6. D	18. B	30. B	42. B	54. B
7. B	19. A	31. C	43. D	55. D
8. C	20. C	32. B	44. B	56. C
9. D	21. C	33. A	45. A	57. A
10. B	22. D	34. B	46. D	58. D
11. C	23. D	35. D	47. D	59. B
12. B	24. B	36. C	48. C	60. C

Part B: Forms Completion

1. D	7. B	13. D	19. D	25. B
2. B	8. C	14. A	20. B	26. B
3. D	9. A	15. C	21. B	27. C
4. C	10. B	16. A	22. C	28. D
5. C	11. D	17. D	23. B	29. C
6. A	12. A	18. A	24. A	30. A

Part C: Coding and Memory

1. B	16. D	31. D	46. D	61. C
2. C	17. B	32. B	47. A	62. B
3. C	18. A	33. A	48. A	63. D
4. A	19. A	34. B	49. C	64. A
5. A	20. D	35. A	50. D	65. C
6. D	21. B	36. B	51. C	66. B
7. A	22. C	37. D	52. B	67. C
8. A	23. D	38. C	53. C	68. C
9. C	24. C	39. A	54. D	69. C
10. C	25. D	40. B	55. B	70. B
11. B	26. B	41. D	56. A	71. A
12. C	27. D	42. C	57. C	72. D
13. C	28. D	43. D	58. D	
14. D	29. C	44. A	59. C	
15. A	30. C	45. B	60. A	

CHAPTER

Practice Test 5

11

Part A: Address Checking

Directions: Part A of this test consists of 60 items for you to complete in 11 minutes. You will be shown a **Correct List** of addresses and ZIP codes alongside a **List to Be Checked**. The two lists should contain the same addresses and ZIP codes, except that the **List to Be Checked** may contain errors.

Each row of information consists of one item. For each item, compare the address and ZIP code in the **Correct List** with the address and ZIP code in the **List to Be Checked**. Determine whether there are **No Errors**, an error in **Address Only**, an error in **ZIP Code Only**, or an error in **Both** the address and the ZIP code. Select an answer from the following four choices:

A. No Errors	B. Address Only	C. ZIP Code Only	D. Both

Mark your answers (A, B, C, or D) on the answer sheet at the end of the chapter.

An answer key is given at the end of the chapter.

Number of Items: 60

Time: 11 minutes

A. No Errors	B. Address Only	C. ZIP Code Only	D. Both

	Correct List			List to Be Checked	
	Address	*ZIP Code*		*Address*	*ZIP Code*
1.	12 Sunset St. Panama City, FL	32403		12 Sunset St. Panama City, FL	34203
2.	693 Easton Ave. Kansas City, KS	66101-5619		693 Easton Ave. Kansas City, MO	66101-5619
3.	6510 Chase St. Peoria, IL	61605		65110 Chase St. Peoria, IL	61650
4.	801 Meridian Ave. Toledo, OH	43607		801 Medina Ave. Toledo, OH	43607
5.	550 Lookout Place Hannibal, MO	63401-0455		5500 Lookout Place Hannibal, MO	63401-0455
6.	2475 Marsha Way Hartford, CT	06105		2475 Marsha Way Hartford, CT	06105
7.	675 W. Sharpe St. Roanoke, VA	24014-4041		675 W. Sharpe Ct. Roanoke, VA	24014-4051
8.	135 Leland Ct. Richmond, KY	40475-7287		135 Lelane Ct. Richmond, KY	40475-7287
9.	185 Ludlow Circle Bloomington, IN	47403-8562		185 Ludlow Circle Bloomington, IN	47003-8562
10.	1556 N. Broad St. Altoona, PA	16601		1556 S. Broad St. Altoona, PA	19901
11.	PO Box 9077 Newark, NJ	07105-9077		PO Box 9077 Newark, NJ	07105-8077
12.	1242 3rd St. Pocatello, ID	83204-7610		1242 3rd St. Pocatello, ID	84304-7610
13.	77040 Elk Crossing Duluth, MN	55801		77040 Elk Crossing Deluth, MN	55801
14.	930 Harrison Dr. Glendale, AZ	85304		930 Harrison Dr. Glendale, AZ	85304
15.	One West Avenue Inglewood, CA	90302-3298		One West Avenue Ingelwood, CA	90302-3298

continued on next page

A. No Errors	B. Address Only	C. ZIP Code Only	D. Both

	Correct List		List to Be Checked	
	Address	ZIP Code	Address	ZIP Code
16.	4000 E. Victory Street Scottsbluff, NE	69361	4000 E. Victory St. Scottsbluff, NE	69316
17.	9227 Fern Glen Springfield, MO	65806-1629	9227 Fern Glen Springfield, MO	65306-1929
18.	5449 Fleet Rd. Spokane, WA	99207	5449 Fleet Rd. Spokane, WA	99207
19.	1418 N. 31st St. Burlington, TX	76519-2945	1418 N. 37st St. Burlington, TX	76519-2945
20.	76 Fell Rd., Suite 201 Portsmouth, VA	23704-7462	76 Fall Rd., Suite 201 Portsmouth, VA	23704-7462
21.	2355 Erringer Rd. Oakland, CA	94607	2355 Erringer Rd. Oakland, CA	84607
22.	3404 Walnut Ave. Joliet, IL	60431	3404 Walnut Ave. Joliet, IL	64631
23.	1710 Bancroft Way Davenport, IA	52802-2743	1710 Bancroft Way Davenport, LA	52802-2743
24.	3079 E. Tulare St. San Antonio, TX	78207	307 E. Tulare St. San Antonio, TX	78507
25.	P.O. Box 9588 Louisville, KY	40214	P.O. Box 9558 Louisville, KY	40214
26.	50 S. Federal Blvd. Leavenworth, KS	66048-3279	50 S. Federal Blvd. Leavenworth, KS	66048-3279
27.	3368 Baltic Ct. Weymouth, MA	02190-9155	3368 Baltic Cir. Weymouth, MA	02910-9155
28.	6305 N. Alta Ave. Saginaw, MI	48603-8629	6305 N. Alda Ave. Saginaw, MI	48603-8629
29.	902 Hiram Blvd. #18 Juneau, AK	99801	902 Hiram Blvd. #18 Juneau, AK	99881
30.	11830 Hillcrest Rd. Rockford, AL	35136	11830 Hillview Rd. Rockford, AL	35256
31.	1511 Davenport Ave. Fargo, ND	58103-5456	1511 Davenport Way Fargo, ND	58103-5456
32.	334 Surrey Rd., Apt. B Harrisburg, PA	17101	334 Surrey Rd., Apt. B Harrisburg, PA	17021

continued on next page

A. No Errors	B. Address Only	C. ZIP Code Only	D. Both

	Correct List		List to Be Checked	
	Address	*ZIP Code*	*Address*	*ZIP Code*
33.	3030 Commerce Ctr. Salem, OR	97306-1165	30300 Commerce Ctr. Salem, OR	97306-1165
34.	2830 W. Colter Ter. Monroe, ME	04951	2830 W. Colter Ter. Monroe, ME	04951
35.	23 Business Park Blvd. New Orleans, LA	70114	23 Busness Park Blvd. New Orleans, LA	70147
36.	3790 Morrell Ln. Johnstown, PA	15901-7047	3790 Morell Ln. Johnstown, PA	15901-7074
37.	1331 E. Wyoming Ave. Salisbury, MD	21801-2759	1331 E. Wyoming Ave. Salisbury, MD	11801-2759
38.	84 Geary Tower San Francisco, CA	94105	84 Geary Tower San Francisco, CA	94105
39.	6053 California Ave. San Diego, CA	92123	6533 California Ave. San Diego, CA	92123
40.	500 University Way Saint Petersburg, FL	33703	550 University Way Saint Petersburg, FL	33703
41.	7502 33rd St. Mankato, MN	56001-0154	7502 33rd St. Mankato, MN	56610-0154
42.	2281 S. Cape Blvd. New Britain, CT	06052-7393	2281 S. Cape Blvd. New Britain, CT	06052-7330
43.	35 Hope Cir. Decatur, GA	30033-3479	35 Hope Cir. Decater, GA	30033-3479
44.	70 St. Paul Place Baton Rouge, LA	70808	70 Saint Paul Place Baton Rouge, LA	70888
45.	3807 N. Garden Rd. Glasgow, KY	42141-0004	3807 N. Gardner Rd. Glasgow, KY	42141-0004
46.	400 W. King Ave. Helena, MT	59601	400 W. King Ave. Helena, MT	59601
47.	5600 Highway 11 North Birmingham, AL	35203-1555	5600 Highway 11 South Birmingham, AL	35703-1555
48.	1991 Main Street Aurora, CO	80013	1911 Main Street Aurora, CO	80013
49.	382 N. Suncoast Blvd. Anchorage, AK	99501	382 N. Suncoast Blvd. Anchorage, AK	88501

continued on next page

A. No Errors	B. Address Only	C. ZIP Code Only	D. Both

	Correct List		List to Be Checked	
	Address	ZIP Code	Address	ZIP Code
50.	P.O. Box 55 Walla Walla, WA	99362-0055	P.O. Box 45 Walla Walla, WA	99329-0055
51.	67 Martin Luther King Dr. Rochester, MN	55902-2656	67 Martin Luther King Dr. Rochester, NY	55902-2656
52.	1023 Mill Run Fayette, MO	65248-1717	1023 Mill Run Fayette, MO	65248-2727
53.	PO Box 10293 Richmond, VA	23223	PO Box 1023 Richmond, VA	23223
54.	1515 Locust Ct. Lancaster, WI	53813-8826	1515 Locust Ct. Lancaster, WI	53813-8826
55.	901 Sand Hill Rd. #7 Carson City, NV	89703	901 Sandy Hill Rd. #7 Carson City, NV	89703
56.	12271 Tyler Place Brattleboro, VT	05301	12271 Tyler Place Battleboro, VT	08301
57.	497 N. Thompson Blvd. Newark, DE	19711-5337	497 N. Thompson Blvd. Newark, DE	19712-5337
58.	9000 SW Parkway Atlanta, GA	30306	9000 SW Parkway Atlanta, GA	30306
59.	440 Black Mountain Rd. Greensboro, NC	27406-3856	440 Black Mountain Dr. Greensboro, NC	27406-3856
60.	118 W. Fifth Street Bridgeport, CT	06604	118 W. Fourth Street Bridgeport, CT	00644

Part B: Forms Completion

Directions: Part B of this test consists of 30 questions for you to complete in 15 minutes. You will be shown a series of forms that are similar to ones used by the U.S. Postal Service. The parts of each form are labeled (for example, 3 and 4a). Each form is accompanied by several questions that test your ability to complete the form properly. For each question, choose the best answer and mark your selection (A, B, C, or D) on your answer sheet.

Go to the next page when you are ready to begin Part B under timed conditions.

An answer key is given at the end of the chapter.

Number of Questions: 30

Time: 15 minutes

Receipt for Registered Mail	
TO BE COMPLETED BY CUSTOMER	
1. Sender	2. Addressee
3. Full Value of Articles (Required): $	
TO BE COMPLETED BY POST OFFICE	

4. Reg. Fee	6. Postage	8. Postal Insurance ☐ Yes ☐ No
5. Handling Fee	7. Return Receipt	9. Total Fee, Postage, and Charges
10. Received By:		11. Date Received

1. Which of these is a correct entry for Box 9?

   (A) "$22.85"

   (B) A check mark

   (C) "Registered"

   (D) "3/18/07"

2. The sender pays for a return receipt. How would you indicate this?

   (A) Enter a dollar amount in Box 5

   (B) Enter the addressee's name in Box 10

   (C) Enter a dollar amount in Box 7

   (D) Enter a check mark in Box 8

3. In which box would a check mark be a correct entry?

   (A) Box 3

   (B) Box 8

   (C) Box 6

   (D) Box 7

4. A person's name is an appropriate entry in each box EXCEPT which?

   (A) Box 10

   (B) Box 2

   (C) Box 1

   (D) Box 11

5. Which of these is an appropriate entry in Box 2?

   (A) "(609) 555-0702"

   (B) "49 Lilac Court"

   (C) "September 2, 2007"

   (D) "$1.75"

6. Who completes Box 10?

   (A) A postal clerk

   (B) The addressee

   (C) The sender

   (D) The sender's agent

Sender's Application for Mail Recall

1. Description of Mailed Item (Check all that apply) ☐ Letter ☐ Express Mail ☐ Approx. Size: _____ x _____ ☐ Package ☐ Special ☐ Color: _____ Delivery	3a. Date Mailed
	3b. Time Mailed A.M. P.M.
2. Identifying Number (Check and complete all that apply) ☐ Certified No. _____ ☐ Registered No. _____ ☐ Insured No. _____ ☐ COD No. _____	4a. Date Appl. Filed
	4b. Time Appl. Filed A.M. P.M.

5. Return Address on Mail	7a. Delivery Address on Mail
6. Check One: ☐ Postage Stamp ☐ Postage Meter Stamp ☐ Other	7b. Check One: ☐ Typewritten ☐ Handwritten ☐ Other

8a. Applicant s Name _____

8b. Applicant's Address _____

8c. Applicant's Telephone Number _____

8d. Signature of Applicant _____

POSTAL USE ONLY	9a. Date Received
	
	9b. Time Received
	                  A.M.
	                  P.M.
		9c. Received by (employee name)

7. Where should the time of mailing be entered on this form?

   (A) Box 3a

   (B) Box 9b

   (C) Box 5

   (D) Box 3b

8. Which of these would be a correct entry in Box 7a?

   (A) A check mark

   (B) "PO Box 3667, Fresno, CA 93704"

   (C) "1 lb. 6 oz."

   (D) "June 21, 2007"

9. A date would be a correct entry in every box EXCEPT which?

   (A) Line 8a

   (B) Line 9a

   (C) Box 3a

   (D) Box 4a

10. Which of these could a check mark in Box 6 indicate?

   (A) A meter stamp is affixed to the mailing envelope

   (B) The delivery address was typewritten

   (C) The article mailed was registered

   (D) The sender did not provide a return address

11. Which of these would be a correct entry for Line 8c?

   (A) A check mark

   (B) "3:30 P.M."

   (C) "(707) 555-1244"

   (D) "08/11/07"

12. Where would you enter the insured number on this form?

   (A) Box 6

   (B) Box 3

   (C) Box 2

   (D) Box 9

13. How would you indicate that the article was received during the morning?

   (A) Circle "A.M." in Box 3b

   (B) Circle "A.M." in Line 9b

   (C) Circle "A.M." in Box 4b

   (D) Enter "A.M." in Box 9a

Signature Confirmation and Receipt		
	TO BE COMPLETED BY SENDER	POST OFFICE USE ONLY

SIGNATURE CONFIRMATION RECEIPT

1a. Sent To (Name): _____

1b. Address: _____
_____

Signature Confirmation Number
4258 0092 1773 8108

2a. Check One:
☐ Priority   ☐ Package Service

2b. Waiver of Signature?
☐ Yes   ☐ No

2c.
Postmark
Here

SIGNATURE CONFIRMATION

3. WAIVER OF SIGNATURE. I authorize that the postal delivery employee's signature suffices as proof of delivery if the item is left in a secure location.

4. Customer Signature

Signature Confirmation Number
4258 0092 1173 8108

14. In which of these lines should a postal employee make an entry?

    (A) Line 4
    (B) Line 3
    (C) Line 2c
    (D) Line 1b

15. Which of these would be a correct entry in Line 1b?

    (A) A check mark
    (B) "Craig Stevens"
    (C) "77 Hadley Rd., Los Angeles, CA 90025
    (D) "Priority"

16. In which of these lines should the sender enter information?

    (A) Line 2b
    (B) Line 1b
    (C) Line 2a
    (D) Line 2c

17. The name "Linnea Rice" is entered in Line 1. What does this indicate?

    (A) The sender is Linnea Rice
    (B) The article is to be sent to Linnea Rice
    (C) Linnea Rice paid postage for the article
    (D) Linnea Rice has waived a signature

18. Which of these types of entries in Line 1a would be correct?

    (A) The signature confirmation number
    (B) The date of mailing
    (C) A description of the article to be mailed
    (D) The addressee's name

Authorization to Hold Mail	
1. Hold Mail For:	2. Beginning Date
1a. Name	3. Ending Date
1b. Street Address	4a. ☐ Do NOT resume delivery until I pick up all accumulated mail.
1c. City, State, ZIP	
5. Customer Signature	4b. ☐ Resume delivery of accumulated and new mail on ending date.
POSTAL USE ONLY	6. Date Received	8. Carrier
	7. Clerk	9. Route Number

19. Where should the customer's name be printed on this form?

    (A) Line 1b
    (B) Box 7
    (C) Line 1a
    (D) Box 3

20. The carrier's route number is 32. How would you indicate this?

    (A) Enter "32" in Box 8
    (B) Enter the carrier's name and number in Box 8
    (C) Enter "32" in Box 9
    (D) Enter "32" in Box 7

21. In which of these would a check mark be a correct entry?

    (A) Box 6
    (B) Box 3
    (C) Line 1b
    (D) Line 4b

22. Which of these would be a correct entry for Box 6?

    (A) A check mark
    (B) "01/29/07"
    (C) "(203) 555-0402"
    (D) "33-987"

23. In which of these boxes should the customer's signature be entered?

    (A) Box 5
    (B) Box 3
    (C) Box 8
    (D) Box 7

Sender's Application for Mail Recall

1. Description of Mailed Item (Check all that apply)	3a. Date Mailed
☐ Letter ☐ Express Mail ☐ Approx. Size: _____ x _____ ☐ Package ☐ Special Delivery ☐ Color: _____	3b. Time Mailed A.M. P.M.
2. Identifying Number (Check and complete all that apply)	4a. Date Appl. Filed
☐ Certified No. _____ ☐ Registered No. _____ ☐ Insured No. _____ ☐ COD No. _____	4b. Time Appl. Filed A.M. P.M.

5. Return Address on Mail	7a. Delivery Address on Mail
6. Check One: ☐ Postage Stamp ☐ Postage Meter Stamp ☐ Other	7b. Check One: ☐ Typewritten ☐ Handwritten ☐ Other

8a. Applicant's Name _____

8b. Applicant's Address _____

8c. Applicant's Telephone Number _____

8d. Signature of Applicant _____

POSTAL USE ONLY	9a. Date Received 9b. Time Received A.M. P.M.	9c. Received by (employee name)

24. Where should the applicant's address be entered on this form?

    (A) Box 2

    (B) Box 9c

    (C) Line 8b

    (D) Box 3b

25. Which of these would be a correct entry in Box 1?

    (A) "Hold for pickup"

    (B) "53304-9002"

    (C) "2 lbs. 1 oz."

    (D) "12 in. x 8 in."

26. The postal employee receiving this form is Julie Baker. Where would you indicate this?

    (A) Box 9c

    (B) Line 9a

    (C) Line 8a

    (D) Box 5

27. Which of these types of entries would be correct in Line 8d?

    (A) A date

    (B) A signature

    (C) An address

    (D) A check mark

28. Which of these would be a correct entry for Line 9a?

    (A) A check mark

    (B) "4:15 P.M."

    (C) "Gary Michalski"

    (D) "02/21/08"

29. Where would you enter the color of the mailing package on this form?

    (A) Box 3

    (B) Box 6

    (C) Box 1

    (D) Box 2

30. Where should the return address be entered on this form?

    (A) Box 5

    (B) Box 8b

    (C) Box 7a

    (D) Box 2

Part C: Coding and Memory

Part C of this test consists of two sections:

- A **Coding Section**, which consists of 36 questions to be completed in 6 minutes
- A **Memory Section**, which consists of 36 questions to be completed in 7 minutes

Both sections test your ability to match one-letter codes to addresses quickly and accurately. The Memory Section also tests your ability to memorize codes and their matching address ranges.

You will use the same **Coding Guide** for both sections of Part C. The first column of the **Coding Guide** shows each **address range**. The second column shows the **delivery route** code (A, B, C, or D) for the address ranges shown in the same row as the code. You may assume that each address range runs continuously (no numbers are skipped) from the lowest to the highest number in the range. Some of the street names appear twice, showing two different address ranges.

Coding Section

This section consists of three segments:

■ **Segment 1** is an introductory exercise consisting of 4 items to be completed in 2 minutes. *Segment 1 is not scored.*

■ **Segment 2** is a practice exercise consisting of 8 items to be completed in 1 1/2 minutes (90 seconds). *Segment 2 is not scored.*

■ **Segment 3** is the actual Coding Section of the test. This segment consists of 36 items to be completed in 6 minutes. *Segment 3 is scored and counts toward your total test score.*

You will use the same Coding Guide for all three segments.

Coding Section—Segment 1

Directions: Segment 1 is an introductory exercise that will familiarize you with the Coding Section and help you learn how to complete it. This segment is *not* scored. Based on the Coding Guide, match each address to a delivery route. Mark your answers on the answer grid at the bottom of this page.

Number of Items: 4

Time Limit: 2 minutes

Coding Guide	
Address Range	*Delivery Route*
1200–2100 Echo Blvd. 400–650 Hyperion Ave. 35–50 Calle Nuevo	A
2101–2500 Echo Blvd. 651–900 Hyperion Ave.	B
9000–15000 Mountain Way 120–220 Third St. South 51–75 Calle Nuevo	C
All mail that does not fall in one of the address ranges listed above	D

	Address	Delivery Code			
1.	13700 Mountain Way	A	B	C	D
2.	4200 Echo Blvd.	A	B	C	D
3.	41 Calle Nuevo	A	B	C	D
4.	2266 Echo Blvd.	A	B	C	D

Sample Answer Sheet

1. Ⓐ Ⓑ Ⓒ Ⓓ   3. Ⓐ Ⓑ Ⓒ Ⓓ
2. Ⓐ Ⓑ Ⓒ Ⓓ   4. Ⓐ Ⓑ Ⓒ Ⓓ

Coding Section—Segment 2

Directions: Segment 2 is *not* scored. It is a practice exercise that will give you experience with the Coding Section under a time constraint similar to the one during the scored Coding Section. Based on the Coding Guide, match each address to a delivery route. Mark your answers on the answer grid at the bottom of this page.

Number of Items: 8

Time Limit: 1 1/2 minutes (90 seconds)

Coding Guide	
Address Range	*Delivery Route*
1200–2100 Echo Blvd. 400–650 Hyperion Ave. 35–50 Calle Nuevo	A
2101–2500 Echo Blvd. 651–900 Hyperion Ave.	B
9000–15000 Mountain Way 120–220 Third St. South 51–75 Calle Nuevo	C
All mail that does not fall in one of the address ranges listed above	D

	Address	Delivery Code			
1.	16 Calle Nuevo	A	B	C	D
2.	529 Hyperion Ave.	A	B	C	D
3.	210 Third St. South	A	B	C	D
4.	2350 Echo Blvd.	A	B	C	D
5.	538 Hyperion Ave.	A	B	C	D
6.	74 Calle Nuevo	A	B	C	D
7.	2430 Echo Blvd.	A	B	C	D
8.	7300 Mountain Way	A	B	C	D

Sample Answer Sheet

1. Ⓐ Ⓑ Ⓒ Ⓓ   4. Ⓐ Ⓑ Ⓒ Ⓓ   7. Ⓐ Ⓑ Ⓒ Ⓓ
2. Ⓐ Ⓑ Ⓒ Ⓓ   5. Ⓐ Ⓑ Ⓒ Ⓓ   8. Ⓐ Ⓑ Ⓒ Ⓓ
3. Ⓐ Ⓑ Ⓒ Ⓓ   6. Ⓐ Ⓑ Ⓒ Ⓓ

Coding Section—Segment 3

Directions: Segment 3 is the *actual scored* Coding Section of the test. Based on the Coding Guide, match each address to a delivery route. Mark your answers on the answer sheet at the end of the chapter.

An answer key for this segment is given at the end of the chapter.

Number of Items: 36

Time Limit: 6 minutes

Coding Guide	
Address Range	*Delivery Route*
1200–2100 Echo Blvd. 400–650 Hyperion Ave. 35–50 Calle Nuevo	A
2101–2500 Echo Blvd. 651–900 Hyperion Ave.	B
9000–15000 Mountain Way 120–220 Third St. South 51–75 Calle Nuevo	C
All mail that does not fall in one of the address ranges listed above	D

Address	Delivery Code			
1. 649 Hyperion Ave.	A	B	C	D
2. 2134 Echo Blvd.	A	B	C	D
3. 35 Calle Nuevo	A	B	C	D
4. 12100 Mountain Way	A	B	C	D
5. 410 Hyperion Ave.	A	B	C	D
6. 320 Third St. South	A	B	C	D
7. 59 Calle Nuevo	A	B	C	D
8. 800 Harper Ave.	A	B	C	D
9. 13250 Mountain Way	A	B	C	D
10. 828 Hyperion Ave.	A	B	C	D
11. 70 Calle Nuevo	A	B	C	D
12. 2004 Echo Blvd.	A	B	C	D
13. 711 Hyperion Ave.	A	B	C	D
14. 202 Third St. North	A	B	C	D
15. 44 Calle Nuevo	A	B	C	D
16. 14446 Mountain Way	A	B	C	D
17. 425 Hyperion Ave.	A	B	C	D
18. 40 Calle Nuevo	A	B	C	D
19. 11405 Mountain Way	A	B	C	D
20. 990 Hyperion Ave.	A	B	C	D
21. 2465 Echo Blvd.	A	B	C	D
22. 180 Third St. South	A	B	C	D
23. 39 Calle Nuevo	A	B	C	D
24. 880 Hyperion Ave.	A	B	C	D
25. 178 Third St. South	A	B	C	D
26. 1950 Mountain Way	A	B	C	D
27. 840 Hyperion Ave.	A	B	C	D
28. 975 Echo Blvd.	A	B	C	D
29. 48 Calle Nuevo	A	B	C	D
30. 460 Hyperion Ave.	A	B	C	D
31. 2479 Echo Blvd.	A	B	C	D
32. 120 Third St. South	A	B	C	D
33. 7900 Mountain Way	A	B	C	D
34. 702 Hyperion Ave.	A	B	C	D
35. 1325 Echo Blvd.	A	B	C	D
36. 47 Calle Canon	A	B	C	D

Memory Section

This section consists of four segments:

- **Segment 1** is a 3-minute study period during which you will attempt to memorize the Coding Guide. *Segment 1 is not scored*, and there are no answers to mark during this segment.
- **Segment 2** is a practice exercise consisting of 8 items to be completed in 1 1/2 minutes (90 seconds). *Segment 2 is not scored.*
- **Segment 3** is a 5-minute study period during which you will attempt to memorize the Coding Guide. *Segment 3 is not scored*, and there are no answers to mark during this segment.
- **Segment 4** is the actual Memory Section of the test. This segment consists of 36 items to be completed in 7 minutes. *Segment 4 is scored and counts toward your total test score.*

You will use the same Coding Guide for all four segments.

Memory Section—Segment 1
Directions: Segment 1 is a 3-minute study period during which you will attempt to memorize the Coding Guide. This segment is *not* scored, and there are no answers to mark during this segment.

Begin the 3-minute study period when you are ready.

Coding Guide	
Address Range	*Delivery Route*
1200–2100 Echo Blvd. 400–650 Hyperion Ave. 35–50 Calle Nuevo	A
2101–2500 Echo Blvd. 651–900 Hyperion Ave.	B
9000–15000 Mountain Way 120–220 Third St. South 51–75 Calle Nuevo	C
All mail that does not fall in one of the address ranges listed above	D

Memory Section—Segment 2

Directions: Segment 2 is a practice exercise that will give you experience coding addresses from memory based on the Coding Guide on the previous page. The Coding Guide is not shown during this segment. Based on the Coding Guide, match each address to a delivery route. Mark your answers on the answer grid at the bottom of this page. This segment is *not* scored.

Turn the page when you are ready to begin Segment 2 under timed conditions.

Number of Items: 8

Time Limit: 1 1/2 minutes (90 seconds)

	Address	Delivery Code			
1.	192 Third St. South	A	B	C	D
2.	629 Hyperion Ave.	A	B	C	D
3.	2338 Echo Blvd.	A	B	C	D
4.	15200 Mountain Way	A	B	C	D
5.	72 Calle Nuevo	A	B	C	D
6.	725 Hyperion Ave.	A	B	C	D
7.	190 Third Avenue	A	B	C	D
8.	1600 Echo Blvd.	A	B	C	D

Sample Answer Sheet

1. Ⓐ Ⓑ Ⓒ Ⓓ   4. Ⓐ Ⓑ Ⓒ Ⓓ   7. Ⓐ Ⓑ Ⓒ Ⓓ
2. Ⓐ Ⓑ Ⓒ Ⓓ   5. Ⓐ Ⓑ Ⓒ Ⓓ   8. Ⓐ Ⓑ Ⓒ Ⓓ
3. Ⓐ Ⓑ Ⓒ Ⓓ   6. Ⓐ Ⓑ Ⓒ Ⓓ

Memory Section—Segment 3

Directions: Segment 3 is a 5-minute study period during which you will again attempt to memorize the Coding Guide. This segment is *not* scored, and there are no answers to mark during this segment.

Begin the 5-minute study period when you are ready.

Coding Guide	
Address Range	*Delivery Route*
1200–2100 Echo Blvd. 400–650 Hyperion Ave. 35–50 Calle Nuevo	A
2101–2500 Echo Blvd. 651–900 Hyperion Ave.	B
9000–15000 Mountain Way 120–220 Third St. South 51–75 Calle Nuevo	C
All mail that does not fall in one of the address ranges listed above	D

Memory Section—Segment 4

Directions: Segment 4 is the *actual scored* Memory Section of the test. The Coding Guide is not shown during this segment. Based on the Coding Guide, match each address to a delivery route. Mark your answers on the answer sheet at the end of the chapter.

Go to the next when you are ready to begin Segment 4 under timed conditions.

An answer key for this segment is given at the end of the chapter.

Number of Items: 36

Time Limit: 7 minutes

	Address		Delivery Code			
37.	2202 Echo Blvd.		A	B	C	D
38.	65 Calle Nuevo		A	B	C	D
39.	590 Hyperion Ave.		A	B	C	D
40.	214 Third St. South		A	B	C	D
41.	1980 Echo Park Blvd.		A	B	C	D
42.	37 Calle Nuevo		A	B	C	D
43.	9650 Mountain Trail		A	B	C	D
44.	2387 Echo Blvd.		A	B	C	D
45.	900 Hyperion Ave.		A	B	C	D
46.	25 Calle Nuevo		A	B	C	D
47.	1460 Echo Blvd.		A	B	C	D
48.	11605 Montauck Way		A	B	C	D
49.	139 Third St. South		A	B	C	D
50.	50 Calle Nuevo		A	B	C	D
51.	1500 Echo Blvd.		A	B	C	D
52.	2220 Third St. South		A	B	C	D
53.	690 Hyperion Ave.		A	B	C	D
54.	12061 Mountain Way		A	B	C	D
55.	57 Third St. South		A	B	C	D
56.	2500 Echo Blvd.		A	B	C	D
57.	52 Calle Nuevo		A	B	C	D
58.	822 Hyperion Ave.		A	B	C	D
59.	2075 Echo Blvd.		A	B	C	D
60.	13855 Mountain Way		A	B	C	D
61.	155 Third St. South		A	B	C	D
62.	1797 Echo Blvd.		A	B	C	D
63.	730 Hyperion Parkway		A	B	C	D
64.	9001 Mountain Way		A	B	C	D

continued on next page

	Address		Delivery Code			
65.	118 Third St. South	*C*	A	B	C	D
66.	2240 Echo Blvd.	*B*	A	B	C	D
67.	67 Campo Nuevo	*D*	A	B	C	D
68.	786 Hyperion Ave.	*a*	A	B	C	D
69.	14800 Mountain Way	*C*	A	B	C	D
70.	35 Calle Nuevo		A	B	C	D
71.	10020 Mountain Way	*C*	A	B	C	D
72.	70 Calle Nuevo		A	B	C	D

Part D: Personal Characteristics and Experience Inventory

Part D consists of a 236-item questionnaire (inventory) on your personal characteristics and experience. You have 90 minutes to complete Part D. This part is scored, but how it is scored is a Postal Service secret. There is no need to prepare for this part of the exam, and therefore it is not included in this practice test. (For more information about Part D, see Chapter 6.)

Practice Test 5 Answer Sheet

The answer sheet given here closely resembles that used on the actual Test 473.

On the front of the answer sheet, you will be asked to fill in personal information similar to the information that you gave when you applied to take the exam. Then you will find spaces—ovals lettered A, B, C, and D—where you are to fill in your answers to Part A, Address Checking, and Part B, Forms Completion, of the exam.

On the other side of the actual answer sheet, you will find similar lettered ovals for you to enter your answers to Part C, Coding and Memory, of the exam. On the answer sheet for Test 473, there will also be spaces for answers to Part D, Personal Characteristics and Experience Inventory, but we have not included that section in this practice exam.

Part A: Address Checking

1. Ⓐ Ⓑ Ⓒ Ⓓ	21. Ⓐ Ⓑ Ⓒ Ⓓ	41. Ⓐ Ⓑ Ⓒ Ⓓ
2. Ⓐ Ⓑ Ⓒ Ⓓ	22. Ⓐ Ⓑ Ⓒ Ⓓ	42. Ⓐ Ⓑ Ⓒ Ⓓ
3. Ⓐ Ⓑ Ⓒ Ⓓ	23. Ⓐ Ⓑ Ⓒ Ⓓ	43. Ⓐ Ⓑ Ⓒ Ⓓ
4. Ⓐ Ⓑ Ⓒ Ⓓ	24. Ⓐ Ⓑ Ⓒ Ⓓ	44. Ⓐ Ⓑ Ⓒ Ⓓ
5. Ⓐ Ⓑ Ⓒ Ⓓ	25. Ⓐ Ⓑ Ⓒ Ⓓ	45. Ⓐ Ⓑ Ⓒ Ⓓ
6. Ⓐ Ⓑ Ⓒ Ⓓ	26. Ⓐ Ⓑ Ⓒ Ⓓ	46. Ⓐ Ⓑ Ⓒ Ⓓ
7. Ⓐ Ⓑ Ⓒ Ⓓ	27. Ⓐ Ⓑ Ⓒ Ⓓ	47. Ⓐ Ⓑ Ⓒ Ⓓ
8. Ⓐ Ⓑ Ⓒ Ⓓ	28. Ⓐ Ⓑ Ⓒ Ⓓ	48. Ⓐ Ⓑ Ⓒ Ⓓ
9. Ⓐ Ⓑ Ⓒ Ⓓ	28. Ⓐ Ⓑ Ⓒ Ⓓ	49. Ⓐ Ⓑ Ⓒ Ⓓ
10. Ⓐ Ⓑ Ⓒ Ⓓ	30. Ⓐ Ⓑ Ⓒ Ⓓ	50. Ⓐ Ⓑ Ⓒ Ⓓ
11. Ⓐ Ⓑ Ⓒ Ⓓ	31. Ⓐ Ⓑ Ⓒ Ⓓ	51. Ⓐ Ⓑ Ⓒ Ⓓ
12. Ⓐ Ⓑ Ⓒ Ⓓ	32. Ⓐ Ⓑ Ⓒ Ⓓ	52. Ⓐ Ⓑ Ⓒ Ⓓ
13. Ⓐ Ⓑ Ⓒ Ⓓ	33. Ⓐ Ⓑ Ⓒ Ⓓ	53. Ⓐ Ⓑ Ⓒ Ⓓ
14. Ⓐ Ⓑ Ⓒ Ⓓ	34. Ⓐ Ⓑ Ⓒ Ⓓ	54. Ⓐ Ⓑ Ⓒ Ⓓ
15. Ⓐ Ⓑ Ⓒ Ⓓ	35. Ⓐ Ⓑ Ⓒ Ⓓ	55. Ⓐ Ⓑ Ⓒ Ⓓ
16. Ⓐ Ⓑ Ⓒ Ⓓ	36. Ⓐ Ⓑ Ⓒ Ⓓ	56. Ⓐ Ⓑ Ⓒ Ⓓ
17. Ⓐ Ⓑ Ⓒ Ⓓ	37. Ⓐ Ⓑ Ⓒ Ⓓ	57. Ⓐ Ⓑ Ⓒ Ⓓ
18. Ⓐ Ⓑ Ⓒ Ⓓ	38. Ⓐ Ⓑ Ⓒ Ⓓ	58. Ⓐ Ⓑ Ⓒ Ⓓ
19. Ⓐ Ⓑ Ⓒ Ⓓ	39. Ⓐ Ⓑ Ⓒ Ⓓ	59. Ⓐ Ⓑ Ⓒ Ⓓ
20. Ⓐ Ⓑ Ⓒ Ⓓ	40. Ⓐ Ⓑ Ⓒ Ⓓ	60. Ⓐ Ⓑ Ⓒ Ⓓ

Part B: Forms Completion

1. Ⓐ Ⓑ Ⓒ Ⓓ	11. Ⓐ Ⓑ Ⓒ Ⓓ	21. Ⓐ Ⓑ Ⓒ Ⓓ
2. Ⓐ Ⓑ Ⓒ Ⓓ	12. Ⓐ Ⓑ Ⓒ Ⓓ	22. Ⓐ Ⓑ Ⓒ Ⓓ
3. Ⓐ Ⓑ Ⓒ Ⓓ	13. Ⓐ Ⓑ Ⓒ Ⓓ	23. Ⓐ Ⓑ Ⓒ Ⓓ
4. Ⓐ Ⓑ Ⓒ Ⓓ	14. Ⓐ Ⓑ Ⓒ Ⓓ	24. Ⓐ Ⓑ Ⓒ Ⓓ
5. Ⓐ Ⓑ Ⓒ Ⓓ	15. Ⓐ Ⓑ Ⓒ Ⓓ	25. Ⓐ Ⓑ Ⓒ Ⓓ
6. Ⓐ Ⓑ Ⓒ Ⓓ	16. Ⓐ Ⓑ Ⓒ Ⓓ	26. Ⓐ Ⓑ Ⓒ Ⓓ
7. Ⓐ Ⓑ Ⓒ Ⓓ	17. Ⓐ Ⓑ Ⓒ Ⓓ	27. Ⓐ Ⓑ Ⓒ Ⓓ
8. Ⓐ Ⓑ Ⓒ Ⓓ	18. Ⓐ Ⓑ Ⓒ Ⓓ	28. Ⓐ Ⓑ Ⓒ Ⓓ
9. Ⓐ Ⓑ Ⓒ Ⓓ	19. Ⓐ Ⓑ Ⓒ Ⓓ	29. Ⓐ Ⓑ Ⓒ Ⓓ
10. Ⓐ Ⓑ Ⓒ Ⓓ	20. Ⓐ Ⓑ Ⓒ Ⓓ	30. Ⓐ Ⓑ Ⓒ Ⓓ

Part C: Coding and Memory

1. Ⓐ Ⓑ Ⓒ Ⓓ	25. Ⓐ Ⓑ Ⓒ Ⓓ	49. Ⓐ Ⓑ Ⓒ Ⓓ
2. Ⓐ Ⓑ Ⓒ Ⓓ	26. Ⓐ Ⓑ Ⓒ Ⓓ	50. Ⓐ Ⓑ Ⓒ Ⓓ
3. Ⓐ Ⓑ Ⓒ Ⓓ	27. Ⓐ Ⓑ Ⓒ Ⓓ	51. Ⓐ Ⓑ Ⓒ Ⓓ
4. Ⓐ Ⓑ Ⓒ Ⓓ	28. Ⓐ Ⓑ Ⓒ Ⓓ	52. Ⓐ Ⓑ Ⓒ Ⓓ
5. Ⓐ Ⓑ Ⓒ Ⓓ	29. Ⓐ Ⓑ Ⓒ Ⓓ	53. Ⓐ Ⓑ Ⓒ Ⓓ
6. Ⓐ Ⓑ Ⓒ Ⓓ	30. Ⓐ Ⓑ Ⓒ Ⓓ	54. Ⓐ Ⓑ Ⓒ Ⓓ
7. Ⓐ Ⓑ Ⓒ Ⓓ	31. Ⓐ Ⓑ Ⓒ Ⓓ	55. Ⓐ Ⓑ Ⓒ Ⓓ
8. Ⓐ Ⓑ Ⓒ Ⓓ	32. Ⓐ Ⓑ Ⓒ Ⓓ	56. Ⓐ Ⓑ Ⓒ Ⓓ
9. Ⓐ Ⓑ Ⓒ Ⓓ	33. Ⓐ Ⓑ Ⓒ Ⓓ	57. Ⓐ Ⓑ Ⓒ Ⓓ
10. Ⓐ Ⓑ Ⓒ Ⓓ	34. Ⓐ Ⓑ Ⓒ Ⓓ	58. Ⓐ Ⓑ Ⓒ Ⓓ
11. Ⓐ Ⓑ Ⓒ Ⓓ	35. Ⓐ Ⓑ Ⓒ Ⓓ	59. Ⓐ Ⓑ Ⓒ Ⓓ
12. Ⓐ Ⓑ Ⓒ Ⓓ	36. Ⓐ Ⓑ Ⓒ Ⓓ	60. Ⓐ Ⓑ Ⓒ Ⓓ
13. Ⓐ Ⓑ Ⓒ Ⓓ	37. Ⓐ Ⓑ Ⓒ Ⓓ	61. Ⓐ Ⓑ Ⓒ Ⓓ
14. Ⓐ Ⓑ Ⓒ Ⓓ	38. Ⓐ Ⓑ Ⓒ Ⓓ	62. Ⓐ Ⓑ Ⓒ Ⓓ
15. Ⓐ Ⓑ Ⓒ Ⓓ	39. Ⓐ Ⓑ Ⓒ Ⓓ	63. Ⓐ Ⓑ Ⓒ Ⓓ
16. Ⓐ Ⓑ Ⓒ Ⓓ	40. Ⓐ Ⓑ Ⓒ Ⓓ	64. Ⓐ Ⓑ Ⓒ Ⓓ
17. Ⓐ Ⓑ Ⓒ Ⓓ	41. Ⓐ Ⓑ Ⓒ Ⓓ	65. Ⓐ Ⓑ Ⓒ Ⓓ
18. Ⓐ Ⓑ Ⓒ Ⓓ	42. Ⓐ Ⓑ Ⓒ Ⓓ	66. Ⓐ Ⓑ Ⓒ Ⓓ
19. Ⓐ Ⓑ Ⓒ Ⓓ	43. Ⓐ Ⓑ Ⓒ Ⓓ	67. Ⓐ Ⓑ Ⓒ Ⓓ
20. Ⓐ Ⓑ Ⓒ Ⓓ	44. Ⓐ Ⓑ Ⓒ Ⓓ	68. Ⓐ Ⓑ Ⓒ Ⓓ
21. Ⓐ Ⓑ Ⓒ Ⓓ	45. Ⓐ Ⓑ Ⓒ Ⓓ	69. Ⓐ Ⓑ Ⓒ Ⓓ
22. Ⓐ Ⓑ Ⓒ Ⓓ	46. Ⓐ Ⓑ Ⓒ Ⓓ	70. Ⓐ Ⓑ Ⓒ Ⓓ
23. Ⓐ Ⓑ Ⓒ Ⓓ	47. Ⓐ Ⓑ Ⓒ Ⓓ	71. Ⓐ Ⓑ Ⓒ Ⓓ
24. Ⓐ Ⓑ Ⓒ Ⓓ	48. Ⓐ Ⓑ Ⓒ Ⓓ	72. Ⓐ Ⓑ Ⓒ Ⓓ

Part D: Personal Characteristics and Experience Inventory

On the actual exam, there would be spaces for the answers to 236 questions here, but we are not including this section in the practice exams or answer sheets.

Answer Key

Part A: Address Checking

1. C	13. B	25. B	37. C	49. C
2. B	14. A	26. A	38. A	50. D
3. D	15. B	27. D	39. B	51. B
4. B	16. D	28. B	40. B	52. C
5. B	17. C	29. C	41. C	53. B
6. A	18. A	30. D	42. C	54. A
7. D	19. B	31. B	43. B	55. B
8. B	20. B	32. C	44. D	56. D
9. C	21. C	33. B	45. B	57. C
10. D	22. C	34. A	46. A	58. A
11. C	23. B	35. D	47. D	59. B
12. C	24. D	36. D	48. B	60. D

Part B: Forms Completion

1. A	7. D	13. B	19. C	25. D
2. C	8. B	14. C	20. C	26. A
3. B	9. A	15. C	21. D	27. B
4. D	10. A	16. B	22. B	28. D
5. B	11. C	17. B	23. A	29. C
6. A	12. C	18. D	24. C	30. A

Part C: Coding and Memory

1. A	16. C	31. B	46. D	61. C
2. B	17. A	32. C	47. A	62. A
3. A	18. A	33. D	48. D	63. D
4. C	19. C	34. B	49. C	64. C
5. A	20. D	35. A	50. A	65. D
6. D	21. B	36. D	51. A	66. B
7. C	22. C	37. B	52. D	67. D
8. D	23. A	38. C	53. B	68. B
9. C	24. B	39. A	54. C	69. C
10. B	25. C	40. C	55. D	70. A
11. C	26. D	41. D	56. B	71. C
12. A	27. B	42. A	57. C	72. C
13. B	28. D	43. D	58. B	
14. D	29. A	44. B	59. A	
15. A	30. A	45. B	60. C	

Part A: Address Checking

Directions: Part A of this test consists of 60 items for you to complete in 11 minutes. You will be shown a **Correct List** of addresses and ZIP codes alongside a **List to Be Checked**. The two lists should contain the same addresses and ZIP codes, except that the **List to Be Checked** may contain errors.

Each row of information consists of one item. For each item, compare the address and ZIP code in the **Correct List** with the address and ZIP code in the **List to Be Checked**. Determine whether there are **No Errors**, an error in **Address Only**, an error in **ZIP Code Only**, or an error in **Both** the address and the ZIP code. Select an answer from the following four choices:

A. No Errors	B. Address Only	C. ZIP Code Only	D. Both

Mark your answers (A, B, C, or D) on the answer sheet at the end of the chapter.

An answer key is given at the end of the chapter.

Number of Items: 60

Time: 11 minutes

A. No Errors	B. Address Only	C. ZIP Code Only	D. Both

	Correct List		List to Be Checked	
	Address	*ZIP Code*	*Address*	*ZIP Code*
1.	1739 Montemar Ct. Saint Paul, MN	55103	1739 Montemar Ct. Saint Paul, MN	55003
2.	687 Morris St. Staten Island, NY	10307-9026	687 Morris Rd. Staten Island, NY	10307-9026
3.	9888 El Collegio Escondido, CA	92025-4362	9889 El Collegio Escondido, CA	92025-4326
4.	850 Roberts Pl. Winston Salem, NC	27104	850 Robertson Pl. Winston Salem, NC	27104
5.	7955 Convoy Street Lima, OH	45804	7955 Convoy Street Lima, OH	48404
6.	PO Box 658962 Sioux City, IA	51105-8962	PO Box 65892 Sioux City, IA	51510-8962
7.	18 Orchard Terrace Evanston, IL	60203-1902	18 Orchard Terrace Evanstown, IL	60203-1902
8.	3836 East Campus Drive Wichita, KS	67228	3836 East Campus Drive Wichita, KS	67238
9.	1550 W. Center Ave. Grand Rapids, MI	49505-5777	1550 N. Center Ave. Grand Rapids, MI	49505-5577
10.	950 Circle Dr. Monterville, WV	26282	950 Circle Dr. Mountville, WV	26282
11.	604 Wright St. Hastings, NE	68901-1657	604 Wright St. Hastings, NE	68901-1757
12.	1691 Rutger Ct. Oklahoma City, OK	73105-0371	1691 Rutger Rd. Oklahoma City, OK	73105-0371
13.	724 Superior Dr. Wausau, WI	54401	724 Superior Dr. Wausau, WI	54401
14.	1022 S. Wilton Pl. Macedonia, IA	51549	1022 S. Wilton Pl. Macadonia, IA	51549
15.	64 Benton Cir. Fairdale, KY	40118	64 Benton Ct. Fairdale, KY	40558

continued on next page

A. No Errors	B. Address Only	C. ZIP Code Only	D. Both

	Correct List		**List to Be Checked**	
	Address	*ZIP Code*	*Address*	*ZIP Code*
16.	5500 Orleans Ave. Huntsville, AL	35801-4789	5500 Orleans Ave. Huntsville, AL	35801-4799
17.	86 Forest Hills St. Gary, IN	46402-9754	86 Forest Hills St. Gary, IN	46402-9754
18.	435 Warren St. Flagstaff, AZ	86001	45 Warren St. Flagstaff, AZ	86001
19.	3316 W. Wisconsin Dr. Saint Cloud, MN	56303-1689	3313 W. Wisconsin Dr. Saint Cloud, MN	56303-1689
20.	5056 Brookpark Rd. Cleveland, OH	44105-2468	5056 Brookpark Rd. Cleveland, OH	41105-2468
21.	244 Oxford Ave, Ste. 9 Los Angeles, CA	90038	244 Oxford Ave, Ste. 9 Los Angeles, CA	90038
22.	9900 Balboa Dr. Richmond, VA	23294	9900 Balboa Richmond, VA	23294
23.	3011 Telegraph Ave. Milwaukee, WI	53204-8753	3011 Telegraph Ave. Milwaukie, WI	53204-3753
24.	P.O. Box 6332 Honolulu, HI	96821	P.O. Box 6332 Honolulu, HI	98621
25.	1585 Fruitvale Pl. Memphis, TN	38118	1585 Fruitvale Pl. Memphis, TN	38818
26.	1303 Ashe Lane Chicago, IL	60660-1628	1303 Asher Lane Chicago, IL	60660-1688
27.	2975 Valmont Rd. Brooklyn, NY	11206-8461	2975 Valmont Rd. Brookline, NY	11206-8461
28.	2039 Katy Rd. #2 Patten, ME	04765-8347	2039 Katy Rd. #2 Patten, ME	04760-8347
29.	2795 Speer Blvd. Lake Charles, LA	70611	2795 Speer Blvd. Lake Charles, FL	77611
30.	315 Castle Court Boston, MA	02114	215 Castle Court Boston, MA	02114
31.	11611 Marsh Ln. Los Angeles, CA	90027-1549	11611 Marsh Ln. Los Angeles, CA	90227-1549
32.	105 Memorial Dr. Dearborn, MI	48128	105 Memorial Rd. Dearborn, MI	48128

continued on next page

A. No Errors	B. Address Only	C. ZIP Code Only	D. Both

	Correct List		List to Be Checked	
	Address	ZIP Code	Address	ZIP Code
33.	5088 Nova St., Apt. 8D Biloxi, MS	39531-4823	5088 Nova St., Apt. 8D Biloxi, MS	39531-4823
34.	4880 Reed Beltway Kansas City, MO	64136	4880 Reed Beltway Kansas City, KS	64136
35.	3033 Cleveland Avenue Philadelphia, PA	19112	3003 Cleveland Avenue Philadelphia, PA	19192
36.	550 Fairburn Rd. Arlington, TX	76017-8477	550 Fairburn Rd. Arlington, TX	76027-8477
37.	5955 N. Oracle Rd. Muscatine, IA	52761-3864	5955 N. Oracle Rd. Muscatine, IA	52761-3864
38.	700 Parsons Ln. Charleston, SC	29405	700 Parson Ln. Charleston, SC	29405
39.	6339 SW Capitol Hwy. Lewistown, MT	59457	6339 SW Capital Hwy. Lewistown, MT	59457
40.	202 Faber Heights Hutchinson, KS	67501	202 Faber Heights Hutchinson, KS	65521
41.	4644 Girard Drive #33 Jacksonville, FL	32206-0001	4644 Girard Drive #33 Jacksonville, FL	32206-0001
42.	24732 Aurora Ave. Omaha, NE	68110-3528	24723 Aurora Ave. Omaha, NE	68110-3528
43.	30 Arthur Rd. Atlantic City, NJ	08401-3883	300 Arthur Rd. Atlantic City, NJ	08401-3833
44.	1009 N. Rush St. Gastonia, NC	28054	1009 N. Rose St. Gastonia, NC	28054
45.	6647 SE Desert Blvd. North Las Vegas, NV	89031-0249	6647 SE Desert Blvd. North Las Vegas, NV	89031-0469
46.	336 Ranchero Drive Fort Worth, TX	76134	336 Ranchero Road Fort Worth, TX	76634
47.	P.O. Box 2237 Evansville, IN	47713-2237	P.O. Box 2237 Evansvile, IN	47713-2237
48.	921 N. 1st St. Urbandale, IA	50322	921 N. 1st St. Urbandale, IA	50377
49.	8580 Camino Del Rio Santa Fe, NM	87505	8550 Camino Del Rio Santa Fe, NM	82505

continued on next page

A. No Errors	B. Address Only	C. ZIP Code Only	D. Both

	Correct List		List to Be Checked	
	Address	ZIP Code	Address	ZIP Code
50.	8999 East Hudson Way Passaic, NJ	07055-3791	8999 West Hudson Way Passaic, NJ	07055-3591
51.	30373 Horseshoe Drive Kings Park, NY	11754-7549	30373 Horseshoe Drive Kings Park, NY	11754-1549
52.	1 Washington Square Tacoma, WA	98406-1470	11 Washington Square Tacoma, WA	98406-1470
53.	4050 Barrows Pkwy. Herndon, VA	22070	4050 Barrows Pkwy. Herndon, VA	22070
54.	1871 West Cochran Ave. Cedar Rapids, IA	52401	1871 West Cochran Cir. Cedar Rapids, IA	52401
55.	141 South 14th St. Ness City, KS	67560-9843	141 South 17th St. Ness City, KS	67560-8943
56.	PO Box 277 Robinette, WV	25607	PO Box 277 Robinette, WV	25807
57.	2701 Fairview Road Lucan, MN	56255-4569	2701 Fairview Road Lucan, MN	56255-4569
58.	50088 W. 53rd St. Cuyahoga Falls, OH	44223-8031	50088 W. 53rd St. Cuyahoge Falls, OH	44223-8031
59.	555 N. Vermont Ave. Villa Park, IL	60181	555 N. Vernon Ave. Villa Park, IL	60181
60.	4200 Farm Hill Road Lexington, KY	40517	4200 Farm Hill Road Lexington, KY	41507

Part B: Forms Completion

Directions: Part B of this test consists of 30 questions for you to complete in 15 minutes. You will be shown a series of forms that are similar to ones used by the U.S. Postal Service. The parts of each form are labeled (for example, 3 and 4a). Each form is accompanied by several questions that test your ability to complete the form properly. For each question, choose the best answer and mark your selection (A, B, C, or D) on your answer sheet.

Go to the next page when you are ready to begin Part B under timed conditions.

An answer key is given at the end of the chapter.

Number of Questions: 30

Time: 15 minutes

Bulk Mailing Certificate

Certificate Fee Schedule

1a. 1 – 1,000 pieces $ _____

1b. Each additional 1,000 pieces (or fraction thereof) $ _____   } Use Current Rate Schedule

2a. Number of Identical Pieces	2b. Mail Class	2c. Postage per Piece	2d. Total Postage
3a. Number of Pieces per Pound	3b. Total Number of Pieces		3c. Bulk Mailing Fee
4a. Mailed By	4b. Mailed For		5. Total Postage and Fees

6. Postmaster's Certificate
I hereby certify that the mailing described above has been received and the number of pieces and the postage is correct.

X _____

(Postmaster)

1. Which of these is a correct entry for Box 1b?
(A) "Bulk"
(B) A check mark
(C) "275.00"
(D) "U.S."

2. In which box could "Marc Cummings" be a correct entry?
(A) Box 4a
(B) Box 1a
(C) Box 5
(D) Box 1b

3. Which of these is an appropriate entry in Box 3a?
(A) "$16.00"
(B) "82 lbs."
(C) "16"
(D) "10/03/06"

4. How would the postmaster certify that the number of pieces is correct?
(A) Enter a check mark in Box 6
(B) Stamp the form with a postmark
(C) Enter her signature in Box 4a
(D) Enter her signature in Box 6

5. Which of these is a correct entry for Box 4b?
(A) "$6.50"
(B) "44935-0087"
(C) "120 Commerce Blvd., Atlanta, GA"
(D) "Orion Corp."

6. The current bulk mailing rate for 1,000 pieces is $55.00. How would you indicate this?
(A) Enter "$55.00" in Box 2c
(B) Enter "55.00" in Line 1a
(C) Enter "$55.00" in Box 5
(D) Enter "55.00" in Box 2a

Customs Dispatch Order and Declaration

1. Sender Information	2. Addressee Information
1a. Name	2a. Name
1b. Street, Apt., or PO Box No.	2b. Street, Apt., or PO Box No.
1c. City, State, ZIP + 4	2c. City, State, ZIP + 4
1d. Country	2d. Country

3a. Contents (Detailed Description)	3c. Qty	3d. Weight lb. oz.	3e. Value (US $)

3b. Check One ☐ Gift ☐ Commercial Sample ☐ Document ☐ Other	3f. Restriction and Other Comments (e.g., subject to quarantine)
4. For Commercial Items Only 4a. Country of Origin _____ ☐ Unknown 4b. HS Tariff No. _____ ☐ Unknown	5. Sender's Signature and Date 6. Delivery (Check One) ☐ Priority/Air ☐ Non-Priority/Surface

7. The item declared weighs 12 pounds. Where would you indicate this?

   (A) Box 3a

   (B) Box 3e

   (C) Box 3d

   (D) Box 3c

8. Where would you indicate that the article declared is subject to quarantine?

   (A) Box 1

   (B) Box 3a

   (C) Box 5

   (D) Box 3f

9. Which of these would be a correct entry for Box 3a?

   (A) A check mark

   (B) "Bottle of wine"

   (C) "$240.00"

   (D) "Michelle Girard"

10. A person's name is a correct entry for every box EXCEPT which?

    (A) Box 5

    (B) Box 6

    (C) Box 2a

    (D) Box 1

11. How would you indicate that the article is sent to France?

    (A) Enter "France" in Box 2d

    (B) Enter "Europe" in Line 4b

    (C) Enter "France" next to "Other" in Box 3b

    (D) Enter "France" in Line 4a

12. Which of these would be a correct entry for Line 2c?

    (A) "Gift"

    (B) "U.S."

    (C) "NY"

    (D) "50"

13. Where should the HS tariff number be entered on this form?

    (A) Box 6

    (B) Line 2b

    (C) Box 3d

    (D) Line 4b

Certified Mail Receipt (Domestic Mail Only)		
TO BE COMPLETED BY SENDER	**OFFICIAL USE**	
1. Sent To	Postage	4.
	Certified Fee	5.
2. Street, Apt. No., or PO Box	Return Receipt Fee	6.
	Restricted Delivery Fee	7.
3. City, State, ZIP + 4		
CERTIFIED MAIL NUMBER 9217 0048 5033 7002	Total Postage and Fees	8.

14. The restricted delivery fee is $3.20. Where would you indicate this?

(A) Box 5

(B) Box 8

(C) Box 7

(D) Box 6

15. All of these would be appropriate entries for Box 3 EXCEPT which?

(A) "Alaska"

(B) "Boston"

(C) "08648-0003"

(D) "Apt. 5"

16. The state to which the article is sent is Illinois. Where would this be indicated on the form?

(A) Line 3

(B) Box 4

(C) Line 1

(D) Line 2

17. Which of these types of entries should the postal employee enter on this form?

(A) A special handling fee

(B) A certified fee

(C) A delivery address

(D) A postmark

18. Which of these would be an appropriate entry on this form?

(A) "10/03/07"

(B) A check mark

(C) "3.30"

(D) A signature

19. Where is the postage indicated on this form?

(A) Box 4

(B) Box 5

(C) Box 6

(D) Box 8

Delivery Confirmation Receipt (Do not use for insured or registered mail.)		
1. (To Be Completed by Sender)	2 – 4 (Post Office Use Only)	
1a. Name	2a. $	Postage
1b. Street, Apt. No., or PO Box No.	2b. $	Delivery Confirmation Fee
1c. City, State, ZIP + 4	2c. $	Total Postage and Fees
DELIVERY CONFIRMATION NUMBER 5011 2974 3310 0993	3. (Check One) ☐ Priority ☐ First Class ☐ Package Services	4. Postmark Here

20. Which of these would be a correct entry for
    Line 1c?

    (A) "San Francisco, CA 94115"

    (B) A check mark

    (C) "1.25"

    (D) "9080 Nantucket Dr."

21. Which of these portions of the form does the
    sender complete?

    (A) Box 3

    (B) Line 2a

    (C) Box 4

    (D) Line 1c

22. The postage is $.57. Where would you indicate
    this?

    (A) Box 2b

    (B) Box 2c

    (C) Box 3

    (D) Box 2a

23. Which type of delivery service can be specified
    on this form?

    (A) Insured

    (B) Registered

    (C) First class

    (D) Express mail

24. Where should the sender's name be entered on
    this form?

    (A) Box 2a

    (B) Line 1b

    (C) Line 1a

    (D) Box 4

25. Which of these entries is correct for Line 2c?

    (A) "11/03/07"

    (B) "6.45"

    (C) "Yolanda Ramirez"

    (D) "2 lb. 8 oz."

Global Direct Notification of Mailing

1. Sender Information 1a. Name _____ 1b. Telephone _____ 1c. Fax No. _____ 1d. Address _____	2. Destination Country
	3. Date Notified
	4. Global Direct ID Number
5a. Mailing Date 5b. Approx. Total Weight 5c. Quantity _____ ☐ Trays _____ ☐ Pallets	6. Return Address ☐ Use my own in-country designated return address ☐ Use the following postal service-provided return address: _____ _____

26. Which of these would be a correct entry for Line 1c?

    (A) "09/14/06"

    (B) A check mark

    (C) "Dennis Grier"

    (D) "(602) 555-4213"

27. Which type of information should be entered in Box 5c?

    (A) A name

    (B) A number

    (C) An address

    (D) A date

28. Where should the sender's ZIP code be entered on this form?

    (A) Line 1d

    (B) Box 4

    (C) Line 1c

    (D) Box 5a

29. The sender wants to designate his own address as the return address. How would the sender indicate this?

    (A) Enter the return address in Box 6

    (B) Enter "See Line 1d" in Box 6

    (C) Enter a check mark in the upper square in Box 6

    (D) Enter "Return address" in Box 6

30. In which of these would the Global Direct ID number be a correct entry?

    (A) Line 1c

    (B) Box 3

    (C) Box 2

    (D) Box 4

Part C: Coding and Memory

Part C of this test consists of two sections:

■ A **Coding Section**, which consists of 36 questions to be completed in 6 minutes
■ A **Memory Section**, which consists of 36 questions to be completed in 7 minutes

Both sections test your ability to match one-letter codes to addresses quickly and accurately. The Memory Section also tests your ability to memorize codes and their matching address ranges.

You will use the same **Coding Guide** for both sections of Part C. The first column of the **Coding Guide** shows each **address range**. The second column shows the **delivery route** code (A, B, C, or D) for the address ranges shown in the same row as the code. You may assume that each address range runs continuously (no numbers are skipped) from the lowest to the highest number in the range. Some of the street names appear twice, showing two different address ranges.

Coding Section

This section consists of three segments:

- **Segment 1** is an introductory exercise consisting of 4 items to be completed in 2 minutes. *Segment 1 is not scored.*
- **Segment 2** is a practice exercise consisting of 8 items to be completed in 1 1/2 minutes (90 seconds). *Segment 2 is not scored.*
- **Segment 3** is the actual Coding Section of the test. This segment consists of 36 items to be completed in 6 minutes. *Segment 3 is scored and counts toward your total test score.*

You will use the same Coding Guide for all three segments.

Coding Section—Segment 1

Directions: Segment 1 is an introductory exercise that will familiarize you with the Coding Section and help you learn how to complete it. This segment is *not* scored. Based on the Coding Guide, match each address to a delivery route. Mark your answers on the answer grid at the bottom of this page.

Number of Items: 4

Time Limit: 2 minutes

Coding Guide	
Address Range	*Delivery Route*
1100–1700 St. James Rd. 11–40 Bradford Court 15000–35000 Route 5 North	A
41–70 Bradford Court 1701–2000 St. James Rd.	B
500–1000 N. Yates Blvd. 35001–55000 Route 5 North 1–100 W. 61st St.	C
All mail that does not fall in one of the address ranges listed above	D

	Address	Delivery Code			
1.	20300 Route 5 North	A	B	C	D
2.	2100 St. James Rd.	A	B	C	D
3.	100 W. 61st St.	A	B	C	D
4.	909 N. Yates Blvd.	A	B	C	D

Sample Answer Sheet

1. Ⓐ Ⓑ Ⓒ Ⓓ   3. Ⓐ Ⓑ Ⓒ Ⓓ
2. Ⓐ Ⓑ Ⓒ Ⓓ   4. Ⓐ Ⓑ Ⓒ Ⓓ

Coding Section—Segment 2

Directions: Segment 2 is *not* scored. It is a practice exercise that will give you experience with the Coding Section under a time constraint similar to the one during the scored Coding Section. Based on the Coding Guide, match each address to a delivery route. Mark your answers on the answer grid at the bottom of this page.

Number of Items: 8

Time Limit: 1 1/2 minutes (90 seconds)

Coding Guide	
Address Range	*Delivery Route*
1100–1700 St. James Rd. 11–40 Bradford Court 15000–35000 Route 5 North	A
41–70 Bradford Court 1701–2000 St. James Rd.	B
500–1000 N. Yates Blvd. 35001–55000 Route 5 North 1–100 W. 61st St.	C
All mail that does not fall in one of the address ranges listed above	D

	Address	Delivery Code			
1.	70100 Route 5 North	A	B	C	D
2.	22 Bradford Court	A	B	C	D
3.	1870 St. James Rd.	A	B	C	D
4.	9 W. 61st St.	A	B	C	D
5.	7460 N. Yates Blvd.	A	B	C	D
6.	45400 Route 5 North	A	B	C	D
7.	51 Bradford Court	A	B	C	D
8.	1620 St. James Rd.	A	B	C	D

Sample Answer Sheet

1. Ⓐ Ⓑ Ⓒ Ⓓ   4. Ⓐ Ⓑ Ⓒ Ⓓ   7. Ⓐ Ⓑ Ⓒ Ⓓ
2. Ⓐ Ⓑ Ⓒ Ⓓ   5. Ⓐ Ⓑ Ⓒ Ⓓ   8. Ⓐ Ⓑ Ⓒ Ⓓ
3. Ⓐ Ⓑ Ⓒ Ⓓ   6. Ⓐ Ⓑ Ⓒ Ⓓ

Coding Section—Segment 3

Directions: Segment 3 is the *actual scored* Coding Section of the test. Based on the Coding Guide, match each address to a delivery route. Mark your answers on the answer sheet at the end of the chapter.

An answer key for this segment is given at the end of the chapter.

Number of Items: 36

Time Limit: 6 minutes

Coding Guide	
Address Range	Delivery Route
1100–1700 St. James Rd. 11–40 Bradford Court 15000–35000 Route 5 North	A
41–70 Bradford Court 1701–2000 St. James Rd.	B
500–1000 N. Yates Blvd. 35001–55000 Route 5 North 1–100 W. 61st St.	C
All mail that does not fall in one of the address ranges listed above	D

	Address	Delivery Code			
1.	120 Bradford Court	A	B	C	D
2.	615 N. Yates Blvd.	A	B	C	D
3.	1111 St. James Rd.	A	B	C	D
4.	16 W. 61st St.	A	B	C	D
5.	50 Bradford Loop	A	B	C	D
6.	28229 Route 5 North	A	B	C	D
7.	400 N. Yates Blvd.	A	B	C	D
8.	24 W. 61st St.	A	B	C	D
9.	1887 St. James Rd.	A	B	C	D
10.	19 Bradford Court	A	B	C	D
11.	54123 Route 5 North	A	B	C	D
12.	1713 St. James Rd.	A	B	C	D
13.	19405 Route 5	A	B	C	D
14.	75 W. 61st St.	A	B	C	D
15.	70 Bradford Court	A	B	C	D
16.	721 N. Yates Blvd.	A	B	C	D
17.	5500 Route 5 North	A	B	C	D
18.	1302 St. James Rd.	A	B	C	D
19.	69 Brickle Court	A	B	C	D
20.	773 N. Yates Blvd.	A	B	C	D
21.	37946 Route 5 North	A	B	C	D
22.	44 Bradford Court	A	B	C	D
23.	91 E. 61st Ave.	A	B	C	D
24.	1949 St. James Rd.	A	B	C	D
25.	42605 Route 5 North	A	B	C	D
26.	1700 St. James Rd.	A	B	C	D
27.	9900 N. Yates Blvd.	A	B	C	D
28.	57 Bradford Court	A	B	C	D
29.	51 W. 61st St.	A	B	C	D
30.	17053 Route 5 North	A	B	C	D
31.	1289 James Rd.	A	B	C	D
32.	38 Bradford Court	A	B	C	D
33.	1120 W. 61st St.	A	B	C	D
34.	32446 Route 5 North	A	B	C	D
35.	1785 St. Joseph Rd.	A	B	C	D
36.	14 Bradford Court	A	B	C	D

Memory Section

This section consists of four segments:

- **Segment 1** is a 3-minute study period during which you will attempt to memorize the Coding Guide. *Segment 1 is not scored,* and there are no answers to mark during this segment.
- **Segment 2** is a practice exercise consisting of 8 items to be completed in 1 1/2 minutes (90 seconds). *Segment 2 is not scored.*
- **Segment 3** is a 5-minute study period during which you will attempt to memorize the Coding Guide. *Segment 3 is not scored,* and there are no answers to mark during this segment.
- **Segment 4** is the actual Memory Section of the test. This segment consists of 36 items to be completed in 7 minutes. *Segment 4 is scored and counts toward your total test score.*

You will use the same Coding Guide for all four segments.

Memory Section—Segment 1

Directions: Segment 1 is a 3-minute study period during which you will attempt to memorize the Coding Guide. This segment is *not* scored, and there are no answers to mark during this segment.

Begin the 3-minute study period when you are ready.

Coding Guide	
Address Range	*Delivery Route*
1100–1700 St. James Rd. 11–40 Bradford Court 15000–35000 Route 5 North	A
41–70 Bradford Court 1701–2000 St. James Rd.	B
500–1000 N. Yates Blvd. 35001–55000 Route 5 North 1–100 W. 61st St.	C
All mail that does not fall in one of the address ranges listed above	D

Memory Section—Segment 2

Directions: Segment 2 is a practice exercise that will give you experience coding addresses from memory based on the Coding Guide on the previous page. The Coding Guide is not shown during this segment. Based on the Coding Guide, match each address to a delivery route. Mark your answers on the answer grid at the bottom of this page. This segment is *not* scored.

Turn the page when you are ready to begin Segment 2 under timed conditions.

Number of Items: 8

Time Limit: 1 1/2 minutes (90 seconds)

	Address	Delivery Code			
1.	35290 Route 5 North	A	B	C	D
2.	1459 St. James Rd.	A	B	C	D
3.	66 Bradford Court	A	B	C	D
4.	501 N. Yates Blvd.	A	B	C	D
5.	150 W. 61st St.	A	B	C	D
6.	1705 St. James Rd.	A	B	C	D
7.	47020 Rural Route 5	A	B	C	D
8.	27 Bradford Court	A	B	C	D

Sample Answer Sheet

1. (A) (B) (C) (D)   4. (A) (B) (C) (D)   7. (A) (B) (C) (D)
2. (A) (B) (C) (D)   5. (A) (B) (C) (D)   8. (A) (B) (C) (D)
3. (A) (B) (C) (D)   6. (A) (B) (C) (D)

Memory Section—Segment 3

Directions: Segment 3 is a 5-minute study period during which you will again attempt to memorize the Coding Guide. This segment is *not* scored, and there are no answers to mark during this segment.

Begin the 5-minute study period when you are ready.

Coding Guide	
Address Range	*Delivery Route*
1100–1700 St. James Rd. 11–40 Bradford Court 15000–35000 Route 5 North	A
41–70 Bradford Court 1701–2000 St. James Rd.	B
500–1000 N. Yates Blvd. 35001–55000 Route 5 North 1–100 W. 61st St.	C
All mail that does not fall in one of the address ranges listed above	D

Memory Section—Segment 4

Directions: Segment 4 is the *actual scored* Memory Section of the test. The Coding Guide is not shown during this segment. Based on the Coding Guide, match each address to a delivery route. Mark your answers on the answer sheet at the end of the chapter.

Go to the next page when you are ready to begin Segment 4 under timed conditions.

An answer key for this segment is given at the end of the chapter.

Number of Items: 36

Time Limit: 7 minutes

	Address	Delivery Code			
37.	40 Bradford Court	A	B	C	D
38.	39372 Route 5 North	A	B	C	D
39.	1020 St. James Rd.	A	B	C	D
40.	510 N. Yates Blvd.	A	B	C	D
41.	30 W. 61st St.	A	B	C	D
42.	16 Bradford Court	A	B	C	D
43.	975 N. Yates Blvd.	A	B	C	D
44.	52100 Route 5 North	A	B	C	D
45.	1200 St. James Rd.	A	B	C	D
46.	37590 W. 61st St.	A	B	C	D
47.	13900 Route 5 North	A	B	C	D
48.	1828 St. James Rd.	A	B	C	D
49.	58 Bradford Court	A	B	C	D
50.	839 N. Yeats Ave.	A	B	C	D
51.	48 W. 73rd St.	A	B	C	D
52.	1541 St. James Rd.	A	B	C	D
53.	63 Bradford Court	A	B	C	D
54.	15190 Route 5 North	A	B	C	D
55.	602 Yates Blvd.	A	B	C	D
56.	1944 St. James Rd.	A	B	C	D
57.	49 Bradford Court	A	B	C	D
58.	2 W. 61st St.	A	B	C	D
59.	1792 St. James Rd.	A	B	C	D
60.	25500 Route 5 North	A	B	C	D
61.	836 N. Yates Blvd.	A	B	C	D
62.	71 Bradford Court	A	B	C	D
63.	30020 Route 5 North	A	B	C	D
64.	46 Bradford Court	A	B	C	D

continued on next page

	Address	Delivery Code			
65.	1900 St. James Rd.	A	B	C	D
66.	50 W. 61st St.	A	B	C	D
67.	690 N. Yates Blvd.	A	B	C	D
68.	50002 Route 5 North	A	B	C	D
69.	11 Bradford Court	A	B	C	D
70.	40990 Route 5 North	A	B	C	D
71.	509 St. James Rd.	A	B	C	D
72.	30 Bradford Court	A	B	C	D

Part D: Personal Characteristics and Experience Inventory

Part D consists of a 236-item questionnaire (inventory) on your personal characteristics and experience. You have 90 minutes to complete Part D. This part is scored, but how it is scored is a Postal Service secret. There is no need to prepare for this part of the exam, and therefore it is not included in this practice test. (For more information about Part D, see Chapter 6.)

Practice Test 6 Answer Sheet

The answer sheet given here closely resembles that used on the actual Test 473.

On the front of the answer sheet, you will be asked to fill in personal information similar to the information that you gave when you applied to take the exam. Then you will find spaces—ovals lettered A, B, C, and D—where you are to fill in your answers to Part A, Address Checking, and Part B, Forms Completion, of the exam.

On the other side of the actual answer sheet, you will find similar lettered ovals for you to enter your answers to Part C, Coding and Memory, of the exam. On the answer sheet for Test 473, there will also be spaces for answers to Part D, Personal Characteristics and Experience Inventory, but we have not included that section in this practice exam.

Part A: Address Checking

1. Ⓐ Ⓑ Ⓒ Ⓓ
2. Ⓐ Ⓑ Ⓒ Ⓓ
3. Ⓐ Ⓑ Ⓒ Ⓓ
4. Ⓐ Ⓑ Ⓒ Ⓓ
5. Ⓐ Ⓑ Ⓒ Ⓓ
6. Ⓐ Ⓑ Ⓒ Ⓓ
7. Ⓐ Ⓑ Ⓒ Ⓓ
8. Ⓐ Ⓑ Ⓒ Ⓓ
9. Ⓐ Ⓑ Ⓒ Ⓓ
10. Ⓐ Ⓑ Ⓒ Ⓓ
11. Ⓐ Ⓑ Ⓒ Ⓓ
12. Ⓐ Ⓑ Ⓒ Ⓓ
13. Ⓐ Ⓑ Ⓒ Ⓓ
14. Ⓐ Ⓑ Ⓒ Ⓓ
15. Ⓐ Ⓑ Ⓒ Ⓓ
16. Ⓐ Ⓑ Ⓒ Ⓓ
17. Ⓐ Ⓑ Ⓒ Ⓓ
18. Ⓐ Ⓑ Ⓒ Ⓓ
19. Ⓐ Ⓑ Ⓒ Ⓓ
20. Ⓐ Ⓑ Ⓒ Ⓓ

21. Ⓐ Ⓑ Ⓒ Ⓓ
22. Ⓐ Ⓑ Ⓒ Ⓓ
23. Ⓐ Ⓑ Ⓒ Ⓓ
24. Ⓐ Ⓑ Ⓒ Ⓓ
25. Ⓐ Ⓑ Ⓒ Ⓓ
26. Ⓐ Ⓑ Ⓒ Ⓓ
27. Ⓐ Ⓑ Ⓒ Ⓓ
28. Ⓐ Ⓑ Ⓒ Ⓓ
28. Ⓐ Ⓑ Ⓒ Ⓓ
30. Ⓐ Ⓑ Ⓒ Ⓓ
31. Ⓐ Ⓑ Ⓒ Ⓓ
32. Ⓐ Ⓑ Ⓒ Ⓓ
33. Ⓐ Ⓑ Ⓒ Ⓓ
34. Ⓐ Ⓑ Ⓒ Ⓓ
35. Ⓐ Ⓑ Ⓒ Ⓓ
36. Ⓐ Ⓑ Ⓒ Ⓓ
37. Ⓐ Ⓑ Ⓒ Ⓓ
38. Ⓐ Ⓑ Ⓒ Ⓓ
39. Ⓐ Ⓑ Ⓒ Ⓓ
40. Ⓐ Ⓑ Ⓒ Ⓓ

41. Ⓐ Ⓑ Ⓒ Ⓓ
42. Ⓐ Ⓑ Ⓒ Ⓓ
43. Ⓐ Ⓑ Ⓒ Ⓓ
44. Ⓐ Ⓑ Ⓒ Ⓓ
45. Ⓐ Ⓑ Ⓒ Ⓓ
46. Ⓐ Ⓑ Ⓒ Ⓓ
47. Ⓐ Ⓑ Ⓒ Ⓓ
48. Ⓐ Ⓑ Ⓒ Ⓓ
49. Ⓐ Ⓑ Ⓒ Ⓓ
50. Ⓐ Ⓑ Ⓒ Ⓓ
51. Ⓐ Ⓑ Ⓒ Ⓓ
52. Ⓐ Ⓑ Ⓒ Ⓓ
53. Ⓐ Ⓑ Ⓒ Ⓓ
54. Ⓐ Ⓑ Ⓒ Ⓓ
55. Ⓐ Ⓑ Ⓒ Ⓓ
56. Ⓐ Ⓑ Ⓒ Ⓓ
57. Ⓐ Ⓑ Ⓒ Ⓓ
58. Ⓐ Ⓑ Ⓒ Ⓓ
59. Ⓐ Ⓑ Ⓒ Ⓓ
60. Ⓐ Ⓑ Ⓒ Ⓓ

Part B: Forms Completion

1. Ⓐ Ⓑ Ⓒ Ⓓ
2. Ⓐ Ⓑ Ⓒ Ⓓ
3. Ⓐ Ⓑ Ⓒ Ⓓ
4. Ⓐ Ⓑ Ⓒ Ⓓ
5. Ⓐ Ⓑ Ⓒ Ⓓ
6. Ⓐ Ⓑ Ⓒ Ⓓ
7. Ⓐ Ⓑ Ⓒ Ⓓ
8. Ⓐ Ⓑ Ⓒ Ⓓ
9. Ⓐ Ⓑ Ⓒ Ⓓ
10. Ⓐ Ⓑ Ⓒ Ⓓ

11. Ⓐ Ⓑ Ⓒ Ⓓ
12. Ⓐ Ⓑ Ⓒ Ⓓ
13. Ⓐ Ⓑ Ⓒ Ⓓ
14. Ⓐ Ⓑ Ⓒ Ⓓ
15. Ⓐ Ⓑ Ⓒ Ⓓ
16. Ⓐ Ⓑ Ⓒ Ⓓ
17. Ⓐ Ⓑ Ⓒ Ⓓ
18. Ⓐ Ⓑ Ⓒ Ⓓ
19. Ⓐ Ⓑ Ⓒ Ⓓ
20. Ⓐ Ⓑ Ⓒ Ⓓ

21. Ⓐ Ⓑ Ⓒ Ⓓ
22. Ⓐ Ⓑ Ⓒ Ⓓ
23. Ⓐ Ⓑ Ⓒ Ⓓ
24. Ⓐ Ⓑ Ⓒ Ⓓ
25. Ⓐ Ⓑ Ⓒ Ⓓ
26. Ⓐ Ⓑ Ⓒ Ⓓ
27. Ⓐ Ⓑ Ⓒ Ⓓ
28. Ⓐ Ⓑ Ⓒ Ⓓ
29. Ⓐ Ⓑ Ⓒ Ⓓ
30. Ⓐ Ⓑ Ⓒ Ⓓ

Part C: Coding and Memory

1. Ⓐ Ⓑ Ⓒ Ⓓ	25. Ⓐ Ⓑ Ⓒ Ⓓ	49. Ⓐ Ⓑ Ⓒ Ⓓ	
2. Ⓐ Ⓑ Ⓒ Ⓓ	26. Ⓐ Ⓑ Ⓒ Ⓓ	50. Ⓐ Ⓑ Ⓒ Ⓓ	
3. Ⓐ Ⓑ Ⓒ Ⓓ	27. Ⓐ Ⓑ Ⓒ Ⓓ	51. Ⓐ Ⓑ Ⓒ Ⓓ	
4. Ⓐ Ⓑ Ⓒ Ⓓ	28. Ⓐ Ⓑ Ⓒ Ⓓ	52. Ⓐ Ⓑ Ⓒ Ⓓ	
5. Ⓐ Ⓑ Ⓒ Ⓓ	29. Ⓐ Ⓑ Ⓒ Ⓓ	53. Ⓐ Ⓑ Ⓒ Ⓓ	
6. Ⓐ Ⓑ Ⓒ Ⓓ	30. Ⓐ Ⓑ Ⓒ Ⓓ	54. Ⓐ Ⓑ Ⓒ Ⓓ	
7. Ⓐ Ⓑ Ⓒ Ⓓ	31. Ⓐ Ⓑ Ⓒ Ⓓ	55. Ⓐ Ⓑ Ⓒ Ⓓ	
8. Ⓐ Ⓑ Ⓒ Ⓓ	32. Ⓐ Ⓑ Ⓒ Ⓓ	56. Ⓐ Ⓑ Ⓒ Ⓓ	
9. Ⓐ Ⓑ Ⓒ Ⓓ	33. Ⓐ Ⓑ Ⓒ Ⓓ	57. Ⓐ Ⓑ Ⓒ Ⓓ	
10. Ⓐ Ⓑ Ⓒ Ⓓ	34. Ⓐ Ⓑ Ⓒ Ⓓ	58. Ⓐ Ⓑ Ⓒ Ⓓ	
11. Ⓐ Ⓑ Ⓒ Ⓓ	35. Ⓐ Ⓑ Ⓒ Ⓓ	59. Ⓐ Ⓑ Ⓒ Ⓓ	
12. Ⓐ Ⓑ Ⓒ Ⓓ	36. Ⓐ Ⓑ Ⓒ Ⓓ	60. Ⓐ Ⓑ Ⓒ Ⓓ	
13. Ⓐ Ⓑ Ⓒ Ⓓ	37. Ⓐ Ⓑ Ⓒ Ⓓ	61. Ⓐ Ⓑ Ⓒ Ⓓ	
14. Ⓐ Ⓑ Ⓒ Ⓓ	38. Ⓐ Ⓑ Ⓒ Ⓓ	62. Ⓐ Ⓑ Ⓒ Ⓓ	
15. Ⓐ Ⓑ Ⓒ Ⓓ	39. Ⓐ Ⓑ Ⓒ Ⓓ	63. Ⓐ Ⓑ Ⓒ Ⓓ	
16. Ⓐ Ⓑ Ⓒ Ⓓ	40. Ⓐ Ⓑ Ⓒ Ⓓ	64. Ⓐ Ⓑ Ⓒ Ⓓ	
17. Ⓐ Ⓑ Ⓒ Ⓓ	41. Ⓐ Ⓑ Ⓒ Ⓓ	65. Ⓐ Ⓑ Ⓒ Ⓓ	
18. Ⓐ Ⓑ Ⓒ Ⓓ	42. Ⓐ Ⓑ Ⓒ Ⓓ	66. Ⓐ Ⓑ Ⓒ Ⓓ	
19. Ⓐ Ⓑ Ⓒ Ⓓ	43. Ⓐ Ⓑ Ⓒ Ⓓ	67. Ⓐ Ⓑ Ⓒ Ⓓ	
20. Ⓐ Ⓑ Ⓒ Ⓓ	44. Ⓐ Ⓑ Ⓒ Ⓓ	68. Ⓐ Ⓑ Ⓒ Ⓓ	
21. Ⓐ Ⓑ Ⓒ Ⓓ	45. Ⓐ Ⓑ Ⓒ Ⓓ	69. Ⓐ Ⓑ Ⓒ Ⓓ	
22. Ⓐ Ⓑ Ⓒ Ⓓ	46. Ⓐ Ⓑ Ⓒ Ⓓ	70. Ⓐ Ⓑ Ⓒ Ⓓ	
23. Ⓐ Ⓑ Ⓒ Ⓓ	47. Ⓐ Ⓑ Ⓒ Ⓓ	71. Ⓐ Ⓑ Ⓒ Ⓓ	
24. Ⓐ Ⓑ Ⓒ Ⓓ	48. Ⓐ Ⓑ Ⓒ Ⓓ	72. Ⓐ Ⓑ Ⓒ Ⓓ	

Part D: Personal Characteristics and Experience Inventory

On the actual exam, there would be spaces for the answers to 236 questions here, but we are not including this section in the practice exams or answer sheets.

Answer Key

Part A: Address Checking

1. C	13. A	25. C	37. A	49. D
2. B	14. B	26. D	38. B	50. D
3. D	15. D	27. B	39. B	51. C
4. B	16. C	28. C	40. C	52. B
5. C	17. A	29. D	41. A	53. A
6. D	18. B	30. B	42. B	54. B
7. B	19. B	31. C	43. D	55. D
8. C	20. C	32. B	44. B	56. C
9. D	21. A	33. A	45. C	57. A
10. B	22. B	34. B	46. D	58. B
11. C	23. D	35. D	47. B	59. B
12. B	24. C	36. C	48. C	60. C

Part B: Forms Completion

1. C	7. C	13. D	19. A	25. B
2. A	8. D	14. C	20. A	26. D
3. C	9. B	15. D	21. D	27. B
4. D	10. B	16. A	22. D	28. A
5. D	11. A	17. B	23. C	29. C
6. B	12. C	18. C	24. C	30. D

Part C: Coding and Memory

1. D	16. C	31. D	46. D	61. C
2. C	17. D	32. A	47. D	62. D
3. A	18. A	33. D	48. B	63. A
4. C	19. D	34. A	49. B	64. B
5. D	20. C	35. D	50. D	65. B
6. A	21. C	36. A	51. D	66. C
7. D	22. B	37. A	52. A	67. C
8. C	23. D	38. C	53. B	68. C
9. B	24. B	39. D	54. A	69. A
10. A	25. C	40. C	55. D	70. C
11. C	26. A	41. C	56. B	71. D
12. B	27. D	42. A	57. B	72. A
13. D	28. B	43. C	58. C	
14. C	29. C	44. C	59. B	
15. B	30. A	45. A	60. A	

Practice Test 7

Part A: Address Checking

Directions: Part A of this test consists of 60 items for you to complete in 11 minutes. You will be shown a **Correct List** of addresses and ZIP codes alongside a **List to Be Checked**. The two lists should contain the same addresses and ZIP codes, except that the **List to Be Checked** may contain errors.

Each row of information consists of one item. For each item, compare the address and ZIP code in the **Correct List** with the address and ZIP code in the **List to Be Checked**. Determine whether there are **No Errors**, an error in **Address Only**, an error in **ZIP Code Only**, or an error in **Both** the address and the ZIP code. Select an answer from the following four choices:

A. No Errors	B. Address Only	C. ZIP Code Only	D. Both

Mark your answers (A, B, C, or D) on the answer sheet at the end of the chapter.

An answer key is given at the end of this chapter.

Number of Items: 60

Time: 11 minutes

A. No Errors	B. Address Only	C. ZIP Code Only	D. Both

	Correct List		**List to Be Checked**	
	Address	*ZIP Code*	*Address*	*ZIP Code*
1.	2943 Cambridge Dr. West York, PA	17404	2943 Cambridge Dr. New York, PA	17404
2.	1321 23rd St. SE Beaumont, TX	77705	1321 22rd St. SE Beaumont, TX	77005
3.	46 Prince St. Oklahoma City, OK	73142-2756	36 Prince St. Oklahoma City, OK	73142-2756
4.	39 Upper Falls Trail Hattiesburg, MS	39401-4492	39 Upper Falls Trail Hattiesburg, MS	39401-4492
5.	76 Babson Circle Terre Haute, IN	47804	76 Babson Circle Terra Haute, IN	47844
6.	577 Monroe Baltimore, MD	21218-1327	577 Monroe St. Baltimore, MD	21218-1327
7.	20 Rochelle Ter. Bozeman, MT	59715-8463	20 Rochelle Ter. Bozeman, MT	59715-8364
8.	1834 Stone Pl. Boles, AR	72926	1834 Stone Pl. Bales, AR	72629
9.	19010 Front Street Cumberland, KY	40823-8937	19010 First Street Cumberland, KY	40823-8937
10.	9 W. Lenski Court Flint, MI	48503	9 W. Lenski Court Flint, MI	45803
11.	PO Box 96837 Youngstown, OH	44510-6837	PO Box 96837 Youngtown, OH	44510-6837
12.	1710 Hayes St. Clarksville, TN	37042-6571	1710 Hayes St. Clarksville, TN	37042-5771
13.	610 Gallagher Rd. Stockton, CA	95206	610 Gallagher Road Stockton, CA	85206
14.	25 Lindsley Dr. Portland, OR	97209	25 Lindsey Dr. Portland, OR	97290
15.	1911 Sanger Ave. Lawrence, KS	66049	1911 Sanger Ave. Lawrence, KS	64069

continued on next page

A. No Errors	B. Address Only	C. ZIP Code Only	D. Both

	Correct List		List to Be Checked	
	Address	*ZIP Code*	*Address*	*ZIP Code*
16.	55 Rockford St. Birmingham, AL	35204-9034	55 Rockford St. Birmingham, AL	35204-9034
17.	2480 3rd Ave., Ste. A Washington, DC	20017-7621	2480 3d Ave., Ste. A Washington, DC	20017-7621
18.	2072 Opal St. Naples, FL	33961	2027 Opal St. Naples, FL	33961
19.	4782 Citrus Ln. #6 Valley City, ND	58072-4581	4782 Citrus Ln. #6 Valley City, ND	58072-4481
20.	1939 Ozark Dr. Independence, MO	64053-3488	1939 Ozark Dr. Independence, MO	64053-3488
21.	9037 Industry Loop Tempe, AZ	85282	9037 Industry Loop Tempe, AZ	88252
22.	P.O. Box 4245 Columbus, OH	43203	P.O. Box 4245 Columbus, OK	42203
23.	1006 Dwight Ct. Bedford, WY	83112-3428	1006 Dwight Ct. Medford, WY	83112-3428
24.	271 S. Orange Ave. Amarillo, TX	79111	271 S. Orange Ave. Amarillo, TX	79111
25.	1113 E. Franklin Indianapolis, IN	46218	1113 S. Franklin Indianapolis, IN	46228
26.	1205 Wheaton Terrace Champaign, IL	61821-8752	1205 Wheaten Terrace Champaign, IL	61821-8752
27.	5915 Forest Ln. Concord, CA	94520-0022	5915 Forest Ln. Concord, CA	94520-0222
28.	1060 Rainbow Road Albuquerque, NM	87107-7882	1060 Rainbow Road Alberqueque, NM	87107-7822
29.	14 Tuscany Circle Johnstown, PA	15902	14 Tuscany Circle Johnston, PA	15902
30.	10300 Gulf St. Apt. A Albertville, AL	35950	10300 Gulf St. Apt. A Albertville, AL	36950
31.	3190 Midstate Hwy. South Bend, IN	46617-1589	3190 Midstate Pkwy. South Bend, IN	46617-1589
32.	3925 Cascade Rd. Vancouver, WA	98661	3925 Cascade Rd. Vancouver, WA	98611

continued on next page

A. No Errors	B. Address Only	C. ZIP Code Only	D. Both

	Correct List		List to Be Checked	
	Address	ZIP Code	Address	ZIP Code
33.	540 W. Prince Rd. Norwich, KS	67118-7651	540 W. Prince Rd. Norwalk, KS	67118-7651
34.	9941 Huron Ln. Warren, MI	48092	9441 Huron Ln. Warren, MI	40292
35.	1941 Broadway Raleigh, NC	27604	1941 Broadway Raleigh, NC	27602
36.	755 Vera Terrace #1 West Orange, NJ	07052-1698	755 Vera Terrace #1 West Orange, NJ	07052-1698
37.	1140 W. Mill Road Cutler, ME	04626-9523	1140 W. Mile Road Cutler, ME	04626-9523
38.	6000 S. Rose Avenue Hyde Park, NY	12538	600 S. Rose Avenue Hyde Park, NY	12588
39.	3320 W. McGraw St. Huntington Beach, CA	92648	3320 W. McGraw St. Huntington Beach, CA	49268
40.	8424 Ruffin Rd. Jackson, MS	39206	8424 Ruffin Rd. Jackson, MS	39206
41.	2307 45th St. Shreveport, LA	71104-8115	2307 54th St. Shreveport, LA	71104-8115
42.	103 Faulkner Avenue Russell, MN	56169-9977	103 Faulkner Avenue Roswell, NM	56196-9977
43.	2005 James Blvd. Charlotte, NC	28205-4528	205 James Blvd. Charlotte, NC	28205-4528
44.	1003 S. Range Street Aberdeen, SD	57401	1003 S. Range Street Aberdeen, SD	57401
45.	P.O. Box 862 New York, NY	10040-0862	P.O. Box 862 New York, NY	10044-0862
46.	1310 San Fernando Rd. Long Beach, CA	90805	1310 San Fernando Blvd. Long Beach, CA	90805
47.	28303 Winkler Avenue Hamilton, CO	81638-1173	28303 Winkler Avenue Hamilton, CO	81638-7173
48.	4203 S. Biscuit Blvd. Cedar Rapids, IA	52404-9178	4203 E. Biscuit Blvd. Cedar Rapids, IA	52404-1978
49.	2184 Sunny Shores Pensacola, FL	32506	2184 Sunny Shores Pensecola, FL	32506

continued on next page

A. No Errors	B. Address Only	C. ZIP Code Only	D. Both

Correct List

	Address	ZIP Code
50.	445 Research Park Albuquerque, NM	87108
51.	773 West 15th Street Chattanooga, TN	37406-1974
52.	1001 Hoover Pkwy. Reno, NV	89512-8583
53.	55 Fairway Drive Norfolk, VA	23513
54.	PO Box 2883 Springfield, IL	62701
55.	3385 E. Baker Avenue Lyons, NE	68038-1467
56.	6165 Forest View Chesapeake, OH	45619
57.	1250 Campus Road Camden, NJ	08103-6629
58.	201 A Street Lexington, KY	40507
59.	300 Roberts Ave. NE Seattle, WA	98117
60.	2480 Rock Creek Blvd. Chapel Hill, NC	27516-4992

List to Be Checked

Address	ZIP Code
445 Research Park Albuquerque, NM	87801
773 West 15th Street Chatanooga, TN	37406-1974
1001 Hoover Pkwy. Reno, NV	89502-8583
55 Fareway Drive Norfolk, VA	23513
PO Box 2888 Springfield, IL	67201
3385 E. Baker Avenue Lyons, NE	68038-1476
6165 Forest View Chesapeake, OH	45619
1250 Campus Drive Camden, NJ	08103-6629
201 A Street Lexington, KY	40507
300 Roberts Ave. NE Seattle, WA	91187
2480 Rock Creek Blvd. Chapel Hill, NC	27516-4992

Part B: Forms Completion

Directions: Part B of this test consists of 30 questions for you to complete in 15 minutes. You will be shown a series of forms that are similar to ones used by the U.S. Postal Service. The parts of each form are labeled (for example, 3 and 4a). Each form is accompanied by several questions that test your ability to complete the form properly. For each question, choose the best answer and mark your selection (A, B, C, or D) on your answer sheet.

Go to the next page when you are ready to begin Part B under timed conditions.

An answer key is given at the end of this chapter.

Number of Questions: 30

Time: 15 minutes

Insured Mail Receipt		
1a. Name	5. ☐ Fragile ☐ Perishable ☐ Liquid	
1b. Street, Apt., or PO Box No.		
1c. City, State, ZIP + 4, Country	6. Insurance Coverage $	
Postage	2. $	
Insurance Fee	3a. $	Postmark Here
Special Handling Fee (Endorsement Required)	3b. $	
Return Receipt Fee (Except for Canada)	3c. $	
Total Postage and Fees	4. $	

1. Which of these would be a correct entry for Box 1b?

   (A) A check mark

   (B) "PO Box 3427"

   (C) "U.S.A."

   (D) "Robert Trudeau"

2. Where is the return receipt fee entered on this form?

   (A) Box 4

   (B) Box 3a

   (C) Box 2

   (D) Box 3c

3. For which of these would it be correct to enter a check mark in Box 5?

   (A) The article requires a return receipt

   (B) The article is liquid

   (C) Insurance coverage is provided

   (D) The article cannot be mailed

4. The item is mailed to Canada. Each of these could be a correct entry EXCEPT which?

   (A) An entry in Box 3c

   (B) An entry in Box 3b

   (C) A check mark in Box 5

   (D) An entry in Box 1c

5. Which of these is a correct entry for Box 6?

   (A) "44129-0125"

   (B) "Paid in full"

   (C) "475.00"

   (D) "Fragile"

6. The postage is $1.27. Where would you enter this on the form?

   (A) Box 1b

   (B) Box 4

   (C) Box 3a

   (D) Box 2

Postage Statement – Priority Mail

1. Permit Holder	2. Mailing Agent (if different from permit holder)
1a. Name:	2a. Name:
1b. Address:	2b. Address:
1c. Telephone Number:	2c. Telephone Number:
3a. Mailing Date:	USPS Use Only
3b. Post Office of Mailing:	

		lb.	oz.
6a. Weight (Single Piece)		lb.	oz.
6b. Number of Pieces			
6c. Total Weight		lb.	oz.
6d. Total Postage			

4. Processing Type
☐ Letters
☐ Parcels
☐ Flats
☐ Other: _____

5. Permit Number

7a. Employee's Name (Print)

7b. Employee's Signature

7c. Date Mailer Notified

7. Where should the mailing agent's name be entered on this form?

(A) Line 1a

(B) Line 7a

(C) Line 2a

(D) Line 7b

8. Which of these would be a correct entry in Line 7a?

(A) "3 lb. 4 oz."

(B) A check mark

(C) "28"

(D) "David Stover"

9. Where would you indicate the post office of mailing?

(A) Line 7c

(B) Line 3b

(C) Line 7a

(D) Line 2b

10. The permit holder's telephone number is (212) 555-4421. Where would you indicate this?

(A) Line 1c

(B) Line 3a

(C) Line 3b

(D) Line 2c

11. Which of these would be a correct entry for Box 5?

(A) "Jennifer Warner"

(B) "88-902"

(C) "07/19/08"

(D) A check mark

12. The weight of a single piece is 2 lb. 6 oz. How would you indicate this?

(A) Enter "2" and "6" in Line 6c

(B) Enter "2 lb. 6 oz." in Line 6b

(C) Enter "2" and "6" in Line 6a

(D) Enter "2 lb. 6 oz." in Line 6d

13. Where would you indicate the number of pieces mailed?

(A) Box 5

(B) Line 6a

(C) Box 4

(D) Line 6b

Return Receipt (Domestic)

SENDER: COMPLETE THIS SECTION

1. Article Sent To:

2. Type of Service
   - [ ] Certified Mail   [ ] Insured Mail
   - [ ] Registered Mail   [ ] COD
   - [ ] Express Mail

3. Article Number:

4. Check here if delivery is restricted: [ ] (extra fee)

COMPLETE THIS SECTION ON DELIVERY

5. Received By (Print Name)

6. Delivery Date

7. Delivered To (check one)
   - [ ] Address shown in Item No. 1
   - [ ] Other (enter address):

8. Signature
   - [ ] Addressee
   - [ ] Other

14. The item was sent to Janice Avery. Where would this be indicated?

    (A) Box 8

    (B) Box 6

    (C) Line 1

    (D) Box 3

15. Which of these would be a correct entry in Box 7?

    (A) An address

    (B) A date

    (C) A name

    (D) A dollar amount

16. A person other than the addressee received the article of mail. Where would this fact be indicated?

    (A) Box 5 only

    (B) Box 8 only

    (C) Box 7 only

    (D) Box 5 and Box 8

17. Which of these would be a correct entry in Box 4?

    (A) "11/16/07"

    (B) A check mark

    (C) "$3.40"

    (D) "Restricted"

18. All of these are appropriate entries in Box 1 EXCEPT which?

    (A) "Pittsburg, PA"

    (B) "PO Box 38892"

    (C) "(707) 555-4471"

    D) "Jeff Friedman"

19. In which of these boxes would a number be a correct entry?

    (A) Box 8

    (B) Line 3

    (C) Box 4

    (D) Box 2

Receipt for Registered Mail		
TO BE COMPLETED BY CUSTOMER		
1. Sender	2. Addressee	
3. Full Value of Articles (Required): $		
TO BE COMPLETED BY POST OFFICE		
4. Reg. Fee	6. Postage	8. Postal Insurance ☐ Yes ☐ No
5. Handling Fee	7. Return Receipt	9. Total Fee, Postage, and Charges
10. Received By:		11. Date Received

20. In which of these boxes should the customer enter information?

    (A) Box 7

    (B) Box 3

    (C) Box 6

    (D) Box 4

21. In which box would "05/08/07" be a correct entry?

    (A) Box 2

    (B) Box 4

    (C) Box 11

    (D) Box 7

22. Which of these is a correct entry for Box 7?

    (A) A check mark

    (B) "N/A"

    (C) "$1.85"

    (D) "11:20 A.M."

23. In which box would a dollar amount be an appropriate entry?

    (A) Box 10

    (B) Box 8

    (C) Box 1

    (D) Box 5

24. Whose name should be entered in Box 10?

    (A) The sender's

    (B) The mail recipient's

    (C) The mail carrier's

    (D) None of the above

25. The customer pays a handling fee of $5.50. How would you indicate this?

    (A) Enter "$5.50" in Box 5

    (B) Enter "$5.50" in Box 4

    (C) Enter a check mark in Box 8

    (D) Enter "Yes" in Box 5

SIGNATURE CONFIRMATION RECEIPT	**Signature Confirmation and Receipt**	
	TO BE COMPLETED BY SENDER	POST OFFICE USE ONLY
	1a. Sent To (Name): _____ 1b. Address: _____ _____	2a. Check One: ☐ Priority ☐ Package Service 2b. Waiver of Signature? ☐ Yes ☐ No 2c. Postmark Here
	Signature Confirmation Number 4258 0092 1773 8108	

SIGNATURE CONFIRMATION	3. WAIVER OF SIGNATURE. I authorize that the postal delivery employee's signature suffices as proof of delivery if the item is left in a secure location.	
	4. Customer Signature	Signature Confirmation Number 4258 0092 1173 8108

26. Where would you indicate that the sender waives a signature upon delivery?

   (A) Line 2d

   (B) Line 2b

   (C) Line 2a

   (D) Line 2c

27. Which of these would be a correct type of entry in Line 4?

   (A) The delivery address

   (B) The signature confirmation number

   (C) The customer's name

   (D) A check mark

28. It would be appropriate for the sender to make an entry in each line EXCEPT which?

   (A) Line 2b

   (B) Line 3

   (C) Line 4

   (D) Line 1a

29. A check mark is used in each of these EXCEPT which?

   (A) Waiver of signature

   (B) Package service

   (C) Priority mail

   (D) Express mail

30. All of these are appropriate entries in Line 1b EXCEPT which?

   (A) "73002-0112"

   (B) "PO Box 99"

   (C) "Watertown, NY"

   (D) "(652) 555-0093"

Part C: Coding and Memory

Part C of this test consists of two sections:

- A **Coding Section**, which consists of 36 questions to be completed in 6 minutes
- A **Memory Section**, which consists of 36 questions to be completed in 7 minutes

Both sections test your ability to match one-letter codes to addresses quickly and accurately. The Memory Section also tests your ability to memorize codes and their matching address ranges.

You will use the same **Coding Guide** for both sections of Part C. The first column of the **Coding Guide** shows each **address range**. The second column shows the **delivery route** code (A, B, C, or D) for the address ranges shown in the same row as the code. You may assume that each address range runs continuously (no numbers are skipped) from the lowest to the highest number in the range. Some of the street names appear twice, showing two different address ranges.

Coding Section

This section consists of three segments:

- **Segment 1** is an introductory exercise consisting of 4 items to be completed in 2 minutes. *Segment 1 is not scored.*
- **Segment 2** is a practice exercise consisting of 8 items to be completed in 1 1/2 minutes (90 seconds). *Segment 2 is not scored.*
- **Segment 3** is the actual Coding Section of the test. This segment consists of 36 items to be completed in 6 minutes. *Segment 3 is scored and counts toward your total test score.*

You will use the same Coding Guide for all three segments.

Coding Section—Segment 1

Directions: Segment 1 is an introductory exercise that will familiarize you with the Coding Section and help you learn how to complete it. This segment is *not* scored. Based on the Coding Guide, match each address to a delivery route. Mark your answers on the answer grid at the bottom of this page.

Number of Items: 4

Time Limit: 2 minutes

Coding Guide	
Address Range	*Delivery Route*
1000–1900 Oswego Drive 250–275 Stanley Ave. SW 5–20 Dover Terrace	A
276–300 Stanley Ave. SW 1901–2000 Oswego Drive	B
15000–20000 Alamo Lane 21–40 Dover Terrace 800–1200 Sinclair Towers	C
All mail that does not fall in one of the address ranges listed above	D

	Address	Delivery Code			
1.	17200 Alamo Lane	A	B	C	D
2.	1150 Oswego Drive	A	B	C	D
3.	297 Stanley Ave. SW	A	B	C	D
4.	1459 Sinclair Towers	A	B	C	D

Sample Answer Sheet

1. Ⓐ Ⓑ Ⓒ Ⓓ   3. Ⓐ Ⓑ Ⓒ Ⓓ
2. Ⓐ Ⓑ Ⓒ Ⓓ   4. Ⓐ Ⓑ Ⓒ Ⓓ

Coding Section—Segment 2

Directions: Segment 2 is *not* scored. It is a practice exercise that will give you experience with the Coding Section under a time constraint similar to the one during the scored Coding Section. Based on the Coding Guide, match each address to a delivery route. Mark your answers on the answer grid at the bottom of this page.

Number of Items: 8

Time Limit: 1 1/2 minutes (90 seconds)

Coding Guide	
Address Range	*Delivery Route*
1000–1900 Oswego Drive 250–275 Stanley Ave. SW 5–20 Dover Terrace	A
276–300 Stanley Ave. SW 1901–2000 Oswego Drive	B
15000–20000 Alamo Lane 21–40 Dover Terrace 800–1200 Sinclair Towers	C
All mail that does not fall in one of the address ranges listed above	D

	Address	Delivery Code			
1.	253 Stanley Rd.	A	B	C	D
2.	20 Dover Terrace	A	B	C	D
3.	193 Oswego Drive	A	B	C	D
4.	15303 Alamo Lane	A	B	C	D
5.	780 Sinclair Towers	A	B	C	D
6.	1437 Oswego Drive	A	B	C	D
7.	21 Dover Terrace	A	B	C	D
8.	271 Stanley Ave. SW	A	B	C	D

Sample Answer Sheet

1. Ⓐ Ⓑ Ⓒ Ⓓ   4. Ⓐ Ⓑ Ⓒ Ⓓ   7. Ⓐ Ⓑ Ⓒ Ⓓ
2. Ⓐ Ⓑ Ⓒ Ⓓ   5. Ⓐ Ⓑ Ⓒ Ⓓ   8. Ⓐ Ⓑ Ⓒ Ⓓ
3. Ⓐ Ⓑ Ⓒ Ⓓ   6. Ⓐ Ⓑ Ⓒ Ⓓ

Coding Section—Segment 3

Directions: Segment 3 is the *actual scored* Coding Section of the test. Based on the Coding Guide, match each address to a delivery route. Mark your answer on the answer sheet at the end of the chapter.

An answer key for this segment is given at the end of the chapter.

Number of Items: 36

Time Limit: 6 minutes

Coding Guide	
Address Range	*Delivery Route*
1000–1900 Oswego Drive 250–275 Stanley Ave. SW 5–20 Dover Terrace	A
276–300 Stanley Ave. SW 1901–2000 Oswego Drive	B
15000–20000 Alamo Lane 21–40 Dover Terrace 800–1200 Sinclair Towers	C
All mail that does not fall in one of the address ranges listed above	D

	Address		Delivery Code			
1.	839 Sinclair Towers		A	B	C	D
2.	291 Stanley Ave. SW		A	B	C	D
3.	17 Dover Terrace		A	B	C	D
4.	2105 Oswego Drive		A	B	C	D
5.	16100 Alamo Lane		A	B	C	D
6.	1090 Sinclair Towers		A	B	C	D
7.	267 Stanley Ave. SW		A	B	C	D
8.	2 Dover Terrace		A	B	C	D
9.	1901 Oswego Drive		A	B	C	D
10.	1112 Sinclair Towers		A	B	C	D
11.	13 Dover Terrace		A	B	C	D
12.	17330 Alamo Lane		A	B	C	D
13.	987 Suncrest Tower		A	B	C	D
14.	1984 Oswego Drive		A	B	C	D
15.	275 Stanley Ave. SW		A	B	C	D
16.	907 Sinclair Towers		A	B	C	D
17.	18350 Alamo Court		A	B	C	D
18.	1709 Oswego Drive		A	B	C	D
19.	39 Dover Terrace		A	B	C	D
20.	825 Sinclair Towers		A	B	C	D
21.	269 Stanley Ave. SW		A	B	C	D
22.	1530 Oswego Blvd.		A	B	C	D
23.	8 Dover Terrace		A	B	C	D
24.	300 Stanley Ave. SW		A	B	C	D
25.	18902 Alamo Lane		A	B	C	D
26.	1890 Oshkosh Drive		A	B	C	D
27.	278 Stanley Ave. SW		A	B	C	D
28.	50 Dover Terrace		A	B	C	D
29.	276 Stanley Ave. SW		A	B	C	D
30.	1004 Sinclair Terrace		A	B	C	D
31.	28 Dover Terrace		A	B	C	D
32.	805 Oswego Drive		A	B	C	D
33.	19478 Alamo Lane		A	B	C	D
34.	1929 Oswego Drive		A	B	C	D
35.	11 Dover Terrace		A	B	C	D
36.	1850 Alamo Lane		A	B	C	D

Memory Section

This section consists of four segments:

- **Segment 1** is a 3-minute study period during which you will attempt to memorize the Coding Guide. *Segment 1 is not scored*, and there are no answers to mark during this segment.
- **Segment 2** is a practice exercise consisting of 8 items to be completed in 1 1/2 minutes (90 seconds). *Segment 2 is not scored*.
- **Segment 3** is a 5-minute study period during which you will attempt to memorize the Coding Guide. *Segment 3 is not scored*, and there are no answers to mark during this segment.
- **Segment 4** is the actual Memory Section of the test. This segment consists of 36 items to be completed in 7 minutes. *Segment 4 is scored and counts toward your total test score*.

You will use the same Coding Guide for all four segments.

Memory Section—Segment 1

Directions: Segment 1 is a 3-minute study period during which you will attempt to memorize the Coding Guide. This segment is *not* scored, and there are no answers to mark during this segment.

Begin the 3-minute study period when you are ready.

Coding Guide	
Address Range	*Delivery Route*
1000–1900 Oswego Drive 250–275 Stanley Ave. SW 5–20 Dover Terrace	A
276–300 Stanley Ave. SW 1901–2000 Oswego Drive	B
15000–20000 Alamo Lane 21–40 Dover Terrace 800–1200 Sinclair Towers	C
All mail that does not fall in one of the address ranges listed above	D

Memory Section—Segment 2

Directions: Segment 2 is a practice exercise that will give you experience coding addresses from memory based on the Coding Guide on the previous page. The Coding Guide is not shown during this segment. Based on the Coding Guide, match each address to a delivery route. Mark your answers on the answer grid at the bottom of this page. This segment is *not* scored.

Turn the page when you are ready to begin Segment 2 under timed conditions.

Number of Items: 8

Time Limit: 1 1/2 minutes (90 seconds)

	Address	Delivery Code			
1.	19990 Alamo Lane	A	B	C	D
2.	1845 Oswego Drive	A	B	C	D
3.	60 Stanley Ave. SW	A	B	C	D
4.	33 Dover Terrace	A	B	C	D
5.	21049 Alamo Lane	A	B	C	D
6.	1939 Oswego Drive	A	B	C	D
7.	255 Stanley Ave. SW	A	B	C	D
8.	289 Stanley Ave. SW	A	B	C	D

Sample Answer Sheet

1. Ⓐ Ⓑ Ⓒ Ⓓ   4. Ⓐ Ⓑ Ⓒ Ⓓ   7. Ⓐ Ⓑ Ⓒ Ⓓ
2. Ⓐ Ⓑ Ⓒ Ⓓ   5. Ⓐ Ⓑ Ⓒ Ⓓ   8. Ⓐ Ⓑ Ⓒ Ⓓ
3. Ⓐ Ⓑ Ⓒ Ⓓ   6. Ⓐ Ⓑ Ⓒ Ⓓ

Memory Section—Segment 3

Directions: Segment 3 is a 5-minute study period during which you will again attempt to memorize the Coding Guide. This segment is *not* scored, and there are no answers to mark during this segment.

Begin the 5-minute study period when you are ready.

<table>
<tr><th colspan="2">Coding Guide</th></tr>
<tr><th>Address Range</th><th>Delivery Route</th></tr>
<tr><td>1000–1900 Oswego Drive
250–275 Stanley Ave. SW
5–20 Dover Terrace</td><td>A</td></tr>
<tr><td>276–300 Stanley Ave. SW
1901–2000 Oswego Drive</td><td>B</td></tr>
<tr><td>15000–20000 Alamo Lane
21–40 Dover Terrace
800–1200 Sinclair Towers</td><td>C</td></tr>
<tr><td>All mail that does not fall in one
of the address ranges listed above</td><td>D</td></tr>
</table>

Memory Section—Segment 4

Directions: Segment 4 is the *actual scored* Memory Section of the test. The Coding Guide is not shown during this segment. Based on the Coding Guide, match each address to a delivery route. Mark your answers on the answer sheet at the end of the chapter.

Go to the next page when you are ready to begin Segment 4 under timed conditions.

An answer key for this segment is given at the end of the chapter.

Number of Items: 36

Time Limit: 7 minutes

	Address		Delivery Code			
37.	283 Stanley Ave. SW		A	B	C	D
38.	31 Dover Terrace		A	B	C	D
39.	1976 Oswego Drive		A	B	C	D
40.	1199 Sinclair Towers		A	B	C	D
41.	292 Stein Ave. SW		A	B	C	D
42.	5 Dover Terrace		A	B	C	D
43.	1958 Oswego Drive		A	B	C	D
44.	17001 Alamo Lane		A	B	C	D
45.	31 Dover Circle		A	B	C	D
46.	277 Stanley Ave. SW		A	B	C	D
47.	1360 Oswego Drive		A	B	C	D
48.	1200 Sinclair Towers		A	B	C	D
49.	12500 Alamo Lane		A	B	C	D
50.	19 Dover Terrace		A	B	C	D
51.	261 Stanley Ave. SW		A	B	C	D
52.	1950 Oswego Drive		A	B	C	D
53.	10 Dover Terrace		A	B	C	D
54.	15150 Alamo Lane		A	B	C	D
55.	964 Sinclair Towers		A	B	C	D
56.	1993 Oswego Drive		A	B	C	D
57.	25 Dover Terrace		A	B	C	D
58.	20000 Alamo Lane		A	B	C	D
59.	250 Stanley Ave. SW		A	B	C	D
60.	7 Clover Terrace		A	B	C	D
61.	258 Stanley Ave. SW		A	B	C	D
62.	40 Dover Terrace		A	B	C	D
63.	17130 Allen Lane		A	B	C	D
64.	1909 Oswego Drive		A	B	C	D

continued on next page

	Address		Delivery Code			
65.	3050 Stanley Ave. SW		A	B	C	D
66.	1001 Sinclair Towers	*C*	A	B	C	D
67.	1045 Oswego Drive	*A*	A	B	C	D
68.	227 Stanley Ave. SW		A	B	C	D
69.	14 Dover Terrace		A	B	C	D
70.	228 Sinclair Towers	*D*	A	B	C	D
71.	280 Stanley Ave. SW		A	B	C	D
72.	72 Dover Terrace		A	B	C	D

Part D: Personal Characteristics and Experience Inventory

Part D consists of a 236-item questionnaire (inventory) on your personal characteristics and experience. You have 90 minutes to complete Part D. This part is scored, but how it is scored is a Postal Service secret. There is no need to prepare for this part of the exam, and therefore it is not included in this practice test. (For more information about Part D, see Chapter 6.)

Practice Test 7 Answer Sheet

The answer sheet given here closely resembles that used on the actual Test 473.

On the front of the answer sheet, you will be asked to fill in personal information similar to the information that you gave when you applied to take the exam. Then you will find spaces—ovals lettered A, B, C, and D—where you are to fill in your answers to Part A, Address Checking, and Part B, Forms Completion, of the exam.

On the other side of the actual answer sheet, you will find similar lettered ovals for you to enter your answers to Part C, Coding and Memory, of the exam. On the answer sheet for Test 473, there will also be spaces for answers to Part D, Personal Characteristics and Experience Inventory, but we have not included that section in this practice exam.

Part A: Address Checking

1. Ⓐ Ⓑ Ⓒ Ⓓ
2. Ⓐ Ⓑ Ⓒ Ⓓ
3. Ⓐ Ⓑ Ⓒ Ⓓ
4. Ⓐ Ⓑ Ⓒ Ⓓ
5. Ⓐ Ⓑ Ⓒ Ⓓ
6. Ⓐ Ⓑ Ⓒ Ⓓ
7. Ⓐ Ⓑ Ⓒ Ⓓ
8. Ⓐ Ⓑ Ⓒ Ⓓ
9. Ⓐ Ⓑ Ⓒ Ⓓ
10. Ⓐ Ⓑ Ⓒ Ⓓ
11. Ⓐ Ⓑ Ⓒ Ⓓ
12. Ⓐ Ⓑ Ⓒ Ⓓ
13. Ⓐ Ⓑ Ⓒ Ⓓ
14. Ⓐ Ⓑ Ⓒ Ⓓ
15. Ⓐ Ⓑ Ⓒ Ⓓ
16. Ⓐ Ⓑ Ⓒ Ⓓ
17. Ⓐ Ⓑ Ⓒ Ⓓ
18. Ⓐ Ⓑ Ⓒ Ⓓ
19. Ⓐ Ⓑ Ⓒ Ⓓ
20. Ⓐ Ⓑ Ⓒ Ⓓ

21. Ⓐ Ⓑ Ⓒ Ⓓ
22. Ⓐ Ⓑ Ⓒ Ⓓ
23. Ⓐ Ⓑ Ⓒ Ⓓ
24. Ⓐ Ⓑ Ⓒ Ⓓ
25. Ⓐ Ⓑ Ⓒ Ⓓ
26. Ⓐ Ⓑ Ⓒ Ⓓ
27. Ⓐ Ⓑ Ⓒ Ⓓ
28. Ⓐ Ⓑ Ⓒ Ⓓ
28. Ⓐ Ⓑ Ⓒ Ⓓ
30. Ⓐ Ⓑ Ⓒ Ⓓ
31. Ⓐ Ⓑ Ⓒ Ⓓ
32. Ⓐ Ⓑ Ⓒ Ⓓ
33. Ⓐ Ⓑ Ⓒ Ⓓ
34. Ⓐ Ⓑ Ⓒ Ⓓ
35. Ⓐ Ⓑ Ⓒ Ⓓ
36. Ⓐ Ⓑ Ⓒ Ⓓ
37. Ⓐ Ⓑ Ⓒ Ⓓ
38. Ⓐ Ⓑ Ⓒ Ⓓ
39. Ⓐ Ⓑ Ⓒ Ⓓ
40. Ⓐ Ⓑ Ⓒ Ⓓ

41. Ⓐ Ⓑ Ⓒ Ⓓ
42. Ⓐ Ⓑ Ⓒ Ⓓ
43. Ⓐ Ⓑ Ⓒ Ⓓ
44. Ⓐ Ⓑ Ⓒ Ⓓ
45. Ⓐ Ⓑ Ⓒ Ⓓ
46. Ⓐ Ⓑ Ⓒ Ⓓ
47. Ⓐ Ⓑ Ⓒ Ⓓ
48. Ⓐ Ⓑ Ⓒ Ⓓ
49. Ⓐ Ⓑ Ⓒ Ⓓ
50. Ⓐ Ⓑ Ⓒ Ⓓ
51. Ⓐ Ⓑ Ⓒ Ⓓ
52. Ⓐ Ⓑ Ⓒ Ⓓ
53. Ⓐ Ⓑ Ⓒ Ⓓ
54. Ⓐ Ⓑ Ⓒ Ⓓ
55. Ⓐ Ⓑ Ⓒ Ⓓ
56. Ⓐ Ⓑ Ⓒ Ⓓ
57. Ⓐ Ⓑ Ⓒ Ⓓ
58. Ⓐ Ⓑ Ⓒ Ⓓ
59. Ⓐ Ⓑ Ⓒ Ⓓ
60. Ⓐ Ⓑ Ⓒ Ⓓ

Part B: Forms Completion

1. Ⓐ Ⓑ Ⓒ Ⓓ
2. Ⓐ Ⓑ Ⓒ Ⓓ
3. Ⓐ Ⓑ Ⓒ Ⓓ
4. Ⓐ Ⓑ Ⓒ Ⓓ
5. Ⓐ Ⓑ Ⓒ Ⓓ
6. Ⓐ Ⓑ Ⓒ Ⓓ
7. Ⓐ Ⓑ Ⓒ Ⓓ
8. Ⓐ Ⓑ Ⓒ Ⓓ
9. Ⓐ Ⓑ Ⓒ Ⓓ
10. Ⓐ Ⓑ Ⓒ Ⓓ

11. Ⓐ Ⓑ Ⓒ Ⓓ
12. Ⓐ Ⓑ Ⓒ Ⓓ
13. Ⓐ Ⓑ Ⓒ Ⓓ
14. Ⓐ Ⓑ Ⓒ Ⓓ
15. Ⓐ Ⓑ Ⓒ Ⓓ
16. Ⓐ Ⓑ Ⓒ Ⓓ
17. Ⓐ Ⓑ Ⓒ Ⓓ
18. Ⓐ Ⓑ Ⓒ Ⓓ
19. Ⓐ Ⓑ Ⓒ Ⓓ
20. Ⓐ Ⓑ Ⓒ Ⓓ

21. Ⓐ Ⓑ Ⓒ Ⓓ
22. Ⓐ Ⓑ Ⓒ Ⓓ
23. Ⓐ Ⓑ Ⓒ Ⓓ
24. Ⓐ Ⓑ Ⓒ Ⓓ
25. Ⓐ Ⓑ Ⓒ Ⓓ
26. Ⓐ Ⓑ Ⓒ Ⓓ
27. Ⓐ Ⓑ Ⓒ Ⓓ
28. Ⓐ Ⓑ Ⓒ Ⓓ
29. Ⓐ Ⓑ Ⓒ Ⓓ
30. Ⓐ Ⓑ Ⓒ Ⓓ

Part C: Coding and Memory

1. Ⓐ Ⓑ Ⓒ Ⓓ
2. Ⓐ Ⓑ Ⓒ Ⓓ
3. Ⓐ Ⓑ Ⓒ Ⓓ
4. Ⓐ Ⓑ Ⓒ Ⓓ
5. Ⓐ Ⓑ Ⓒ Ⓓ
6. Ⓐ Ⓑ Ⓒ Ⓓ
7. Ⓐ Ⓑ Ⓒ Ⓓ
8. Ⓐ Ⓑ Ⓒ Ⓓ
9. Ⓐ Ⓑ Ⓒ Ⓓ
10. Ⓐ Ⓑ Ⓒ Ⓓ
11. Ⓐ Ⓑ Ⓒ Ⓓ
12. Ⓐ Ⓑ Ⓒ Ⓓ
13. Ⓐ Ⓑ Ⓒ Ⓓ
14. Ⓐ Ⓑ Ⓒ Ⓓ
15. Ⓐ Ⓑ Ⓒ Ⓓ
16. Ⓐ Ⓑ Ⓒ Ⓓ
17. Ⓐ Ⓑ Ⓒ Ⓓ
18. Ⓐ Ⓑ Ⓒ Ⓓ
19. Ⓐ Ⓑ Ⓒ Ⓓ
20. Ⓐ Ⓑ Ⓒ Ⓓ
21. Ⓐ Ⓑ Ⓒ Ⓓ
22. Ⓐ Ⓑ Ⓒ Ⓓ
23. Ⓐ Ⓑ Ⓒ Ⓓ
24. Ⓐ Ⓑ Ⓒ Ⓓ

25. Ⓐ Ⓑ Ⓒ Ⓓ
26. Ⓐ Ⓑ Ⓒ Ⓓ
27. Ⓐ Ⓑ Ⓒ Ⓓ
28. Ⓐ Ⓑ Ⓒ Ⓓ
29. Ⓐ Ⓑ Ⓒ Ⓓ
30. Ⓐ Ⓑ Ⓒ Ⓓ
31. Ⓐ Ⓑ Ⓒ Ⓓ
32. Ⓐ Ⓑ Ⓒ Ⓓ
33. Ⓐ Ⓑ Ⓒ Ⓓ
34. Ⓐ Ⓑ Ⓒ Ⓓ
35. Ⓐ Ⓑ Ⓒ Ⓓ
36. Ⓐ Ⓑ Ⓒ Ⓓ
37. Ⓐ Ⓑ Ⓒ Ⓓ
38. Ⓐ Ⓑ Ⓒ Ⓓ
39. Ⓐ Ⓑ Ⓒ Ⓓ
40. Ⓐ Ⓑ Ⓒ Ⓓ
41. Ⓐ Ⓑ Ⓒ Ⓓ
42. Ⓐ Ⓑ Ⓒ Ⓓ
43. Ⓐ Ⓑ Ⓒ Ⓓ
44. Ⓐ Ⓑ Ⓒ Ⓓ
45. Ⓐ Ⓑ Ⓒ Ⓓ
46. Ⓐ Ⓑ Ⓒ Ⓓ
47. Ⓐ Ⓑ Ⓒ Ⓓ
48. Ⓐ Ⓑ Ⓒ Ⓓ

49. Ⓐ Ⓑ Ⓒ Ⓓ
50. Ⓐ Ⓑ Ⓒ Ⓓ
51. Ⓐ Ⓑ Ⓒ Ⓓ
52. Ⓐ Ⓑ Ⓒ Ⓓ
53. Ⓐ Ⓑ Ⓒ Ⓓ
54. Ⓐ Ⓑ Ⓒ Ⓓ
55. Ⓐ Ⓑ Ⓒ Ⓓ
56. Ⓐ Ⓑ Ⓒ Ⓓ
57. Ⓐ Ⓑ Ⓒ Ⓓ
58. Ⓐ Ⓑ Ⓒ Ⓓ
59. Ⓐ Ⓑ Ⓒ Ⓓ
60. Ⓐ Ⓑ Ⓒ Ⓓ
61. Ⓐ Ⓑ Ⓒ Ⓓ
62. Ⓐ Ⓑ Ⓒ Ⓓ
63. Ⓐ Ⓑ Ⓒ Ⓓ
64. Ⓐ Ⓑ Ⓒ Ⓓ
65. Ⓐ Ⓑ Ⓒ Ⓓ
66. Ⓐ Ⓑ Ⓒ Ⓓ
67. Ⓐ Ⓑ Ⓒ Ⓓ
68. Ⓐ Ⓑ Ⓒ Ⓓ
69. Ⓐ Ⓑ Ⓒ Ⓓ
70. Ⓐ Ⓑ Ⓒ Ⓓ
71. Ⓐ Ⓑ Ⓒ Ⓓ
72. Ⓐ Ⓑ Ⓒ Ⓓ

Part D: Personal Characteristics and Experience Inventory

On the actual exam, there would be spaces for the answers to 236 questions here, but we are not including this section in the practice exams or answer sheets.

Answer Key

Part A: Address Checking

1. B	13. D	25. D	37. B	49. B
2. D	14. D	26. B	38. D	50. C
3. B	15. C	27. C	39. C	51. B
4. A	16. A	28. D	40. A	52. C
5. D	17. B	29. B	41. B	53. B
6. B	18. B	30. C	42. D	54. D
7. C	19. C	31. B	43. B	55. C
8. D	20. A	32. C	44. A	56. A
9. B	21. C	33. B	45. C	57. B
10. C	22. D	34. D	46. B	58. A
11. B	23. B	35. C	47. C	59. C
12. C	24. A	36. A	48. D	60. A

Part B: Forms Completion

1. B	7. C	13. D	19. B	25. A
2. D	8. D	14. C	20. B	26. B
3. B	9. B	15. A	21. C	27. C
4. A	10. A	16. D	22. A	28. A
5. C	11. B	17. B	23. D	29. D
6. D	12. C	18. C	24. B	30. D

Part C: Coding and Memory

1. C	16. C	31. C	46. B	61. A
2. B	17. D	32. D	47. A	62. C
3. A	18. A	33. C	48. C	63. D
4. D	19. C	34. B	49. D	64. B
5. C	20. C	35. A	50. A	65. D
6. C	21. A	36. D	51. A	66. C
7. A	22. D	37. B	52. B	67. A
8. D	23. A	38. C	53. A	68. D
9. B	24. B	39. B	54. C	69. A
10. C	25. C	40. C	55. C	70. D
11. A	26. D	41. D	56. B	71. B
12. C	27. B	42. A	57. C	72. D
13. D	28. D	43. B	58. C	
14. B	29. B	44. C	59. A	
15. A	30. D	45. D	60. D	

Appendix

USPS Hotline Numbers

The hotline numbers listed below by state provide the USPS vacancy numbers needed when applying to take Test 473. They were up to date at the time of the preparation of this book.

Alabama

Birmingham
(205) 521-0214

Mobile
(251) 694-5921

Montgomery
(334) 244-7551

Alaska

None

Arizona

Phoenix
(602) 223-3624

Tucson
(520) 388-5191

Arkansas

(501) 945-6665

California

Anaheim
(714) 662-6375

Bakersfield
(661) 392-6261

Fresno
(559) 497-7636

Los Angeles
(323) 586-1351

Oakland
(510) 251-3040

Redding
(530) 223-7571

Sacramento
(916) 373-8448

San Bernardino–Riverside
(909) 335-4339

San Diego
(858) 674-0577

San Francisco
(415) 550-5534

San Jose
(408) 437-6986

San Luis Obispo–Santa
Barbara–Ventura
(805) 278-7668

Santa Ana
(626) 855-6339

Stockton–Modesto
(209) 983-6490

Van Nuys
(661) 775-7014

Colorado

Colorado Springs
(719) 570-5316

Denver and general
(877) 482-3238

Connecticut

(860) 524-6120

Delaware

(856) 933-4314

District of Columbia

(301) 324-5837

Florida

Jacksonville (north Florida)
(904) 359-2737

Miami (south Florida)
(888) 725-7295

Orlando (central Florida)
(888) 725-7295

Pensacola
(850) 434-9167

Tallahassee
(850) 216-4248

Tampa–Sarasota–Ft. Myers
(800) 533-9097

Georgia

Atlanta
(770) 717-3500

Macon
(478) 752-8465

Savannah
(912) 235-4629

Hawaii

Oahu
(808) 423-3690

Idaho

Boise (southern Idaho)
(208) 433-4415

Illinois

Bedford Park
(708) 563-7496

Carol Stream (northern Illinois)
(630) 260-5200

Chicago
(312) 983-8522

Peoria
(309) 671-8835

Springfield
(217) 788-7437

Indiana

(317) 870-8500

Iowa

(515) 251-2061

Kansas

Topeka
(785) 295-9164

Wichita
(316) 946-4596

Kentucky

(502) 454-1625

Louisiana

(888) 421-4887

Maine

(207) 941-2064 or (207) 828-8520

Maryland

(410) 347-4320

Massachusetts

Boston
(617) 654-5569

Springfield
(413) 731-0425

Other areas
(978) 664-7665

Michigan

Detroit
(888) 442-5361

Royal Oak
(248) 546-7104

Minnesota

(877) 293-3364

Western region only
(888) 725-7854

Mississippi

(228) 831-5438 or (601) 351-7099

Missouri

Gateway district (St. Louis)
(314) 436-3855

Kansas City
(816) 374-9346

Montana

(406) 657-5763

Nebraska

(402) 473-1669 or (402) 348-2523

Nevada

Las Vegas and southern Nevada
(702) 361-9564

Reno and northern Nevada
(775) 788-0656

New Hampshire

(603) 644-4065

New Jersey

Bellmawr
(856) 933-4314

Elizabeth, Newark
   (northern New Jersey)
(908) 820-8450 or (866) 665-3562

New Brunswick, Edison
   (central New Jersey)
(732) 819-4334

New Mexico

(505) 346-8780

New York

Albany
(518) 452-2445

Buffalo
(716) 846-2478

Long Island
(631) 582-7530

New York City (Manhattan, Bronx)
(212) 330-3633

New York City (Queens, Brooklyn,
Staten Island)
(718) 529-7000

Syracuse
(315) 452-3616

White Plains (Westchester)
(914) 697-5400

North Carolina

Charlotte
(704) 393-4490

Fayetteville
(910) 486-2321

Raleigh, Durham, Greensboro
(866) 839-7826

North Dakota

(888) 725-7854

Ohio

Akron–Canton
(330) 996-9530

Cincinnati
(513) 684-5449

Cleveland and northern Ohio
(216) 443-4210

Columbus
(614) 469-4356

Dayton
(937) 227-1146

Oklahoma

(405) 553-6159

Oregon

Eugene
(541) 341-3625

Portland
(503) 294-2270

Pennsylvania

Harrisburg (central region)
(717) 257-2191

Philadelphia
(215) 895-8830

Pittsburgh
(412) 359-7516

Rhode Island

None

South Carolina

Columbia and other regions
(803) 926-6400

Greeneville
(864) 282-8374

South Dakota

(888) 725-7854

Tennessee

Chattanooga
(423) 499-8348

Knoxville
(865) 558-4540

Memphis–Jackson
(901) 521-2550

Nashville
(615) 885-9190

Texas

Corpus Christi
(361) 886-2281

Dallas
(214) 760-4531

Fort Worth
(817) 317-3366

Houston
(713) 226-3872

San Antonio–Laredo
(210) 368-8400

Utah

(801) 974-2209

Vermont

None

Virginia

Merrifield (northern region)
(703) 698-6561

Norfolk
(757) 629-2225

Richmond
(804) 775-6290

Washington

Seattle
(206) 442-6240

Spokane and eastern region
(509) 626-6896

Tacoma
(253) 471-6148

West Virginia

(304) 561-1266

Wisconsin

Green Bay
(920) 498-3831

Madison (south and central regions)
(608) 246-1268

Milwaukee
(414) 287-1835

Wyoming

(including northern Colorado)
(877) 482-3238